S0-BCS-333

SELLING WITH EMOTIONAL INTELLIGENCE

5 SKILLS FOR

BUILDING STRONGER CLIENT

RELATIONSHIPS

MITCH ANTHONY

Dearborn™
Trade Publishing
A **Kaplan Professional** Company

This publication is designed to provide accurate and authoritative information in regard to the subject matter covered. It is sold with the understanding that the publisher is not engaged in rendering legal, accounting, or other professional service. If legal advice or other expert assistance is required, the services of a competent professional should be sought.

Vice President and Publisher: Cynthia A. Zigmund
Acquisitions Editor: Mary B. Good
Senior Project Editor: Trey Thoelcke
Interior Design: Lucy Jenkins
Cover Design: Design Solutions
Typesetting: the dotted i

© 2003 by Mitch Anthony

Published by Dearborn Trade Publishing, a Kaplan Professional Company

All rights reserved. The text of this publication, or any part thereof, may not be reproduced in any manner whatsoever without written permission from the publisher.

Printed in the United States of America

04   05   10 9 8 7 6 5 4 3 2

Library of Congress Cataloging-in-Publication Data

Anthony, Mitch.
    Selling with emotional intelligence : 5 skills for building stronger client relationships / Mitch Anthony.
        p.   cm.
    Includes index.
    ISBN 0-7931-6128-2 (6×9 hc)
        1. Selling—Psychological aspects.   2. Emotional intelligence.   I. Title.
HF5438.8.P75A58 2003
658.85′01′9—dc21   2003000917

Dearborn Trade books are available at special quantity discounts to use for sales promotions, employee premiums, or educational purposes. Please call our Special Sales Department to order or for more information at 800-245-2665, e-mail trade@ dearborn.com, or write to Dearborn Trade Publishing, 30 South Wacker Drive, Suite 2500, Chicago, IL 60606-7481.

DEDICATION

This book is dedicated to my brother and trusted friend, Mark Anthony, a tested and proven sales professional who opened a golden door of thought and opportunity in my life. We have yet to see just where this door will lead.

CONTENTS

Acknowledgments vi
Introduction vii

1. Introduction to EQ—Five Critical Areas of Awareness 1
2. Moving from *Me* to *We* 10
3. Understanding Your Personality DNA 22
4. Critical Mass for Sales Success 34
5. Applied Critical Mass 44
6. Hotheads and Seeing Red 54
7. Six Seconds of Sabotage—From Anger to Danger 62
8. The Viral Spiral of Emotion 71
9. How to Prevent and Contain Negative Outbursts 78
10. Solving the Stress Mess 83
11. Feeling Helpless or Taking Charge 89
12. Redefining Optimism 97
13. Sources of Discouragement 107
14. Finding Motivators That Last 116
15. Winning the Emotional Tugs-of-War—The Power of Positive Intent 126
16. Risking Rejection—Getting Past No 135
17. The Face You See—The Face You Show 145
18. Developing Emotional Radar—The Powers of Observation 154
19. Shifting Gears—Four Critical Selling Adjustments 164
20. The Power of Curiosity—Overcoming the Narcissistic Urge 176
21. Emotional Archeology—Mastering the Art of the Irresistible Question 185
22. It's Not about You 195
23. The "Likability" Quotient 202
24. Reducing Stress in Confrontation 212
25. Masters in Conflict 221
26. Negotiating Emotion 231
27. Seven Habits of the Emotionally Competent 242

Bibliography 253
Index 256

ACKNOWLEDGMENTS

Every project I undertake starts and ends with thanks to my wife, partner, chief editor, guide, and friend—Debbie. You know what you do. No words of mine could sufficiently describe your value. You caress each chapter, paragraph, sentence, word, and punctuation mark to assure that your husband is understood and properly stated.

I wish to thank "the chief," James Amburgey, for his diligent research and ability to mine the appropriate quote.

Thanks to my literary agent, Laurie Harper, for always telling the truth. When she says my idea is worth pursuing, I know that I can believe her. When she says I am headed down the wrong road, I know I'd better believe her. Thank you, Laurie, for pointing me to my "own voice."

Thanks to Don Hull and Mary Good at Dearborn for priming the pump and convincing me of the necessity of this work. The words you posted by your computer, Don, spoke volumes to me.

I would like to acknowledge the work of Daniel Goleman who has done a great service to our world by expanding the definition of what constitutes intelligence. It is Goleman's framework that I have attempted to translate into the realm and language of sales, and I am sure that I could never do justice to the tremendous insights he has given in his book, *Emotional Intelligence*.

Finally, I said every work begins and ends with thanks to my wife. So, Deb, thanks again.

"Only that day dawns to which we are wide awake."

—HENRY DAVID THOREAU

Have you ever met someone who is really smart but really stupid? Of course you have. Now, ask yourself what they are lacking. Common sense? People smarts? Relational insight? Can't see the forest for the trees? The individual you thought of probably is quite intelligent but lacks in what author Daniel Goleman calls *emotional intelligence.*

Goleman's landmark work demonstrated that emotional intelligence (EQ) has a far greater weighting on a person's potential for success (85 percent) than does IQ (15 percent). Those findings turned historical academic assumptions about success attributes on their head—and went a long way toward affirming common sense. Success is, in large part, due to how well we manage emotion.

When reading Daniel Goleman's book, *Emotional Intelligence,* in the mid-1990s, I was struck with the relevance of his insights for those in the sales profession. I initially developed a sales training program based upon these principles (the ARROW Program) and consequently, through the encouragement of an editor, was sold on the idea of writing this book. I am convinced that nowhere are the dramas of emotional intelligence played out more vividly than on the sales stage.

One of the inexorable truths of competition is that when clients have a choice, they choose the option with the least amount of emotional exhaustion and annoyance. The more competitive an environment is, the more emotional intelligence—or the lack thereof—is brought into sharp focus. At such times, vendors bringing any degree of emotional annoyance will be brought face-to-face with their own manners and approaches. That awareness will come either through personal introspection—or through their boss's inspections.

The pleasantness of the purchasing process depends largely upon our skill of making people feel at ease both with us and the process we are introducing. Some salespeople have acquired and refined these skills, while others seem clueless. Because of the possibility of having clueless precede us in the selling process, sales professionals must deal constantly with a degree of "sales baggage" with every client or potential client. Consequently, when you mention the word *selling* or *salesperson,* you get a broad range of emotional reactions, the worst of which are feelings of manipulation resulting from chicanery and hyperbole.

SELLING BY ANY OTHER NAME

Emotional intelligence in selling begins with the recognition that one must meet emotional agendas beyond the buy-and-sell transaction for a buyer to be satisfied with the transaction. Our skill level in the field of human emotions must keep pace with our expertise in our field of commerce. The reticence that many clients have about dealing with people who sell is quite likely from having done business with individuals who either did not clearly understand these emotional factors or who understood their importance but used them exploitatively.

MY AGENDA

When I asked my wife how she felt about the word *selling* and the people who *sell,* her answer was instructive. "It depends on how much I want what they're selling. If I want it, and they know what they are talking about and are not pushy, then I like the process and the people selling. But, if I'm not sure I want it, or they don't know what they're talking about, or they are trying to push something on me, then I don't like it (or them) at all."

My wife's answer reveals critical dynamics that lead to an emotional connection (or disconnection) between buyer and vendor. Her response reveals three levels of judgment.

1. *Emotional desire.* ("If it is what *I* want")
2. *Intelligence.* ("If they know what they are talking about")
3. *Emotional approach.* ("If they are not pushy")

This reply is instructive for sales professionals because it reflects a *satisfaction filter* that clients use when entertaining sales approaches. A client requires intelligence at three levels: "Do you know me?", "Do you know your stuff?", and "Do you know how to approach me?"

This book will largely deal with the intelligence required to satisfy the first and last questions. Do you know me? Do you know how to approach me? Sandwiched between wanting the facts and the rationale for buying your product are the emotional agendas that must be met with every client. These two critical levels of satisfaction cannot be met without *emotional intelligence*. We must master this dynamic of human interaction—known as emotion—to keep negativity from sabotaging our relationships and our attitude toward the work we do.

AWARE OF WHAT?

An engineer, doctor, or accountant can often get by without a high degree of emotional intelligence because of the quantitative or scientific nature of their work. However, the sales professional cannot afford such an oversight. The sales professional who fails to be aware of emotional dynamics will soon be combing the want ads. The sales professional must attempt to be keenly aware at all times. Awareness is the hinge that swings open the doors of access both to individuals and corporations.

To master emotional challenges, we must possess awareness at many levels. Not only should our eyes be open, but they must also look in many directions. The function of the cerebral mind is to criticize, decipher, judge, negotiate, and control. Awareness, however, is a "big mind" function that helps us to know, sense, and accept ourselves and others. This mindfulness function helps us to receive input from others and respond appropriately as well as merge and connect with others smoothly.

Much of what you read in this text could be called "people sense" or basic emotional intelligence; however, some very intelligent people forget these basics on a daily basis—and it ends up costing them dearly. No matter what product, service, or idea you sell, you are in the people business, and the following people rules apply.

1. *You must constantly prove and reprove yourself.* People possess varying degrees of suspicion about sales professionals (and sales processes) until they see enough evidence to remove that suspicion. It takes time to prove yourself.
2. *People expect you to figure them out.* People have specific emotional agendas that must be met. They want to be understood, and they want to be approached on their terms. If you don't take the time to figure them out, they will go elsewhere.
3. *This is not about you.* The only reason anyone is talking to you is to meet their own needs, wants, and wish lists—to get their problems solved. Don't allow yourself, in your occasional lapses into self-

concern, to forget this fact for a second. If you think that this is about you, you won't last long.

THE GAME IS WHEEL OF FORTUNE— THE WORD ON THE BOARD IS *SE—ING*

Our clue is that this word describes what a sales professional must be looking to do every hour of every day with every client to achieve success. Which letter(s) would you like? A good majority of contestants in the sales profession would ask for the letter *L* and spell *selling*. However, the emotionally intelligent answer would be to ask for an *R* and a *V* and spell *serving*. Within that dichotomy lies the foundation upon which emotional intelligence can be built.

Is it even possible to think of serving others before serving myself, when I so clearly have something to gain by selling? The question I'd like to propose is, "Why would any sales professional *want* to sell any product or service to a client who did not truly want or need that particular product or service?" To make a quick buck? The odds are that, sooner or later, clients will discover this motive, and their anger will turn the short-term financial gain into a long-term loss of clientele. Emotional intelligence is an imperative in our relationships with clients. Today's client has developed a keen sense in sniffing out self-interest.

IT'S THE RELATIONSHIP

I recently ran into Greg, a fellow who years ago worked for Larry, a friend of mine who is a seasoned sales veteran. I had not seen Greg in years, and our conversation quickly turned to Larry, whose mantra has always been, "It's all about the relationship."

Greg said, "Back when I worked for Larry, I never really believed him about everything being about the relationship. I thought the best way was to show the client what I knew and what I could do. But now, in my new career, I see how right Larry was. It really *is* all about the relationship. People have to come to a place where they feel comfortable with me as a person. I just wished I would have believed it earlier."

Larry's mantra, though simple, is hard to improve upon. "It's all about the relationship." And it takes emotional intelligence to build that relationship and to keep it working.

CHAPTER ONE

INTRODUCTION TO EQ
Five Critical Levels of Awareness

"Being aware is more important than being smart."

—PHIL JACKSON

Doors open and close in our lives because of emotional intelligence—or its absence. Nowhere is this truth more evident than in the sales profession. Sales professionals must straddle the fine emotional lines between being:

- Assertive but not pushy
- Conversational but not overly loquacious
- Energetic but not tempestuous (manic)
- Callous to rejection but sensitive to concerns
- Empathetic but not absorbing

Think of any doors that have been slammed in your face and assess the approach you used. Was your approach emotionally intelligent? Probably not. More than likely, someone took offense at your approach, took a hold of the door handle, and . . . slam! Conversely, look at the doors that have been opened and that have paid dividends. Chances are your approach was different. You played your cards right—a metaphor for emotional intelligence at the strategic level—and reaped rewards for doing so.

A door of awareness in your brain swings open and closes in synchronicity with the doors that open and close in the material world. That door of awareness stands between your emotional and rational self. When this door is closed, the emotional part of the brain can sabotage and pollute your every effort. The rational part of your brain will then begin to rationalize every word and deed you used to sabotage and pollute your own efforts. With this door of awareness closed, we make poor decisions, and we expend rational energy in justifying those decisions.

When this door of awareness in the brain is opened, however, the emotional and rational sectors of the brain begin to act in harmony. The emotional part of the brain becomes subservient to the rational. Emotional energy is channeled in healthy and productive manners, and you become a much easier person for others to deal with because you are more at ease with yourself.

The doors to success are opened by being aware of the issues that can and do derail us in our pursuits and relationships. Five key areas to be aware of if you want to succeed in a sales career are:

1. *Awareness*
2. *Restraint*
3. *Resilience*
4. *Others* (empathy)
5. *Working with others* (building rapport)

To begin this awareness process (and to provide a point of reference), I have created the *ARROW Profile*. This self-assessment will allow you to gauge your strength in these five key areas of emotional intelligence. The acronym ARROW serves as a metaphor for what stands between us and our targets.

FLY STRAIGHT TO REACH YOUR GOALS

In sales, the sales professional's goals are constantly emphasized. Everyone is concerned with targets—the company has its goals, and the employees have their individual goals. By what means or skill set will we reach that target? One critical skill set is our ability to navigate the emotional landscape with clients and to keep our own negative emotions in check.

Think of goals as our target, and think of our emotional competencies as the arrow that will help us to reach that target. If our arrow is crooked or broken, no amount of strength training, concentration on taking aim, hype, and motivation about the target will help us reach it. Without a straight arrow, everything else is futile and will only lead to frustrated archers and target providers (companies). Let's now reach into our psychological quiver and check the state of our arsenal.

Take a moment to complete the ARROW profile in Figure 1.1 then plot it in Figure 1.2. Next to each question, write the number under the "Self" column that best describes you. Use the scale of one to five, where one means never, three means some of the time, and five means all of the time. Some people by nature underestimate their strength in the five categories, while others overestimate. To attain a more realistic picture of your EQ, have some-

FIGURE 1.1 ARROW Self-Assessment

Directions: Next to each question, place a number between 1 and 5, as per the scale below.

1	2	3	4	5
Never		Some of the time		All of the time

SELF — 180°

A TOTAL
1. I am aware of why certain people like me.
2. I am aware of the things I do that offend or annoy others.
3. I am comfortable with who I am.
4. When in an uncomfortable situation, I can identify the emotion I am feeling.
5. I am aware of which emotions cause me the most trouble.
6. I am aware of why certain people are uncomfortable around me.
7. I am aware of the areas I need to work on.
8. I am aware of the effects my moods have on others.

R TOTAL
1. I can find a solution when I am upset.
2. I am able to wait for something that I really want.
3. I can quickly pull myself out of negative moods.
4. I am able to express my anger to others in a proper manner.
5. I can talk honestly about issues that hurt or frustrate me.
6. I avoid taking out my stress on others.
7. I can remain calm when provoked.
8. I am able to persevere with unpleasant tasks.

R TOTAL
1. I am able to refocus when others let me down.
2. I am able to accept events I cannot control.
3. I believe that mistakes are an opportunity to learn.
4. I examine myself rather than blaming others.
5. I am able to laugh at my mistakes.
6. I am able to put my failures behind me.
7. I maintain a positive and optimistic attitude.
8. I am able to persevere when treated unfairly.

O TOTAL
1. I can easily sense what others are feeling.
2. I respond sensitively to the feelings of others.
3. I can sense what others are motivated by.
4. I am interested in other people's perceptions and opinions.
5. I look past my feelings to other people's feelings.
6. I can easily tell when people's words and body language do not agree.
7. I like spending time getting to know people.
8. I make an effort to listen when people are expressing their problems.

W TOTAL
1. People feel at ease around me.
2. I am good at communicating with people.
3. I am good at resolving conflicts with others.
4. I am able to get people to work well together.
5. I am good at articulating thoughts and feelings.
6. I try to encourage and inspire other people.
7. I can remain friendly, even when in disagreement.
8. I am able to work well with people of differing opinions and values.

FIGURE 1.2 ARROW Profile

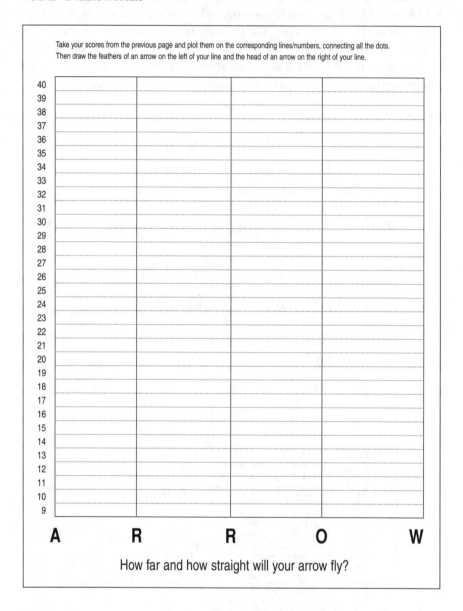

Take your scores from the previous page and plot them on the corresponding lines/numbers, connecting all the dots. Then draw the feathers of an arrow on the left of your line and the head of an arrow on the right of your line.

40
39
38
37
36
35
34
33
32
31
30
29
28
27
26
25
24
23
22
21
20
19
18
17
16
15
14
13
12
11
10
9

A   R   R   O   W

How far and how straight will your arrow fly?

one with whom you work closely write his estimation of you under the "180°" column. Then, take the average of the two scores.

Following are descriptions of the five competencies this book will cover to help you excel in emotional intelligence. Each section of the book is dedicated to the development of one of the five competencies (as it relates to sales success). These five competencies are what you measured in yourself in the ARROW Profile. These areas include personal awareness, re-straint, resilience, empathy, and building rapport.

Personal Awareness

The first section of the book dissects the issue of awareness. It looks at how awareness affects your relationships with clients and coworkers and your suitability for the selling profession. Introspection leads to awareness, which usually leads to improvement. Some of the questions I address in the first two chapters of this section are:

- What emotional factors differentiate the good sales professional from the great sales professional?
- Why do I have an easier time connecting with some people and a more difficult time connecting with others?
- Why do some personality styles cause me an inordinate amount of stress and tension?
- Do some aspects of my personality and approach act as a turnoff to others?
- How do I recognize and compensate for the natural liabilities in my personality makeup?

Awareness means we are willing to see ourselves from *outside* of our-selves. We must be willing to capture a portrait of the perceptions others have of us before we can bridge the relationship gaps in our business.

We must also become aware of our strengths and learn to put those strengths in the driver's seat. We discuss, as the famed coach John Wooden put it, how not to, "let the things you are not good at get in the way of the things you are good at."

The last two chapters on awareness, "Critical Mass for Sales Success" and "Applied Critical Mass," address the emotional makeup (the intangi-bles) of sales professionals who excel year in and year out and always seem to be at the top of their game. These chapters give you a psychological benchmark against which to measure your attitude and approach as you work toward higher levels of selling success.

Restraint

Have you ever had one of those nights where you beat yourself up over something you wished you hadn't said that day? Is there a memory that causes you to cringe with embarrassment because of an emotional outburst that seemed justified at the time because you were all stirred up? You blew your top, and like a bottle of coke opened after shaking, there was no way to take it back. We've all had these moments in our lives because of a lack of restraint skills.

In the second section of this book, I discuss the "stress mess" that we create in our lives by not having a game plan for managing our moods, events, stressful situations, and challenging people. Relational progress can be quickly sabotaged and wiped out in those few seconds where we lose it. Once we become aware of what is going on chemically and emotionally in our brains at those moments, we are better prepared to manage feelings of anger, hostility, disrespect, and embarrassment.

In this section I also explore the *viral spiral* that occurs when we fail to properly manage negative emotions. If we are not aware of how our negative emotions impact others, our relationships are adversely affected. And, because of the strain on our relationships, new issues rapidly develop, causing relationships to deteriorate into this downward viral spiral. Without restraint, we can allow ourselves to be dragged down into a virtual cesspool of negative emotions.

Restraint is the powerful emotional skill that keeps destructive emotions in check. Restraint also prevents us from barging ahead in situations that require patience—not pushing too fast or getting ahead of clients. Those who possess restraint and continue to nurture this skill move to unprecedented levels of self-confidence and relationship-building skills. We all know that negative emotions cannot be entirely avoided. There will always be people who manage to tick us off. However, the degree to which we are affected by their actions (our reaction) is regulated by our own emotional intelligence.

Resilience

Does any career require the same degree of resilience as the sales profession? Each day in this profession you are expected to endure rejection, disappointment, inaccessibility, runarounds, difficult characters, and slashed budgets (sometimes all before noon) and come back smiling and energized for the next "opportunity."

No doubt some people are equipped with thicker skin than others, but that does not mean that resilience is strictly a gift of genetics. While a degree of resilience seems to be imprinted by nature, a large degree of resilience—or the lack thereof—is a *learned behavior* of attitude, logic, and response.

Resilience may be the single most important emotional factor affecting success in a sales-oriented career. Without resilience, we quickly fall prey to self-sabotaging messages that grow from the soil of failure and disappointment. In Chapter 13, "Sources of Discouragement," I reveal how to sift through the various sources of discouragement in your life and how to rebound from each with optimism.

Optimism is the spinal column to and from which all nerves of resilience flow. In Chapter 12, "Redefining Optimism," I present a much-needed redefinition of the term and expose the many misconceptions about optimism. As a result, you will be better equipped to insulate your attitude from the daily bombardments of pessimism and cynicism, which only serve to sour relationships and cause you to fall short of your goals.

This section also explains the difference between intrinsic and extrinsic motivation and demonstrates why top sales professionals are intrinsically motivated individuals. Extrinsically motivated sales professionals are quick to lose motivation, experience burnout, and are more susceptible to feelings of insignificance with their work. Chapter 14, "Finding Motivators That Last," reveals the chief intrinsic motivators utilized by successful sales pros and how they can help you achieve at greater levels and avoid the pitfalls of burnout.

Empathy

Empathy, a cornerstone of emotional intelligence, is a highly misunderstood term. When people think of the word *empathy*, they usually think first about sympathy and compassion. However, the concept of empathy is much broader in scope than simply feeling for or with someone. Empathy is about understanding what people want and understanding the other person's situation. Empathy is about being able to pick up on and read the signals that people are sending in the course of a discussion.

I like to define empathy as *emotional radar*. Those who have developed this skill are able to read between the lines of dialogue and discern a client's motivations. This sense of emotional radar is what some would call political smarts—the ability to recognize the payoffs that will make each party feel good about the transaction at hand.

This section of the book not only guides you on how to read between the lines, but it also teaches you how to read body language and tonal language. Subtle but reliable signals, advertised in the face, eyes, posture, and rhythms of speech, expose what people really think about what you are saying. This observational skill is an indispensable tool in the empathy arsenal.

Once we learn to overcome the *narcissistic urge*—the impulse that constantly tries to bring attention and recognition back to ourselves—we begin to develop keen intuitive senses that comprise the emotional competency known as empathy. This narcissistic urge (common to all people) may be our worst enemy in the process of building productive relationships. Chapter 20, "The Power of Curiosity," explores how others have overcome the narcissistic urge and gained a reputation for being understanding, insightful, and wise with their client base.

Building Rapport

Once sales professionals are trained in a particular product or industry, their entire success rides not on their ability simply to regurgitate what they have been taught, but on their ability to build rapport with others and persuade them to act. This is true as well for sales managers, who direct the efforts of a sales force. The quality of managing and leading others hinges on the emotional skill set of building rapport.

Chapter 23, "The Likability Quotient," provides feedback from groups who were asked to say specifically what they like and do not like in meeting and getting to know others. *Likability* is surprisingly quantifiable and is imperative to building the long-term rapport necessary for successful business relationships. How successful can business relationships be if key contacts cringe every time they see sales reps coming?

Every personality uniquely challenges how we tailor our approach and presentation. Dealing with the quirks and idiosyncracies of each particular style takes constant adjustment. I have spent years researching this phenomenon within the sales industry. Each of the core personality styles has a unique emotional agenda that must be met to catch and keep their interest.

Chapters 25 and 26, "Masters in Conflict" and "Negotiating Emotion," address some of the most challenging circumstances for emotional intelligence, conflict scenarios, and negotiations—dealing with rigid views and heightened sensitivities. These chapters provide practical tips for diffusing negative emotions and understanding the people with whom we are attempting to make peace or make a deal.

Plenty of sales professionals are terrific at building rapport—until that rapport is threatened. At that point, they go MIA (missing in action), because the negative flip side of the winsome personality is to run for the hills and avoid conflict when anything negative gets in the way. To enjoy lasting success in the sales profession, a person must possess the emotional aptitude to successfully navigate through disagreements, misunderstandings, and opposing points of view.

Lead, Don't Manage

Chapter 15, "Winning the Emotional Tugs-of-War," and Chapter 27, "Seven Habits of the Emotionally Competent," are founded on the philosophy that we *manage* processes but we *lead* people. It is dangerous to make decisions and establish agendas without asking, "How will this idea play out emotionally?" Emotionally intelligent people understand the import of that question and proceed with a high regard for emotional impact and consequences.

The topic of emotions is a complex landscape, but there are simple rules for becoming a positive emotional force. The first and foremost of these rules is to keep your eyes and ears open. Become an observer of yourself first. We start this journey by looking into our personality DNA and sketching a word portrait of how others see our strengths . . . and our weaknesses.

CHAPTER TWO

MOVING FROM *ME* TO *WE*

"There is a certain type of purchaser that absolutely drives me up a tree. The sort that obsesses over meaningless detail, doesn't respond to anything I say, and never wants to pull the trigger. I'm sure I've lost many sales with these people because of my barely concealed annoyance. I think they sense it and become tenser than they already are. If I was better at masking my agitation or had a better game plan for managing this type, I'm sure it would lead to much greater volume."

—M.V. BOYENGA, Manufacturer's Representative

The Principles of Emotional Intelligence

- Awareness of our individual personality style will help us avoid annoying others of opposite styles.
- Awareness of why certain types of people grate on our nerves will help us to be emotionally prepared for them.
- Understanding why we react the way we do is the first step toward changing the way we react.

Understanding the inherent strengths and challenges in our own personality and making necessary adjustments is a giant leap toward developing emotional intelligence. We must gain a clear understanding of how our personality impacts others and is perceived by others. We must also learn to recognize the type of personality we are attempting to communicate with, so that we do not unwittingly arouse negative emotional reactions and shut down the communication process. Emotional intelligence is a matter of knowing yourself, knowing those around you, and knowing the adjustments you need to make. This process allows us to move from a *me* to a *we* mind-set.

This chapter is about how to make the critical emotional connection with others. Many times we find ourselves in situations similar to fitting a three-prong plug into a two-prong outlet—no matter how hard we try, there will be no connection and certainly no positive electrical flow. The same holds true in developing critical connections with clients to develop an "emotional flow" that leads to trust and loyalty. The only way this happens is when we begin truly to understand the important role that personality plays in establishing this connection.

Many sales professionals only communicate at the superficial level of product features and benefits with a one-size-fits-all mentality. This shallow approach creates a weak psychological footing upon which to build client trust. As the illustration in Figure 2.1 shows (MVP Model), your communication can go from superficial to profound by first addressing your clients' values and motives for buying, and then ultimately addressing their *core personality*—the foundation from which all their decisions and reactions are based.

FIGURE 2.1 MVP Model

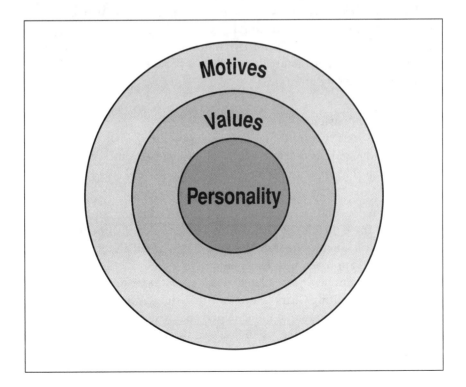

Awareness of our own personality's impact and greater concern for the comfort level of our clients is the bedrock for success in communication. These two objectives, when realized, will minimize miscommunication, misunderstanding, and negative interaction with clients and serve as a basis for strengthened trust and improved relationships. This course, for many, has become a foundational communication skill for managing client expectations, reactions, and behaviors. Moving from me to we means we put our clients first by understanding each client and the manner in which she wishes to be approached.

THE TEAM DYNAMIC

Years ago, I participated in the Meyer–Briggs personality profile study. After the course, when I was asked to explain "what I was," I had difficulty articulating what I had learned. The information, I felt, was brilliant but needed simplification. I began to search out other systems that were simpler in their terminology. Each system I reviewed had one flaw that bothered me—they were all egocentric in their approach.

These systems basically answered one question, namely "Who am I?", as if that was the end of the discussion. It was for this reason that I decided to create a new system called TEAM Dynamics. I designed this system to explore the quadrant personality theory from a broader perspective that answers all the following questions:

- What is my style?
- What is your style, and how do I recognize it?
- What dynamic is created when our two personalities interact, and how can I leave a positive emotional impression?

By moving beyond the egocentric focus, we find many applications for this study of the dynamics of personality. The emotionally intelligent sales professional will quickly integrate this knowledge of self and personality dynamics into his approach with each client.

This theme will be revisited later in this book under different contexts. In Chapter 19, "Shifting Gears—Four Critical Selling Adjustments," I reveal the body language signals that indicate personality style and the specific adjustments you need to make when you see these signals. In Chapter 25, "Masters in Conflict," I explore the topic of how to manage tension and conflict that is based on clashing personalities.

HOW TO TAKE THE PROFILE (SAMPLE)

By filling out the profile in Figure 2.2 you will discover your own personality style. It is important to remember that there is no right or wrong style—the profile simply reflects your specific personality makeup.

For each set, choose the word or phrase that *best* describes you and write a *4*. Then, in the same set, choose the word or phrase that describes you next best and write a *3*. Then choose the next word or phrase that best describes you and write a *2*. Finally choose the last word or phrase in the set, the one that least describes you, and write a *1*. Complete the process for all 12 sets. Add up the numbers for each letter (A, B, C, and D) and record the totals. Note: The numbers for each letter total should be no less than 12 and no greater than 48, and the total of all the letters should add up to 120.

For best results, do not spend a lot of time on each answer—go with your first instinct. You may feel a sense of tension at times when you are forced to choose between two sets of words or phrases that may describe you. This sense of tension is an integral part of the exercise.

THE PERSONALITY AXIS

While each personality style has many features—both positive and challenging—each personality has a simple and understandable axis around which it revolves. Understanding this *personality axis* or "spinal column" of the personality is a good first step toward understanding your own and others' personalities. The axis points for the four personalities are as follows.

The Togetherness Axis—Feelings

First and foremost in the mind of the togetherness personality are the issues revolving around sensitivity. How will others feel? How will this affect them? Did you show me respect and kindness? The higher your number on the Togetherness line, the more prominent this feature will be in your personality.

The Enterpriser Axis—Results

Enterprisers are most happy when they are accomplishing something and achieving results. They want to control their own destiny and are frus-

FIGURE 2.2 TEAM Dynamics Personality Awareness Profile

Directions: *Place the appropriate number next to each descriptive phrase.*

1	2	3	4

Least → *Most*

A _3_ True to friends		A _3_ Understanding
B _1_ Innovator		B _2_ Takes charge
C _4_ Thinks things through		C _1_ Accurate
D _2_ Energetic		D _4_ Achiever
A _3_ Thoughtful of others		A _2_ Giving
B _1_ Daring		B _4_ Does own thing
C _2_ Wants all information		C _1_ Cautious
D _4_ Laughs easily / Witty		D _3_ Articulate
A _3_ Will do as instructed		A _1_ Humble
B _1_ Risk taker		B _4_ Refuses to give up
C _4_ Wants things exact		C _3_ Likes routines
D _2_ Persuasive		D _2_ Leads the pack
A _1_ Listens and remains calm		A _1_ Flows with the crowd
B _4_ Wants to win		B _4_ Strong personality
C _2_ Deliberate		C _3_ Dependable
D _3_ Enthusiastic		D _2_ Interesting
A _1_ Hides feelings		A _1_ Does not rock the boat
B _2_ Courageous		B _2_ Speaks openly and boldly
C _4_ Has high standards		C _4_ Plays by the rules
D _3_ Likes to talk		D _3_ Gets others involved
A _3_ Friendly to others		A _2_ Wants others involved
B _2_ Decisive		B _4_ Results driven
C _1_ Wants order		C _1_ Difficult time deciding
D _4_ Outgoing		D _3_ Optimistic

Add up totals for each and record in the box below.

TOTALS: A = [24] B = [31] C = [30] D = [35]

FIGURE 2.3 TEAM Dynamics Personality Awareness Profile Graph

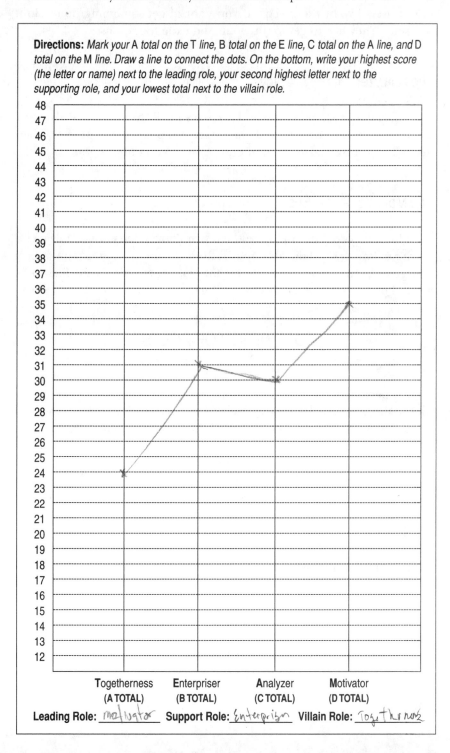

Directions: *Mark your A total on the T line, B total on the E line, C total on the A line, and D total on the M line. Draw a line to connect the dots. On the bottom, write your highest score (the letter or name) next to the leading role, your second highest letter next to the supporting role, and your lowest total next to the villain role.*

	Togetherness	Enterpriser	Analyzer	Motivator
	(A TOTAL)	(B TOTAL)	(C TOTAL)	(D TOTAL)

Leading Role: _maltugtor_   **Support Role:** _Enterprisn_   **Villain Role:** _Tog, thr nok_

trated and unhappy when they are not in control. Individualistic in nature, Enterprisers live by the creed, "If you want to get something done, do it yourself." They like to get to the point and expedite results.

The Analyzer Axis—Accuracy

Analyzers desire precision and accuracy in all they do. They like a linear and predictable process and want to see compliance with process. Their desire for accuracy leads to an intense desire to do things right.

The Motivator Axis—Energy

Motivators gravitate to where the fun and joy of life exists. They take a more random, less predictable approach to life and have great amounts of energy to burn. They love to be on the go, enjoy action, and like to be around people who exude positive energy.

DEFINITION OF ROLES

There is a proper and an improper way to interpret your own or another's personality profile. The improper way to interpret a profile is to look at the highest letter (in this case, T) and assume that the Togetherness profile description comprehensively defines the individual in question. This sort of interpretation, while indicative of a personality tendency, can oversimplify the individual's personality.

The proper approach for interpretation (see Figure 2.3) is to look closely at the top letter (leading role), the second letter (supporting role), and the bottom letter (the villain role).

While some people will have just one definitive role (see sample), a majority of people will have two roles that stand apart. The most common combinations for leading and supporting roles are A–T (Analyzer–Togetherness), E–M (Enterpriser–Motivator), T–M (Togetherness–Motivator), and E–A (Enterpriser–Analyzer). See Figure 2.4.

The more uncommon combinations for leading and supporting roles are E–T and M–A, which is the rarest combination. More information on the dynamics of these combinations is covered in our section on sample patterns. Following are definitions of the leading, supporting, and villain roles that will help you to understand your own personality pattern and the patterns of your clients, employees, and coworkers.

FIGURE 2.4 Sample Personality Patterns

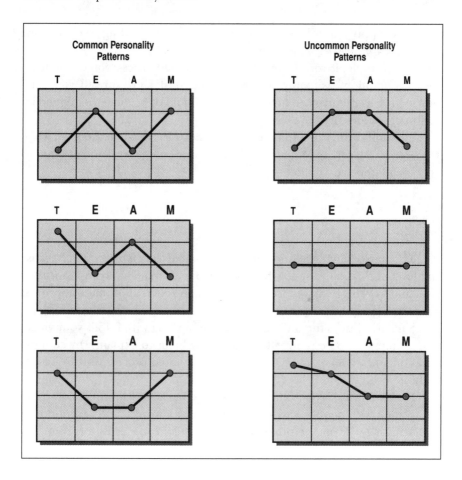

Leading Role

Your leading role is *the most reliable predictor of how you will act and react on a daily basis.* Your leading role can also be described as the comfort zone for your personality.

If you are performing work or fulfilling roles that are congruent with your leading role, you feel minimal stress. The opposite is also true, however. If your work requires tasks and playing roles that are not congruent with your leading role, you will feel higher levels of work-related stress.

An example would be the person with a leading role of Analyzer being in a position that required snap decisions. Another example would be someone with a leading role of Enterpriser who has to deal with detailed paperwork or slow and bureaucratic processes.

Supporting Role

Your supporting role is the complement to your leading role and *plays a major part in your responses to stress and pressure.*

For example, if your supporting role is Togetherness, you will tend to seek cooperation, sympathy, and help when under pressure. If your supporting role is Enterpriser, however, you will tend to become the rugged individualist under pressure.

The supporting role Analyzer will grow cautious and methodical, while the supporting role of Motivator will raise your energy level and attempt to coach and persuade others.

Villain Role

This personality style *causes the most stress and tension in your life.* Because the level of this role is so low in your personality makeup, communicating with and working with a person of your villain role is an unnatural process for you.

Similarly, just as the individual you are working with fulfills your villain role, you may also be their villain role. This helps to explain why communication and understanding can be such a strained process for two people with opposing villain roles.

For example, if your villain role is Togetherness, you will become easily agitated with people who seek unnecessary approval and respond with oversensitivity. If, on the other hand, your villain role is Enterpriser, you will struggle with people who take charge and speak bluntly.

If your villain role is Analyzer, you will be easily annoyed by people who are very cautious, slow down processes, and overthink every matter that comes their way. Finally, if your villain role is Motivator, you will grow tense around people who are talkative, effervescent, and impulsive.

PREDICTABILITY—SIGNIFICANCE OF YOUR NUMBERS

The predictability of your personality or another individual's personality hinges on the level of the numbers on the TEAM Dynamics grid. In our sample in Figure 2.5, although both participants mapped out as high *E,* there would be significant disparities in the predictability of their behavior.

FIGURE 2.5 Enterpriser Contrast

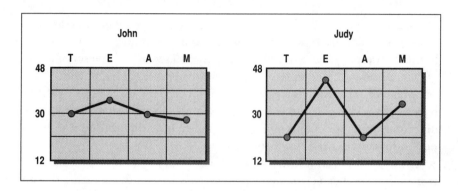

In this case, John (E-35) and Judy (E-44) could claim that their leading role is *E,* but their work style and behavior will profoundly differ because of the *level* of the Enterpriser element.

John's style would be to take charge only when he felt the other person or the group wanted him to. His leadership would be cooperative and empathic in nature.

Judy, however, would most likely take charge regardless of what others thought about it. In Judy, the E is a highly pronounced and definitive feature of her personality.

A 30 on any letter is the middle of the road, or equator, for that particular role. Once you get to around eight points higher or lower (38 or more, 22 or less) on any letter, you will fall into predictable behavior and response patterns.

Although there are four basic personality styles, each person is a unique recipe of those four basic ingredients. Each of us has within us all four personality roles to some degree—whether high or low—and is capable of responding in each role when necessary.

For example, a person with a 16 on the Analyzer line will dislike detail and usually avoid it, but they are capable of becoming quite analytical if necessary. When sensitivity is called for, we can shift into the *T* side of our personality no matter how low it may be. When results and action are called, we can shift into our *E* mode. When caution and careful planning are called for, we can shift into our *A* mode. And, when energy and optimism are called for, we can shift into our *M* mode.

Having a high number in one or two personality areas is a clear indicator of communication style and response to stress or pressure. *One caveat: Personality patterns are not a predictor of a person's values, beliefs, or temperament.*

POLAR OPPOSITES/ORIGINS OF CONFLICT

Much of the conflict we face is personality based. Our personality style in large part defines how we view people and events and how we respond to them. Two people of varying personality styles view a single set of events and come away with completely opposite stories of what happened.

Many of the conflicts we face are simply rooted in personality differences. I am not wrong and you are not wrong—we simply perceive matters differently than our clients and, consequently, have different sets of priorities on how to resolve those conflicts.

Figure 2.6 illustrates the opposite polarities of the four personalities. Ironically, it has been estimated that upwards of 75 percent of married couples are personality polar opposites. And why do we tend to marry our polar opposites? Maybe at the time we were bored with our own personality and wanted to experience a different style. Then one day we wake up, look at our polar-opposite mate, and say, "So, you're going to be like this everyday?"

FIGURE 2.6 TEAM Dynamics

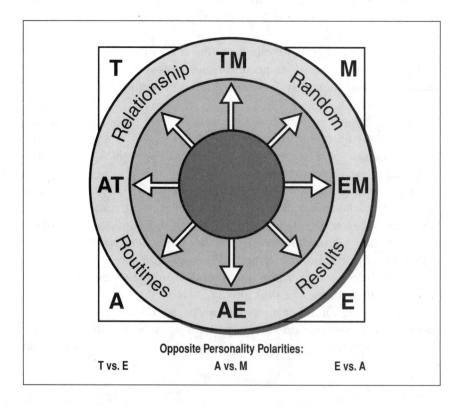

Opposite Personality Polarities:

T vs. E   A vs. M   E vs. A

A monumental leap in our ability to resolve conflict is understanding that much of our conflict is rooted in personality. People are simply following the blueprint of their own personality—just as we are.

Much of our disconnection with clients, the lack of cooperation, and inability to persuade boils down to seeing matters from the other person's perspective. In the next chapter, "Understanding Your Personality DNA," I explain the strengths, challenges, areas of improvement, and common relational liabilities for each of the four personalities. Once you understand these factors, your EQ skills will improve as you begin reviewing liabilities and viewing situations through the eyes of the client. The thought process of moving from me to we begins by recognizing that, on the basis of core personality differences, what works for me doesn't necessarily work for you.

3

UNDERSTANDING YOUR PERSONALITY DNA

*"An appealing personality is not something grafted on from
without. It is not like a coat of paint applied to a building or
cosmetics used on the face. It is expressed through the body, the
mind, the heart, and the spirit. Although some persons seem to
have been born with an exceptionally appealing personality, no one
has a monopoly on it."*

—EDITH JOHNSON

*"Men have yet to learn the value of human personality. The fact
that a person is white, or black, or yellow, of one race or another,
of this religion or that—these things are not all-important. It is the
human personality that should come first."*

—JOHN R. VANSICKLE

The Principles of Emotional Intelligence

- Developing broader emotional appeal hinges, in part, on personality self-awareness.
- Each of our personality styles has predictable strengths and challenges.
- Each individual possesses quirks of personality that can become relational liabilities.

You and I have no more control over the way our personalities instinctively react to people and processes than we do over the color of our eyes or the shape of our noses. The same fact holds true for our clients and customers. Every action, communication, and response is driven by our personality DNA—a psychological blueprint that directs temperament and behavior. This personality DNA plays a leading role in determining the types of people and processes we are uncomfortable with. Once we come to an awareness of our own personality DNA, we realize why we instantly click with some personalities and clash with others. We also realize why some processes drive us crazy, while we seem to revel in others.

The fact that our personality is blueprinted does not mean that we cannot adjust our behavior, communication, and responses. In fact, becoming aware of our personality DNA makes it easier for us to recognize where we need to adjust. We need to throttle back certain aspects of our personality when we are around certain types of clients, because those features will rub them the wrong way. With clients who match our own personality style, however, we need to let those particular features of our personality shine.

Awareness is needed in three specific areas.

1. Who we are
2. Who our clients are
3. The adjustments we need to make in our communication to build better connections

Success comes when we are aware enough to recognize how our personality plays out to others and know how to temper the features of our personality in given situations.

Emotionally intelligent individuals are highly cognizant of their unique personality challenges and inherent relational liabilities. In relationship building, this personal awareness is 80 percent of the battle. Many people keep making the same relational errors over and over and just don't seem to get it. On the other hand, being aware of your personality DNA will pay rich dividends, because it will help you play to your strengths, avoid your liabilities, and focus on the areas in which you can improve. Following is such an agenda for each personality style.

THE TOGETHERNESS PERSONALITY

Strengths

The Togetherness personality (see Figure 3.1) has a feeling-oriented mode of relating. They are always striving to keep consensus, harmony, and teamwork. When conflicts arise, they are likely to play the peacemaker's role by saying, "Let's please try to get along."

FIGURE 3.1 Togetherness Traits

Strengths:
- Strives for cooperation and consensus
- Keeps everyone involved
- Peacemaker
- Kind and caring
- Supportive and encouraging
- Amiable/Tactful

Challenges:
- Wants to please everyone
- Has difficulty making decisions
- Has trouble standing up for feelings
- Easily offended
- Can be overly passive

Self-Improvements
- Stop apologizing for opinions/ideas
- Take events in stride
- Focus on handling criticism with more emotional detachment
- Make feelings clear
- Ask for clear directions

The Togetherness style is led by a sense of caring and constantly tries to play the affirmer and encourager. Such people take a warm, personable approach and strive to avoid offending others. They are by nature understanding and responsive listeners.

Togetherness people always try to show respect to others and expect the same in return. They have their radar up for genuineness, sincerity, and amiability—and tend to shy away from those who do not display these characteristics.

Challenges

The Achilles heel of the Togetherness personality is the need to please everyone. By Achilles heel, I mean an inherent characteristic of personality that causes a high percentage of our personal stress and relational frustration. I know of one Enterpriser personality whose idea of a good practical joke is to call a Togetherness friend at 9:00 PM and say that "so and so" is mad at him. Because of his people-pleasing tendencies, the Togetherness personality won't be able to sleep all night! Enterprisers, on the other hand, would sleep like babies knowing someone was upset with them.

Because of the tendency of the Togethernesss personality to want to please everyone, these individuals often have a difficult time making decisions. They don't want anyone to be upset with the decisions they make. They also have trouble standing up for their own feelings. I often say (tongue in cheek) that you can never quite trust the smiles of Togetherness clients because they can smile benignly at you—and simultaneously plan your assassination. They are unlikely to tell you how they really feel and are most likely to tell you what they think you want to hear.

Following is a list of the common relational liabilities for the Togetherness personality.

- People-pleasing tendencies
- Procrastination
- Aversion to candor and straightforwardness
- Oversensitivity
- Fear of rocking the boat
- Propensity for following the crowd
- Lack of assertiveness
- Overseriousness
- Need for constant affirmation

Areas for Improvement

One of the first areas Togetherness individuals need to work on is dealing with issues in a more objective manner. They can bog down processes by overplaying the consensus card or by letting themselves be too easily offended. The Togetherness personality must learn to not take every disagreement personally and try to handle criticism with a higher degree of emotional detachment. A person's comment may simply be about improving the process—it's not necessarily a personal attack. The Togetherness person needs to work on stronger assertiveness skills. They often punctuate their ideas with physical and tonal question marks, as if to say, "I'm sorry . . . is it OK to say that?" They should practice speaking with more conviction and resolve.

THE ENTERPRISER PERSONALITY

Strengths

The Enterpriser personality style (see Figure 3.2) is results oriented, and their strengths reflect that dynamic. Enterprisers are competitive in nature,

FIGURE 3.2 Enterpriser Traits

Strengths:
- Results oriented
- Competitive
- Time-conscious
- Candid
- Risk taker
- Thrives on pressure

Challenges:
- Impatient with people and processes
- May compromise quality for speed
- Overly individualistic
- Can be abrasive/tactless
- Autocratic tendencies

Self-Improvements
- Show more patience with people/processes
- Articulate more encouragement and support
- Make sure others see ideas before moving
- Listen
- Get help for detail work
- Get others involved
- Treat people with respect

and they like to win. They are time-conscious and like to get as much done as they can in as little time as possible. Consequently, they are quite good at juggling projects and at multitasking.

Enterprisers are risk takers and agents for change. Their motto is, "If it isn't broke, *break it.* We've had it long enough." Enterprisers tend to be innovative thinkers.

Another unique feature of Enterprisers is their ability to thrive under pressure. Enterprisers excel in pressure-packed situations, whereas such circumstances bring out tension and chaos in the other personalities. I often tell audiences that if they are ever in a burning building, they should follow the Enterprisers out, because they will find the most expeditious route out of the building. You don't want to follow the Togetherness individuals, because they'll be apologizing to everyone that they aren't leaving with. You don't want to follow the Analyzers, because they'll be trying to explain the fire marshal's code to the letter as well as lining up everybody in alphabetical order. You definitely don't want to follow the Motivators, because they'll be cooking hotdogs and marshmallows and making signs that read, "Burn, baby, burn!"

Enterprisers also tend to be practical, resourceful, and industrious. Enterprisers simply want to get things done. Their emotional radar is looking for both competence and confidence in the people they work with.

Challenges

The Achilles heel of the Enterpriser personality is impatience with people and processes. Processes just never seem to move at the speed Enterprisers desire. Consequently, Enterprisers begin to get frustrated and begin pushing harder. They tend toward abrasion, harshness, and tactlessness in the name of, "Hey, you wanted the truth, didn't you?"

Because of their impatience, they often approach tasks in an overly individualistic manner, not wanting to be slowed down by indecisive people and status quo protectors (think gatekeepers here). Enterprisers also tend to be autocratic, because they are happiest when they are in charge. I asked a group of Enterprisers why they felt the compulsion to take over every situation, and one member of the group answered in a quintessential Enterpriser fashion, "Look," he said, "I'll make this real simple. People are sheep. Get it?"

Following is a list of common Enterpriser relational liabilities.

- Bluntness/Insensitivity
- Impatience
- Autocratic manner/Condescending
- Lack of affirmative input
- Propensity for giving ultimatums
- Overly confrontational
- Misguided competitiveness
- Poor listening skills
- Compulsion for quick completion
- Frustrated with risk-averse personalities
- Sarcasm

Areas of Improvement

The Enterpriser needs to reach out and get others involved. As one Enterpriser put it, "Being a rugged individualist can lead to a lonely existence." Enterprisers would be wise to remember that although others may slow the process, they may enrich it as well.

Enterprisers need to be careful to display more respect, tact, and diplomacy. Some things may be true—but are just not worth saying. They need to soften the harsh and blunt nature of their communications. Enterprisers need to help others see the vision before they move forward—offering them the needed encouragement along the way (without sarcasm).

Enterprisers need remember that their multitasking often offends the Togetherness personality, who prefers a more personal focus. Stories of fast-moving, hard-charging sales professionals offending Togetherness clients are manifold.

Finally, Enterprisers need to get help with the detail work, the small stuff that makes big things happen. Enterprisers are most comfortable dealing with the big picture and tend to become frustrated or negligent if they do not get help with the small stuff.

THE ANALYZER PERSONALITY

Strengths

Analyzers are accuracy-oriented—they want to get things right (see Figure 3.3). They are often the keepers of the coin purse and protectors of the process in place. Consequently, they are sticklers for proof, data, and evaluation. They tend to focus on facts about things and about people. They are quality-conscious and have very high standards, first for themselves and secondly for others they work with. They have a hard time understanding people who don't do their best to do things right.

It would be safe to say that everything as we know it in this world would self-destruct if not for the Analyzer personality. They are the architects and engineers who design, the specialized builders, the editors and specialists that make sure things are done and made right. Without the Analyzers, we would lose quality control.

Analyzers ask good questions, plan things out carefully, and are conscientious about following procedures. They are generally industrious and tenacious and try to stay logical in their approach. The Analyzer's emotional radar is up for predictability and accuracy.

Challenges

The Achilles heel of Analyzers is their propensity toward skepticism. Their skepticism serves them well in process development but not in the people department. They are often guilty of "snatching defeat out of the jaws of victory," telling people how and why they will fail and who will be responsible.

FIGURE 3.3 Analyzer Traits

Strengths:
- Accurate
- Seeks proof and validation
- Plans projects in a step-by-step manner
- Focuses on facts
- Quality-conscious
- Sets high standards for self/others

Challenges:
- Tends toward pessimism
- Can be critical/Judgmental
- Has difficulty with spontaneity
- Rigid
- Suffers from paralysis by analysis
- Can be impersonal

Self-Improvements
- Open up to new ideas and ways of doing things
- Accept people for who they are
- Display more warmth and affection
- Restrain judgment
- Work on stress management
- Streamline communications

Analyzers also tend to be critical and judgmental. They see the world in black-and-white and have little patience with those who meddle in gray areas.

Two words you never want to say to an Analyzer are, "Hurry up." Neither do you want to imply it. They immediately begin to suffer a condition known as paralysis by analysis. Stress hormones freeze out their cognitive abilities when their time frames shrink. They don't believe you can do something well and do it fast.

Analyzers also tend to be rigid in their approach. It's difficult for them to change their way of thinking. They work vigorously to defend their present point of view and take a defensive tone when you try to bring change. Analyzers can also be so consumed with facts, details, and processes that they neglect being personable. As a result, relationships begin to suffer.

Following is a list of common Analyzer relational liabilities.

- Resistant to change/Slow to change view
- Pessimistic views
- Defensive

- Self-justifying
- Propensity for criticizing and judging
- Tension and loss of composure under pressure
- Intellectual arrogance
- Values processes over people
- Impersonal approach/appearance

Areas of Improvement

The greatest need for Analyzers is to increase their flexibility—both with processes and with people. It is important to open up to new ideas and new ways of doing things and not to panic when people or processes go off the linear track. Many Analyzers need to work on their stress management skills, because they tend to become quite tense and frustrated when matters exit the realm of predictability.

Analyzers often need to improve their people skills as well. They need to remember that it is OK to smile, laugh, and show some enthusiasm. They should work at restraining their judgment, accepting people as they are, and displaying more warmth and affection.

THE MOTIVATOR PERSONALITY

Strengths

This personality style (see Figure 3.4) is quite common in the realm of sales. Motivators are energy oriented. Because Motivators are social creatures by nature, they like to deal with people who are fun-loving, flexible, and friendly. They like to take a playful and random approach to life and projects.

Motivators enjoy conversing, mixing with people, persuading others, and inspiring others toward their goals. They are naturally gifted at building excitement and enthusiasm. Motivators have a spontaneous nature and have an easy time making changes in midstream. Motivators also like a lot of variety and are easily bored with monotonous tasks.

Motivators are optimistic by nature and tend to see the possibilities more than the obstacles in every situation. Because Motivators tend to have their radar tuned to positive energy in others, they are quickly repelled by criticism, skepticism, and cynicism. Motivators like to keep energy levels up. Because they are naturally charismatic, articulate, and charming in their approach, their emotional radar is tuned to friendliness and flexibility.

FIGURE 3.4 Motivator Traits

Strengths:
- Enthusiastic/High energy
- Likes variety
- Tries to create an amicable atmosphere
- Persuasive/Articulate
- Spontaneous
- Laughs easily/Fun-loving
- Flexible
- Optimistic

Challenges:
- Impulsive
- Lacks discipline and follow-through
- Gets bored easily
- Can have several projects going at once, but few are complete
- Overlooks analysis
- Whimsical; may easily forget earlier commitments
- Overuses enthusiasm
- Has an aversion to small type

Self-Improvements:
- Plan and see projects to the end
- Be careful in making commitments
- Get organizational support
- Listen and restrain commentary
- Don't take credit where it is not due

Challenges

The Achilles heel of Motivators is impulsiveness. They are often guilty of leaping before they look. Many Motivators live by the motto, "Ready, fire, aim!" They often pull the trigger prematurely. Contrarily, the Togetherness personality's approach would be "Ready, aim, fire, because that's the way you're supposed to do it." The Analyzer would say, "Ready, aim . . . aim . . . aim . . . have we run this past compliance yet?" And the Enterpriser would skip the "Ready" and just say, "Fire!"

Motivators often have trouble with freedom of thought (foot-in-mouth disease) and blurt words out they later wish they hadn't. This happens because Motivators literally think out loud. Motivators also tend to oversell when under pressure, dominate conversation, and have trouble focusing when someone else is talking.

Many Motivators struggle with organizational and detail issues—they have an aversion to paperwork and fulfillment issues. They like to start better than they like to finish.

Motivators can also be quite whimsical, which leads to making promises and commitments they easily forget. This can and does lead to many relational conflicts. Once conflicts arise, Motivators tend to avoid confronting them.

Following is a list of common Motivator relational liabilities.

- Easily bored
- Impulsiveness
- Lack of follow-through
- Empty promises and shallow commitments
- Disorganization
- Flattery
- Aversion to confronting conflict
- Inappropriate speech/Obnoxious behavior
- Dominating conversations
- Overzealous appetite for attention and recognition
- Persuasive manipulation to achieve objectives
- Lack of discipline and self-restraint
- Taking credit for the work of others

Areas of Improvement

Motivators need to exercise discipline in fulfilling promises, sticking with projects and tasks, and following through on communication. For many Motivators, it would be wise to employ assistance with organization and detail work.

Motivators need to think through their ideas before promoting them. They need to be careful not to garner credit that should go to another person. Motivators also need to concentrate on getting past image and projecting more sincerity with people.

READING AND ADJUSTING

In Chapter 18, "Developing Emotional Radar," I discuss how to read visual and verbal signals to know exactly which personality we are dealing with. Before we can adjust our communication to connect with each client's personality DNA, we must first learn the signals that tip off the specific personality style.

Emotionally intelligent sales professionals quickly learn to work on their challenges and common relational liabilities—a descriptor for emotionally intelligent behavior.

We are what we are, but we can adjust. In Chapter 19, "Shifting Gears: Four Critical Selling Adjustments," I discuss the personality "gears" we can shift into to help customers feel comfortable in our presence. Once you master this art, the rest is simply about helping your clients get what they want.

SELLING WITH EQ

- Emotionally intelligent individuals are aware of their inherent weaknesses as well as strengths.
- Through awareness and vigilance, emotionally intelligent individuals can keep their quirks of personality from mushrooming into offenses.
- Emotionally intelligent individuals improve their emotional appeal by checking their impulses of temperament.

CHAPTER FOUR

CRITICAL MASS FOR SALES SUCCESS

*"Things should be made as simple as
possible but not any simpler."*

—ALBERT EINSTEIN

The Principles of Emotional Intelligence

- The intangibles in emotional makeup separate good producers from great producers.
- Focusing on specific emotional factors can expedite the learning curve to success.
- Teachability is the emotional feature that will help you surpass people with superior talents.

I knew when I finished talking that this insurance executive was going to either think I was completely mad or be ready to embark on a fascinating expedition. Before Larry Foster and I met face-to-face for the first time, he had described in numerous conversations over the phone his frustrations on how to help his people perform and produce at higher levels.

An enigma had been piquing Larry's curiosity for many years. "Why," he wondered aloud, "do we get so easily fooled by applicants for sales positions into believing that certain types are going to be successful, and yet a significant percentage of these people never fulfill their promise?" Part of

Larry's problem was that he had been extremely successful in the sales field (leading the nation in sales for seven consecutive years with his company) and was consequently promoted to a regional management position. It pained him to see people squander away their talents, skill, and training in mediocre accomplishments. From this vantage point, he began to see a pattern in unfulfilled potential that became a vexing riddle to him.

Like every company, Larry's firm had a battery of written tests (personality, sales aptitude, honesty, etc.) they would give to applicants to screen for the "right stuff." Larry noted that these instruments were far from bulletproof and, in fact, when compared later with an individual's actual production in the field, showed a predictability rate of somewhere between 50 and 75 percent. This meant that somewhere between one-fourth to one-half of the prime candidates had failed to produce as the written and interview indicators predicted they would.

The next layer of frustration in his sale management efforts were those individuals who possessed more than enough raw talents and skills to succeed and were, in fact, somewhat successful, but who clearly were not optimizing their talents. These people could be described as above average and even good in their production levels, but they all possessed the tools to be great. They were clearly underachieving, considering their talents and potential.

Larry's interest, as illustrated in Figure 4.1, was to discover and articulate the factors responsible for propelling people of equal talents to superior levels of production. Why are some people of equal talents consistently great while others are consistently good? What features separate the consistently good from the consistently average?

Larry was convinced that the interviewing and training processes could improve, so he began looking for the attributes that caused individuals to escalate beyond their peers. In his search for these attributes, he began to look beyond pat answers like "superior work ethic," "driven," and "motivated." What exactly were these people driven and motivated by? What was their work ethic rooted in? Were other important intangibles overlooked because of the industry's collective assumptions of the ingredients that make a successful sales professional? Larry's haunting suspicion was that if they did not get better at identifying the intangibles, they would continue to make the same recruiting, training, and managing mistakes.

This was the problem Larry presented, and I could only hope he would have the imagination necessary to listen to the odd vantage point I hoped to introduce.

FIGURE 4.1 Bridging the Gap from Good to Great

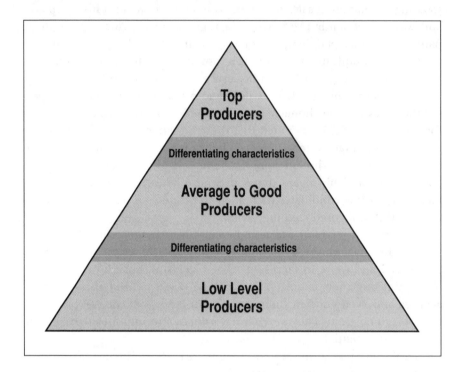

"RELATIVELY SPEAKING"

I suggested to Larry that his problem was an old one in the sales profession and that the chances were not good that we would come up with any new answers by looking at it through the same old perspectives. Sometimes the best way to assail an old problem is to attack it through a new paradigm that, on the surface, seems disconnected but forces creative thinking.

With this preface, I told Larry that I thought Einstein had solved his problem long ago. I wish I had a photograph of the expression on Larry's face when I drew $E=MC^2$ on his marking board. Fortunately, Larry had the patience and interest to hear out my loose interpretation of how Einstein's Law of Relativity might hold clues to his riddle. I told Larry that, in very simple terms, Einstein explained for us how energy is created.

- E = Energy
- M = Critical Mass
- C^2 = Motion (in this case the speed of light squared)

If we were to translate this law of physics so it corresponded to the universe of sales, we would say that energy—or productivity—is the desired result, with two inputs—critical mass and motion. Training, motivating, and managing people and their processes create activity—or motion. Most companies invest the most time, energy, and resources in trying to create motion. While these areas are important, we need to pay more attention to *critical mass*. If individuals are not working with the right stuff at the emotional level, their efforts to produce more will frustrate both their employers and themselves—and not increase productivity.

The leading question needs to be, "What sort of critical mass are you working with in the first place?" Does this individual have the psychological and emotional makeup to succeed and be refined in the crucible of professional sales? The heat of that crucible reveals what sort of critical mass exists—whether it be dross or a precious metal. You can train, motivate, and manage dross, but at the end of the day you will only have trained, somewhat motivated, and frustratingly managed dross.

The attributes constituting the psychological critical mass needed for sales success should be a starting point for producing results, not an afterthought. A metaphor for the correct critical mass is: Rocks will always have more impact than sponges, no matter how hard you push. From a sales management point of view, the harder you have to push, the less likely it is that you have the right critical mass to begin with.

Larry was intrigued with the idea of looking at an old problem through a new lens—with $E=MC^2$ as our formula. We decided to study and define the critical mass intangibles in the psychological makeup of top-level producers that differentiated them from lower performers. After those features were clearly articulated, we would compare them with the interview tools the company was using. We would determine how well those tools were geared for detecting critical mass attributes.

The question in both of our minds that begged for satisfaction was this, "What intangibles constitute the gap between great and good salespeople?"

APPEARANCES CAN FOOL

Before we could get a handle on critical mass, we first had to determine what it was not. We began by culling out the features in a sales professional that companies look for but do not necessarily guarantee success. In Figure 4.2, I have listed the features that organizations look for in a hire.

If I described an individual who is sharp in appearance, possesses good social manners, is intelligent and articulate, has an outgoing personality, is energetic, is a hard worker, and on top of it all, has industry experience, we

FIGURE 4.2 Getting to the Core of Sales Success

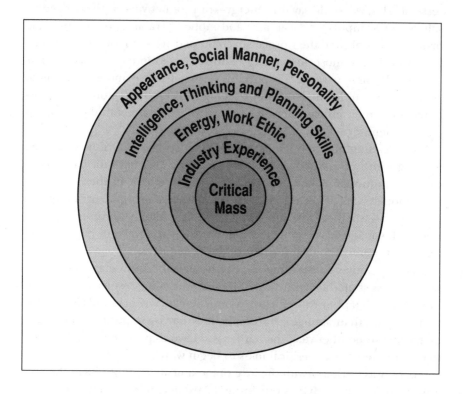

would probably all agree that this person would make a good sales professional. What Larry and I discovered, however, was that these features often prove to be red herrings, because a significant percentage of those in the organization who possessed these desirable features failed to perform.

One way to explain this phenomenon of great appearances yet mediocre performances is that attributes in the persona of success must exist a layer below the surface of these descriptors. Otherwise, everyone fitting this description would be a sure success. We surmised that these attributes would probably not be as easy to describe or define, but we were determined to try, because these attributes were the critical mass we were looking for.

DEFINING THE ATTRIBUTES

Over a period of several weeks, Larry assessed the character, approach, attitude, and behavior of each person in his division. The first layer of assessment was concerned with those people in the top tier (top producers) and was followed by assessments of people in the second tier (average-to-good producers) and in the third tier (low-level producers) of performance. Descriptors related to organization, selling skills, product knowledge, communication skills, and servicing standards were not included, because these were viewed as trainable competencies. In searching for critical mass, we were looking for features that were native to the individual—natural attributes and competencies that cannot be taught (but can be encouraged).

The next step was to interview the subjects themselves. We began by interviewing the salespeople in the top tier. We asked them to describe the intangibles that made them successful in their careers. We then asked the sales managers, who worked with them on an everyday basis, to describe the intangibles for success they observed in these top performers. We did not give the descriptors that Larry or the performers themselves had used to describe their attributes. We encouraged everyone we interviewed to describe (in depth) the features that set each individual apart as a person and as a performer.

After we received their feedback, we categorized the descriptions we harvested into simple, understandable terms. We discovered that categorizing their input was fairly easy to accomplish, because the descriptions seemed to flow into four basic classifications. The four categories of critical mass that emerged from these descriptions were:

1. Competitive drive
2. Achievementality
3. Teachability
4. Wit

In Figure 4.3, I have listed the various components that go into forging each of these cornerstones for sales success. It is no secret that great salespeople are competitive by nature, but the descriptions we heard of top achievers demonstrated that there is more to competitive drive than meets the eye.

Critical Mass Component #1: Competitive Drive

The ingredients we found that indicate a high level of competitive drive include:

- *Resourceful.* Demonstrates competitive drive with limited resources and limiting circumstances.

FIGURE 4.3 Critical Mass Components

$$E = MC^2$$
Energy = Critical Mass x Speed (of Enlightenment)

The Critical Mass Components

1. Competitive Drive

- Is resourceful *(competes with circumstances)*
- Loves to win / hates to lose *(competes with others)*
- Deals well with pressure *(competes with stress)*
- Possesses self-confidence *(competes with self)*
- Is resilient *(competes with failure)*

2. Achievementality

- Does their homework *(about their company/industry)*
- Desires to earn
- Stays focused
- Is goal oriented
- Takes responsibility / makes excuses

3. Teachability

- Desires to learn
- Desires to improve
- Teaches others
- Learns from errors
- Has awareness of knowledge needed

4. Wit

- Uses self-deprecating sense of humor
- Utilizes spontaneous wit *(thinks on their feet)*
- Diffuses tension
- Responds constructively to conflict
- Adjusts to difficult personalities

- *Loves to win/hates to lose.* Demonstrates desire and comfort in competing with others.
- *Good under pressure.* Embraces competitive challenge provided by stressful circumstances.
- *Self-confident.* Likes to compete with self (not to be confused with "paper lion" characteristics such as smugness, arrogance, or conceit, which are usually signs of chocolate-covered insecurity).

- *Resilient.* Takes a competitive posture toward failure, adversity, and negative circumstances.

Critical Mass Component #2: Achievementality

This is a term we created to indicate the following emotional/psychological profile. The ingredients that make up achievementality include:

- *Does homework.* Initiates a rapid rise up the learning curve to expedite success.
- *Desire to earn.* Often views earnings as measuring stick of progress.
- *Focused/Goal oriented.* Not easily distracted from goals by management, adversity, and negative results.
- *High standards.* Has expectations for self and for treatment of clients that transcends the status quo.
- *Takes responsibility.* Not programmed in a way that looks for excuses for failing. Tends to view self as being in control of own destiny, in spite of any obstacles.

Critical Mass Component #3: Teachability

The following features constitute teachability.

- *Desires to learn.* Applies self to the study of product, industry, and the decision-making dynamics of clients.
- *Desires to improve.* Fanatical about personal growth and self-improvement.
- *Knowledge awareness.* Understands the necessary issues for reaching the next level of success
- *Learns from errors.* Views failures and setbacks as an experiment or game and makes concerted effort to extract meaningful lessons from those circumstances.
- *Teaches others.* Helps and teaches others (characteristic of true students).

Critical Mass Component #4: Wit

The final critical mass category represents the following features of personality and makeup.

- *Quick on one's feet.* Goes with the flow (not a slave to scripts) in regards to the whims of the client.
- *Self-deprecating sense of humor.* When in error, beats others to the punch (not given to oversensitivity and defensiveness).
- *Humor/Humility connection.* Does not take self too seriously; as a result, enters into less conflict and is more skilled in managing conflicts.
- *Ready wit, but prudent sense of humor.* Diminishes tension and changes perspectives with sense of humor (understands when and where humor is appropriate).
- *Adjusts to difficult personalities.* Navigates around and through difficult individuals by use of wit.

DRIVING SUCCESS FROM THE INSIDE OUT

Human resources expert Angie Koppen is convinced that companies are being led down a path of disappointment when they focus all their efforts on building *competencies* (specific skills). The rationale she offers is that, while it is true that competencies can be taught, if they are taught to an individual who does not possess the internal attributes that drive success in that job, you are simply dressing up a pig for the dance. Koppen states, "Success is driven from the *inside out.* Any model that does not first appraise the internal attributes necessary to succeed in that specific career will fall short." What Koppen is referring to is critical mass—energy created by putting the proper mass into motion.

Yet, how often have you seen this principle violated in the realm of professional sales? I cannot count the number of people I have conversed with who struggled in sales careers and have to face the reality that possibly they do not possess the emotional critical mass necessary to succeed in this realm. I specifically remember Bill, who had gone from being a counselor to a sales professional, and was struggling with the competitive pressure and productivity expectations. When I asked Bill why he entered a career in sales, he told me, "I was burned out counseling troubled people. I wanted to make more money, and I like being around people." Some friend of Bill's had told him that he was a people person, a good talker, and that he would do well in sales. Descriptors such as *people person* and *good talker* are classic examples of red herrings that fool sales organizations.

Bill could be trained with sales skills and competencies until the world ends. However, no training could erase the fact that his nature was averse to swimming upstream in the competitive rapids of the sales profession. If Bill had seen the descriptors of critical mass that are necessary for success in the sales realm *before* he took the job, he quite possibly would have recognized that, although he was good in regards to teachability, and fair in regards to wit, he was average at best in terms of competitive drive and achievementality. This is not to diminish the importance of building competencies but to emphasize that competencies are secondary in importance to attributes.

In viewing these descriptions of the intangibles that constitute critical mass, most sales professionals would instinctively agree that these personal features are resident in the best of the best. The question is, "Can you succeed in sales without being brilliant in all four categories?" Without a doubt, we believe you can. We found manifold examples of individuals who were strong in two or three categories and were experiencing success. But these same individuals were quick to admit that they could see how the characteristics they were not particularly strong in had restricted their level of success. Now they knew where to place their focus.

This awareness is the key to raising personal productivity. Recognizing that success is driven from the inside out will help you to focus on the one factor that is always in your control—yourself. Your personal productivity increases as you put your critical mass into motion.

In the next chapter, I will discuss some of the ways that critical mass can be applied to your sales organization on both a personal and a corporate level.

SELLING WITH EQ

- Build success from the inside out. Focus on the internal attributes that take you to the next level of success.
- Commit yourself to learning about your product, industry, and clients.
- Focus your competitive energy on breaking personal barriers. Go beyond expectations in all you do.

CHAPTER FIVE

APPLIED CRITICAL MASS

"The doorstep to the temple of wisdom is the
knowledge of our own ignorance."

—CHARLES H. SPURGEON

The Principles of Emotional Intelligence

- Awareness of the critical mass attributes affects the success level of sales professionals, which ultimately affects their sales organizations.
- Development of a system for recognition and application of the critical mass attributes helps individuals perform at a higher level.
- Recognition of the critical mass attributes helps sales organizations do a better job of recruiting, training, and managing their people.

After seeing the dramatic impact of critical mass factors on individual success, Larry and I became interested in the impact of these attributes upon sales organizations. One issue we were curious about was how a *critical mass deficiency* affects the difficulty of a sales manager's job. On the surface, it would seem that if a sales professional was lacking in the critical mass factors, that any person managing that individual would experience some frustration.

To gauge the prevalence of this frustration factor, Larry and I decided to ask the sales managers to rank the difficulty of managing each account executive in terms of time required, messes they had to clean up, and the stress of dealing with this particular individual. The sales managers ranked each account executive on a scale of one to ten with *one* being the easiest to work with and *ten* being the most difficult. The purpose of this exercise was to see if an account executive's critical mass rating correlated with the stress level related to managing this person.

Once we gathered this information, we presented all the criteria we had compiled on critical mass for sales success. Each manager intuitively agreed with the categories that were developed. We then asked the managers to fill out a *Critical Mass Report Card* (see Figure 5.1) for each account executive he or she managed. They were to rank each person subjectively on the four categories of critical mass on a grade-point type scale. An *A* equaled a 4.0, a *B* equaled a 3.0, etc.

The correlation we found was instructive but not surprising. In short, we found that the person who scored as average in critical mass was twice

FIGURE 5.1 Critical Mass Report Card

Directions: Grade yourself (or your employees) in the four components of critical mass. (4 is the highest—1 is the lowest). Add totals for each component and divide by 5 to find out your Critical Mass GPA.

Competitive Drive	Grade	Achievementality	Grade
1. Resourceful?	4 3 2 1	1. Does their homework?	4 3 2 1
2. Loves to win / Hates to lose?	4 3 2 1	2. Desires to earn?	4 3 2 1
3. Deals well with pressure?	4 3 2 1	3. Stays focused?	4 3 2 1
4. Self-confident?	4 3 2 1	4. Goal oriented?	4 3 2 1
5. Resilient?	4 3 2 1	5. Takes responsibility for actions (doesn't make excuses)?	4 3 2 1
Add total then divide by 5	_____	**Add total then divide by 5**	_____
Teachability	**Grade**	**Wit**	**Grade**
1. Desires to learn?	4 3 2 1	1. Has self-deprecating sense of humor?	4 3 2 1
2. Desires to improve?	4 3 2 1	2. Thinks on their feet (spontaneous wit)?	4 3 2 1
3. Teaches others?	4 3 2 1	3. Diffuses tension?	4 3 2 1
4. Learns from errors?	4 3 2 1	4. Responds constructively to conflict?	4 3 2 1
5. Is aware of knowledge needed for self-improvement?	4 3 2 1	5. Adjusts to difficult personalities?	4 3 2 1
Add total then divide by 5	_____	**Add total then divide by 5**	_____

as difficult to manage as the person who ranked high in critical mass. In fact, we later discovered that a low critical mass rating resulted in more stress not just for the sales manager, but for the account executive as well. It only made sense that low critical mass ratings would cause high degrees of stress for individuals engaged in careers requiring psychological and emotional intangibles that they did not come by naturally.

Our discussions of critical mass factors for sales success with groups of sales managers provoked some interesting questions, including:

- Why don't we pay more attention to these four attributes when we are interviewing for sales positions?
- Wouldn't it be helpful to make account executives aware of these intangibles as keys to their success?
- Would it be helpful and instructive to have account executives fill out a critical mass report card on themselves?

CHALLENGING OUR OWN ASSUMPTIONS

After we completed our $E=MC^2$ experiment, we had to decide what we could or should do with the information and observations we had gathered. The first thing we realized, by virtue of presenting this information to others, was that one of our original assumptions when we began this study was wrong. We commenced this experiment with the idea that the critical mass intangibles we were looking for were organic in a person's nature and could not be taught. The reaction we witnessed with managers and account executives taught us, however, that this was not so much a nature vs. nurture issue as it was an awareness issue.

It is true that, by nature, some people are more competitive, achievement oriented, teachable, and more fluid of wit than others. But we also noticed that once people became *aware* that these factors bred success, they began to pay more attention to these factors and, consequently, improved themselves.

We began to hear account executives make comments such as:

- "I really need to focus on lightening up in stressful situations and displaying wit. I've got it, but I just never thought of using it in those predicaments."
- "I need to work on holding myself to higher standards and keep focused when things go wrong."
- "I now realize that I have been so competitive that I became unteachable. I took input and criticism as a threat. I think my lack of teach-

ability has held me back. I now realize that my desire to learn is just as important as my desire to earn."

Their comments convinced us of the value of this discussion on critical mass for sales success. This information resonated at an intuitive level for ambitious sales professionals. Awareness of the necessary attributes for sales success challenged these professionals to look into their critical mass mirrors and identify the areas where they needed to focus—and the facts they needed to accept about their personal makeup. These professionals also recognized that their most successful peers were strong in all four suits of critical mass intangibles. This experience taught people where to focus their attitudes, thoughts, and emotional energies.

ALMOST FAMOUS

When we looked at the productivity charts, we noticed a number of talented individuals who kept bumping their heads against the top-level ceiling. They were good performers, talented people, who just couldn't seem to get over the hump to the top level of productivity. Larry Foster and I wrestled away many conversational hours with questions as to why this was the case. Were any of the critical mass components more important or more often linked to top-tier success? We decided that we would go through a process of elimination to answer this question.

We focused on the *almost famous* crowd—perennial members of the Vice President's Club. They were doing good, but not great. We reviewed their critical mass report cards one by one to see if they were consistently lacking in one field or another. In this review, our question about going from good to great was answered.

Every person at the top or near-top had noticeable competitive drive. All had, to varying degrees, the elements that make up achievementality. The other two aspects, teachability and wit, were hit-and-miss. But we discovered that teachability had a greater bearing on preventing an individual from moving up. For example, we found people at the top who were not necessarily strong in wit but made up for it with extreme strength in competitive drive, achievementality, and teachability. We did not, however, find people at the very top who were unteachable. The next layer down was crammed with competitive and witty achievers who had hit a wall of progress. Because of a lack of teachability, they had not—and would not—address the issues and deficiencies that held them back.

The irony was that, because of their lack of awareness, they had no idea if they were even teachable or not. They characterized their attitude and behavior as "independent," which really meant, "I don't like listening to other people," or, "I've got my own way of doing things," or, "I'll figure it out on my own." More often than not, however, they were unable to "figure it out on their own."

THE DIFFERENCE BETWEEN BEING TALENTED AND BEING A CHAMPION

On a flight home from Detroit, I was seated next to a former coach of the Detroit Red Wings, who now acts as a scout for the organization. Curious about the critical mass components that a professional hockey scout looks for, I asked what features were most important to him when considering a top draft pick. I was intrigued by his answer.

He replied, "Like every other team, we're looking for great athletes. Great athletes are a combination of strength, speed, and agility. But to be real honest with you, strength, speed, and agility are a dime a dozen. The most important component for us is what I would call coachability. We have seen too many kids who have all the physical gifts but won't listen to coaching. They have experienced enough success doing things their way that they refuse to listen to anyone else's way. If you want athletes, you recruit strength, speed, and agility. But if you want champions, you recruit athletes with coachability."

The first idea that stirred in me from this conversation was a close parallel between the critical mass for sales success and the critical mass for athletic success. Before the scout brought up coachability, he talked about strength, speed, and agility. The strength of sales professionals comes from their competitive drive. Their speed in achieving results is due to achievementality. The feature that enables us to wrangle out of difficult situations is due to wit—intellectual and emotional agility.

What I found most amazing from his comments was that his organization had come to the same conclusion that we had regarding the ceiling between good and great. There is no doubt that teachability (or coachability) is the emotional hinge upon which the door of potential swings.

FINDING AND ADDRESSING WEAKNESSES

People at the top had, at some point in their careers, identified and addressed the weaknesses that were holding them back from fulfilling the potential they felt within. It is worth noting that these individuals chose introspection over blaming others or external obstacles. This is the achieve-mentality aspect—placing responsibility for success upon oneself. Some of these people intuitively recognized their weak spots and sought out help. Others, however, had their weaknesses pointed out by a manager or peer, yet possessed the humility of mind (teachability) not to argue and get the answers they needed to make progress.

Are you maximizing your potential? Or do you have this gnawing sense that certain fields of weakness or ignorance are impeding your progress? The teachable individual starts with this humble premise in mind and asks himself, "What areas in my nature, personality, behavior, or professional approach could be holding me back?"

Following are some of the skills that are critical to success in sales. Are there areas where you need help? If so, what have you done to address them?

- Breaking the ice with new prospects
- Organizational skills
- Managing paperwork
- Client research
- Competition research
- Product and industry knowledge
- Closing skills
- Negotiating skills
- Preparing presentations
- Delivering presentations
- Timely follow-through
- Dealing with conflict

KNOW WHERE YOU ARE WEAK

Only rarely does an individual master all of these fields of knowledge and skill, but top producers seek ways to shore up their weak spots. This augmenting process, more often than not, involves asking for help and enlisting the services of others who can cover our liabilities. This, of course, is not possible until we are keenly aware of our own weaknesses. Chances are that a degree of on-the-job frustration and stress will take place before this awareness arrives.

My brother Mark has been a sales professional for over 15 years. When he first started selling specialty insurance products, he knew nothing about the product, clientele, industry—or sales in general. The company that hired him paid him the compliment of sending him to their worst-producing territory in Peoria. He applied himself on the learning curve and hit the ground running. Mark made a good living his first couple of years in the business but felt a growing sense of frustration with the pace of progress in his career and with the extraordinary demands on his time.

On a weekend visit with my brother, I asked him why he thought he was feeling stressed. He immediately began to vent his frustrations regarding the difficulty of seeing so many prospects, completing so much paperwork, and making the President's Club. He felt stressed about how to produce more without killing himself in the process.

I felt stressed just looking at the disheveled piles of binders and paperwork lying around his apartment! Mark admitted that he suspected organization was not his strong suit (noting that he had two colors of socks on that morning, I was inclined to agree) and asked if I had any ideas on how to organize his business to reduce the stress levels. I began immediately to inquire about:

- How far spread out geographically his territory was
- How much time the selling cycle took for each of the products he sold
- What he tried to accomplish on a typical appointment

I guided the inquiry down this path because I had come to the conclusion in my experiences as a counselor and then a consultant that a high degree of stress that people experience in their lives can be traced back to the manner in which they manage their time. When I asked Mark to describe what his job felt like, he characterized it as "constantly putting out fires."

Up to this point, he had convinced himself that there was no time to get organized with such a busy and unpredictable fire-fighting schedule (demonstrating how disorganization ultimately becomes its own excuse for not taking time to organize). Mark had now reached the breaking point where he was willing to confront head-on his personal shortcomings. At this point, I decided to dive headfirst into the discombobulated bowels of random activity that he liked to refer to as a "schedule."

I asked him to describe in detail the past two weeks of his schedule. As he recounted the past two weeks, I was grateful that I was sitting with my brother and not a client—a client would not have been quite so forgiving of the laughing fits I could not restrain. In his first day, he drove three hours to an appointment. Two days later he drove down the exact same road one-and-a-half hours to see someone he had driven by twice two days before. This was just the beginning of a comedy of scheduling errors. One month later, he was scheduled to go back to the client three hours away to see someone else in the same business.

There was no synchronicity between his management of time and territory. The process was random, hinging on which fire needed to be put out first. In other words, deadlines (renewal dates) were driving the entire process. His stress was compounded by the fact that he didn't usually become conscious of the deadline until 30 days before it arrived.

After calling me a few expletive deleteds for laughing at his schedule, he suggested we roll up our sleeves and figure out a more efficient method for scheduling his business. After an entire weekend, we succeeded in scheduling his business for the next year. We scheduled specific days each week for setting appointments and calling on clients and prospects, leaving ample time for process and paperwork. And, most important, he would no longer drive right by potential appointments while traveling to meetings three hours away.

Another important decision Mark made was to hire part-time administrative help to manage communication and paperwork. By the end of our planning, Mark's stress level had remarkably ebbed—his demeanor showed it. What neither of us could foresee, however, was that the change would soon be visible in his production. In the next year, Mark went from the middle of the pack to number one in the nation for his company, and he had the honor of receiving the first of what would be many President's Club plaques.

Here is a perfect example of how awareness and teachability can help a sales professional take a quantum career leap. Mark possessed the interpersonal skills necessary to succeed in sales but needed help on the process side. Mark's teachability kept the door open for him to improve and move to the next level in his career. Just as important as facing his weakness was the step of hiring help to handle the things he hated doing.

While this book deals with some of the interpersonal issues mentioned in the list of necessary skills, there will be other skills for which each of us will need to seek help. Being teachable includes a willingness to admit where we need help as well as a willingness to seek out the help we need.

INTERVIEWING FOR CRITICAL MASS

Larry was convinced that his company's interviewing and screening process was hit or miss in regards to detecting critical mass attributes. Consequently, we developed interview questions for each cornerstone to hone in on an individual's competitive drive, achievementality, teachability, and wit. Figure 5.2 shows the questions we developed for picking up on the attributes that comprise critical mass.

FIGURE 5.2 The Critical Mass Interview

Component 1: Competitive Drive

Question: Describe your life in college. What did you do when money was tight? (lifestyle / resourcefulness)

Question: Have you ever won a contest? Tell me about it. (desire to win)

Question: Tell me about a time when your back was truly against the wall. How did you handle the situation? (dealing with pressure)

Question: There are only 9 of these jobs in my region and 190 in the country. Why should you have it? (self-confidence)

Component 2: Achievementality

Question: Tell me everything you know about this company. (does homework)

Question: What is the most money you have made? Why only that much? (desire to earn)

Question: What did you like least about your last job? How did you stay focused? (staying focused)

Question: Tell me about a significant goal you've achieved in your life. How did you do it? (goal oriented)

Question: In your life, tell me of a goal you had and did not achieve. Why? (taking responsibility vs. making excuses)

Component 3: Teachability

Question: What subject would you like to learn about? Why haven't you yet? (curiosity, desire to learn)

Question: Tell me about an area you were not good at on your last job. How did you overcome it? (desire to improve)

Question: Tell me about an area in which you taught others how to improve a process or do a job better. (has taught others)

Question: Tell me about a big mistake you made. How did you work it out? (learns from errors)

Question: Talk to me about one subject you know the most about. (knowledge awareness)

Component 4: Wit

Question: If I told you that I changed the title of this job to "Big Dope," tell me why you would qualify for it. (self-deprecating sense of humor)

Question: If you were giving a presentation in front of a client and five key decision makers, and your crown fell out on the table, what would you do? (spontaneous wit/thinks on their feet)

Question: The first client you visit tells you to "Get out!" and that your company is a piece of crap. How do you respond? (diffusing tension)

APPLYING E=MC²

An entire book could and may one day be written about how these critical mass factors relate to sales success. For the discussion of emotional intelligence, I felt an introduction to the concepts was imperative for the sake of awareness. Sales professionals who want to succeed can only focus on success factors when they become *aware* of them.

Those of you who have experienced success in sales intuitively recognize that these critical mass components are the same factors that have made you successful, although you may not have used the same terminology to describe these attributes. Hopefully, reading about these attributes affirms what you already knew at the gut level.

If you have felt frustration with moving to the next level of success, it is my hope that learning about and applying the critical mass attributes described in this book will open a pathway of awareness, helping to transport you to that next level.

SELLING WITH EQ

- Make a total commitment of internal and external resources to make yourself as successful as possible.
- Address every weakness in your approach, career plan, and organization.

CHAPTER SIX

HOTHEADS AND SEEING RED

"Most powerful is he who has himself in his own power."

—SENECA

The Principles of Emotional Intelligence

- Recognition of the brain's emotional circuitry can help us control negative emotions.
- Restraint is the necessary skill that keeps us from sabotaging our successes and relationships.
- Those who lack restraint suffer amplified effects from anger, stress, and frustration.

Lester's grip was tight around the steering wheel; in fact, he gripped the wheel as if it were sitting in proxy for the neck of his client, whom he wanted to choke right now. His boss had been on him to start collecting on delinquent accounts. This large account was much needed revenue for the first-quarter sales goals. The client had been continually putting him off, and today, Lester was in no mood for another lame explanation.

Lester marched directly to the owner's office and, muffling his frustration, asked the assistant if the check was ready. The owner's assistant replied, "I think he said he could give it to you in two days, because he has been waiting on an account payable that is late."

At this, Lester snapped, "This is getting ridiculous! How many stories do I have to hear about this damn check!" As he was venting, Lester was trying to stop his tongue from moving but couldn't. He flushed with both anger and embarrassment that he had blown his fuse at someone who was powerless to change the situation. To make matters worse, Lester looked to the right—and there was the owner, standing in his doorway, staring directly at him. Lester tried to apologize but he knew the damage had been done.

Three months later, the owner canceled his business.

Lester's lost account was a casualty of what author Daniel Goleman termed the "amygdala hijack." The amygdala is the emotional center in the brain that, when overloaded with emotion, can trigger an irrational, emotive response. Who doesn't have a hundred stories of words or actions delivered in the heat of passion that we later recall with embarrassment and regret? Our personal memory banks are stocked with radical examples of such incidents.

It is in these moments—where impulsivity overrides rationality—that we do the most harm to ourselves and to the people and things we care most about. For example, one person says something he shouldn't to someone he truly cares about. Another breaks something that she treasures. Another begins to spiral into some sort of self-destructive behavior. All have temporarily been taken hostage as their brains suffer from emotional overload.

Goleman compares the amygdala to an alarm company that stands ready to send out emergency calls to the police, fire, and ambulance crews. Once an alarm is sounded, such as anger or fear, urgent messages are dispatched to every other part of the brain. The body's fight or flight hormones are secreted, the motion centers are put on alert, and the cardiovascular system, muscles, and gut are tensed. Other circuits send out a flow of norepinephrine, which makes all senses more alert and literally sets the brain on edge. The heart rate and blood pressure escalate and breathing slows, while the face muscles are locked into a frozen posture animated by the emotion that triggered the response. We all know what happens at this point: we either say or do something we will soon regret, or we catch ourselves in time and make the conscious decision not to respond irrationally.

Neuroscientist Joseph Ledoux was the first to discover the "electronic backroads" in the brain that lead to the amygdala hijack phenomenon—popularly known as "losing it." Ledoux discovered that when your brain receives information through seeing or hearing, information is sent along different pathways within the brain. The main path the information travels on is toward the neocortex, where we can begin to process the information.

What Ledoux found was a "neural back alley," where the information reaches the emotion center *before* it has a chance to be fully processed in the neocortex. The result? We act before we think. When we react to the impulsive emotion in the amygdala, we spring into action before the cerebral side of our brain has a chance to deliver a more rational battle plan. Soon after we act out impulsively, the cerebral sends a map showing the pothole in the road that we have already fallen into. Now we feel shame along with our anger.

The functions of the amygdala are quite useful when we are in a threatening situation that requires an instinctive reaction—where stopping to think would cause further harm. For example, we see a car heading for a child and, without thinking, spring into action or scream out. But we are disserved by the amygdala when we allow it to act when we really need to be thoughtful.

WHAT DOES THIS REMIND ME OF?

"I used to get really upset when I would pose a question to someone and the person would roll his eyes up to the ceiling. I would start turning red and flushing and feel like my head was heating up. One day after this happened in front of a client, I started analyzing why I reacted like this. I realized that whenever people rolled up their eyes, it reminded me of my father who used to roll his eyes up as a way of telling me that my question or comment was stupid. Consequently, I flushed with anger because I felt self-conscious and stupid every time it happened. One day I was reading an article about body language and learned that a lot of people roll their eyes to the ceiling when they are in deep thought. My client didn't think my question was stupid, he was just thinking about it!" —Rachel C., Account Manager

Many of the emotionally charged reactions we experience are the result of emotional information stored in our amygdala from early experience. If, for example, a tattooed young man driving a red pickup truck once tried to drive you off the road, your amygdala will send a surge of rage every time you see a tattooed young man, a red truck, or that particular stretch of road.

One part of your brain, the hippocampus, remembers the exact context of the incident, while the amygdala remembers the emotion of the incident. In Rachel's account, she was simply reacting to an emotional souvenir from her past. The problem was that the context was completely different, and her emotional memory failed to recognize this fact. Goleman calls this phenomenon the "out-of-date neural alarm." The amygdala associates one element of what is happening now with something that happened long ago, calls it a match, and frantically demands that we react now the way we did in the past. Goleman described it as a "sloppy circuit," because it calls for action before full confirmation of the facts. This is partly what we mean when we talk about the difficulty of communicating with people carrying emotional baggage.

If I were walking down the street and saw an old high school classmate, one part of my brain would tell me who this person is, while the amygdala would remind me that I didn't particularly like this individual. Some people have trouble because they advertise these emotions when they feel them and consequently begin heating up and seeing red. When the emotional part of our brain offers us an emotional souvenir, we need the necessary restraint to keep from speaking, reacting, or displaying that emotion with our facial or body language.

THE BORDER PATROL

Now that we have identified the chief cranial culprit—the amygdala— we need to be aware of the restraint mechanisms for keeping its influence in check. When you get an emotional signal for an anxious, impulsive response, one that demands immediate outlet, be assured that the amygdala has hatched the plan. The other end of our emotional brain, however, has a switch that dampens the fires of rage and reaction. This area is right behind the forehead and is called the prefrontal lobes. I like to think of it as the emotional brain's border patrol—keeping offensive actions and words in check. Maybe this is why people are often seen tapping their foreheads when trying to regain emotional composure. They are trying to kick the border patrol into action.

For example, a coworker walks up to you and offers an unsolicited critique of your work. Your amygdala suddenly registers all the emotions related to previous offenses from this individual and rants for you to give her a piece of your mind right here and now. What keeps you from doing it?

The prefrontal border patrol arrests the perpetrating words or rebuttal— often just in the nick of time—and begins to file a report on the ramifications and emotional complications such a reaction would initiate. If you listen at this point, the report will become all the clearer as the emotional fog begins to lift. You then display a proper and controlled response and walk away from the offending party.

Some readers at this point are thinking, "Yeah, that sounds great. I wish it happened that way more often. But the fact is, I often find myself saying or doing before the border patrol can stop me." The first key to restraint is being aware of what is happening in your emotional circuitry, and the second key is waiting long enough for the border patrol to help you out of the situation. Your brain is designed to help you through these situations, if you restrain your initial impulse.

> "When an emotion triggers, within moments the prefrontal lobes perform what amounts to a risk/benefit ratio of myriad possible reactions, and bet that one of them is best. For animals, when to attack, when to run. And for we humans . . . when to attack, when to run—and also when to placate, persuade, seek sympathy, stonewall, provoke guilt, whine, put on a façade of bravado, be contemptuous, and so on . . . through the whole repertoire of emotional wiles." —Daniel Goleman, *Emotional Intelligence*

THE ONE-MINUTE EMOTIONAL MANAGER

Our emotional systems are designed to feel and navigate the correct course through our feelings. We have problems when we respond without restraint. This impulsivity soon becomes a pattern of public performance that is repeated over and over to the same poor reviews, resulting in both social and self-condemnation. In the next chapter, "Six Seconds of Sabotage," I offer ideas on how to manage that critical time frame between the amygdala getting hijacked and the border patrol making the official arrest.

A switch in the left side of the prefrontal lobe has the ability to turn off negative emotional surges. We simply need to allow the initial rush to pass, giving this switch time and permission to activate. This switch is like the corrective parent that reprimands childish tantrums and suggests more appropriate responses. The success of the reprimand hinges in large part on the history of training with the child. If we have a history of spouting, venting, reacting, and making hair-trigger responses, the child—amygdala—will be more difficult to train.

Responsibility follows awareness in the necessary disciplines of emotional intelligence. In the case of restraint, responsibility is defined as accepting actions and reactions as something we are responsible for. Restraint is an area where many people try to avoid or resist responsibility, because they have ample opportunity to point to those who provoked the negative emotions and place the blame on their shoulders. As long as people look outwardly for excuses, they lack the discipline to restrain self-sabotaging behaviors.

Assuming that we accept responsibility for what we do and say when our amygdalas undergo a temporary hijacking, we must install a short-term management system for controlling our worst negative impulses. I've met many people who, excelling in the skill of restraint, use clichés or acronyms as the first step in their emotional management system.

For example, the HALT acronym taught by Alcoholics Anonymous recommends restraint, especially in times when we are *h*ungry, *a*ngry, *l*onely, or *t*ired. This is a wise impediment to emotional impulsivity, as we are all emotionally vulnerable in these states.

I remember golfing with a fellow who was playing horribly but displaying extraordinary restraint, and I asked him, "How do you keep your cool so well?"

He answered, "Whenever I feel the urge to blow up, I remember my ABCs—*a*ttitude-*b*ehavior-*c*ontrol. My attitude will affect my behavior. My behavior will affect my control. Once I lose control, I have no hope of fixing the problem, and I end up embarrassing myself."

I got the feeling as he explained his restraint model that he had learned this lesson the hard way.

We all need to find a way to keep our hands on the emotional steering wheel when our emotions are raging and disturbed. Control in the first moments is critical to a safe landing. This section of the book will discuss mechanisms for dealing with disturbing emotions, managing stress, and keeping our perspectives through emotional upsets. Prior to setting these mechanisms in place, each of us must discover our level of awareness in the form of an "amygdala checkup." Once you identify specific arenas of emotional vulnerability, you are halfway home to forming the habit of restraint.

Take a moment to complete the Restraint Rubric in Figure 6.1. This tool will help you identify the types of upset to which you are most vulnerable. In the next chapter, I discuss how to keep your anger from escalating into danger during the "Six Seconds of Sabotage."

SELLING WITH EQ

- When upset, remember what is happening at a chemical level in your brain and how vulnerable you are at that moment.
- Give yourself ample time to allow your emotional border patrol to kick into action.
- Develop a focus thought that you can utilize for your cooling off period.

FIGURE 6.1 ARROW Restraint—The Self-Control Rubric

Directions: *Read each statement and circle the number that best describes you.*

⬅━━━━━━━━━━━━━━━━━━━━━━━━━━━━━━━━━━━━━━➡

When someone is annoying me, I . . .

1   (2)   3   4   5

Give them a piece of my mind   Walk away

When I am angry, I . . .

1   2   (3)   4   5

Start yelling and acting out   Get alone and process

When I am stressed, I . . .

1   2   (3)   4   5

Take it out on others   Create a plan to resolve situation

When others reject or ignore me, I . . .

1   2   3   (4)   5

Become depressed   Consider it their loss

When confronted with rudeness, I . . .

1   (2)   3   4   5

Become rude with them   Stay calm; fix problem

When confronted with aggression, I . . .

1   (2)   3   4   5

Raise the aggression level   Diffuse the situation

When confronted with blame, I . . .

1   2   (3)   4   5

Immediately defend myself   Hear out accusation,
                                        calmly explain perspective

Directions: *Read each statement and circle the number that best describes you.*

When I feel an impulse to buy, I . . .

1   2   3   (4)   5

Buy it now   Give myself time to think it through

When I get an impulse to act out negatively, I . . .

1   2   (3)   4   5

Remove myself from the circumstances   Go with the moment

When presented an opportunity for quick gain, I . . .

1   2   3   (4)   5

Jump on it   Seek counsel

When it comes to delaying gratification, I . . .

1   2   3   (4)   5

Usually give in   Can easily discipline self

When I feel underprepared, insecure, or incompetent, I . . .

1   2   3   (4)   5

Bluff my way through it   Ask for help or more time

Add Total: | 36 |

12   18   24   30   (36)   42   48   54   60

Victim of the   Hands on the Emotional
Amygdala Hijack   Steering Wheel

CHAPTER SEVEN

SIX SECONDS OF SABOTAGE
From Anger to Danger

*"The verbal expression of animosity toward others calls
forth certain hormones from the pituitary, adrenal,
thyroid, and other glands, an excess of which can
cause disease in any part of the body."*

—DR. S. I. MCMILLEN

"Anger is never without a reason, but seldom a good one."

—BENJAMIN FRANKLIN

The Principles of Emotional Intelligence

- Understanding the physiology of anger can help us wait out the chemical storms that arouse irrational and irritated responses.
- Taking responsibility for our anger leads to taking responsibility for our reactions.
- Developing a "diffusion response" allows our body chemistry to regulate and keeps us from embarrassing responses.

Lynn was driving down the road for a visit to a top account when her cell phone rang. It was her manager, Victor, reminding her for the fourth time that she needed to push harder with this account on a new product offering. He told her if she got the account, it would give a good bump to her numbers for the quarter.

Lynn listened as long as she could to his redundant, sermonic spiel, and then her frustration came spewing forth, "*&^%$$# it, Vic, this is not the type of account you push on. Go sell it yourself if you're so good at it. And cut the crap about being concerned about my numbers, it's your %$^&^##$ numbers you're concerned about, not mine!" Just then she saw the traffic stopped dead in front of her. She slammed on her brakes and missed backending the BMW in front of her by an inch.

Her entire body started shaking. "I'VE GOT TO GO!" she yelled into the phone and turned it off. She pounded the steering wheel over and over, cursing herself, "You #$%^^ idiot! You ^%$%$& idiot!" When the light turned green she pulled her car over into a vacant lot and tried to process what had just happened to her. This kind of thing didn't happen to her that often, but it happened too often for her own good.

She tried to sort out the many layers of anger she was feeling. She was angry with the client for not giving her a chance to propose this idea. She was angry with her boss for his self-centeredness and his haranguing approach to solving this problem, but, most of all, she was angry with herself for losing control. She pondered the damage she had done to her chances for a promotion—which only increased her self-loathing.

"Just get a grip," she told herself and picked up the phone to try to make amends with her boss.

FAST AND FURIOUS

We have all experienced these embarrassing moments when after the dust settles, we shake our heads and ask, "Why did I do that?" We need to understand that our emotional system operates with much more rapidity and certainty than our rational system. In fact, brain research indicates that our emotions get about a six-second head-start on our rational functions. As we have all discovered, a great deal of damage can happen in those six seconds.

While the rational mind offers a deliberate analysis of the situation, the emotional mind works in a more streamlined and simplistic manner. The time between feeling the negative emotion and the eruption can be almost instantaneous. The emotional mind will react to first impressions and mobilize us to respond, without taking time to question the need for reaction or reflecting on how to react. Although every person can express this quick and sloppy response, most have learned degrees of restraint—often through embarrassing trial and error.

To stay in control of anger, rage, and hostility, it is important to develop three levels of awareness.

1. Be aware of the body's automatic electrochemical responses when it senses a threat.

2. Be aware of the physical signs indicating we are vulnerable to anger at the moment.

3. Be aware of responses that have worked in the past for diffusing the chemistry of anger.

Anger can be brought on by any number of annoyances or perceived threats. The shoddy emotional response thinks nothing of swinging at an expensive vase to kill an annoying fly, or of pounding the horn and shaking a fist at a clueless driver, or of giving verbal ventilation to every agitated thought. Restraint alone keeps us from harming property, others, and ourselves with hair-trigger reactions. Restraint, however, is no mystery. Restraint is the awareness (and regulation) of what is going on inside us, where the dangerous impulses can lead, and how to escape the angry rush.

PHYSIOLOGY OF ANGER

How aware are you of what is happening with your body when you are caught in the emotional spectrum between annoyance and anger? Try to answer the following questions about how your body responds to disturbing emotions.

When I am agitated or annoyed, I . . .

- Tap on the table
- Shake my leg up and down
- Purse my lips
- Narrow my eyes
- Pace the floor
- Breathe long and drawn out
- Breathe short and fast
- Bite my lip
- Grind my teeth
- Clench my fists
- Tighten my grip (on steering wheel, etc.)

When I am really angry . . .

- My stomach tenses
- My stomach hurts
- My head heats up
- My head hurts
- My neck stiffens

- My ears flush
- I experience dizziness, disorientation
- I sense certain muscles tensing up
- My breathing becomes difficult
- My eyesight is affected
- My hearing is affected
- My hands ball up
- I feel the urge to hit, kick, or throw things

In unscientific terms, what is happening in your brain and body is a literal heating up. A rush of chemicals brought on by rage triggers physical responses throughout the body. The chief trigger for anger is the sense of being endangered. This can be brought on by an outright physical threat or by a symbolic threat to our dignity or self-image. Typically, these threats are felt when we are treated rudely, talked down to, insulted, ignored, patronized, or subjected to any other action implying we are not important.

For the sake of restraint, we must try to understand that these automatic chemical responses—designed to protect us—can do us great harm when misapplied. We are simply experiencing the arousal of the catecholamine and adrenocortical systems (chemical reactions) in our brains, and if we recognize this fact, we can wait it out and rise above it. The first phase of the emotional rush to overcome is the initial six-second rush—the time between information reaching the emotional control center and, later, the rational control center.

Brain researcher, Dolf Zillman, in *The Handbook of Mental Control*, explained that the first rush gives us a huge energy lift to prepare us for a "vigorous course of action." This rush can last for minutes and prepares our bodies for a quick fight. The answer here is simple: *do* or *say* nothing until your body's chemistry normalizes.

ANGER'S SECOND WAVE

After the initial rush of emotion, our rational processes surface, and we begin to think of ways and reasons for cooling off. During this period of thought and analysis, however, we continue to feel the resurgence of heated emotions demanding an outlet in action. During this period, the brain arouses the adrenocorticol system and keeps us in a state of readiness to fly off at the slightest provocation. This is why we are much more vulnerable to a fit of rage if we have been previously irritated or provoked by another situation beforehand. For example, normally you might not be angry with your kids being loud and silly, but if you had a stressful day at work, your brain's chemical system is in a readiness state. You are now in a perfectly vulnerable spot for an emotional hijacking.

This second rush can be more difficult to deal with because it can last for days—if we continue to ponder the thoughts and circumstances that provoked the reaction. I can remember situations that caused me to feel angry for days at a time, from my first waking moment to my last. It was not until I could find some perspective, which allowed me to view the situation through another lens, that the anger's chemical train was derailed. This explains why it is so vitally important to talk out frustrations and hostilities with a trusted friend. The input friends bring can help us change our focus and, subsequently, the chemistry that upsets our body and emotions.

Get in touch with what your body is telling you. Anger is not only bad for relationships, it is harmful to your body. If you feel symptoms in your body, then your chemistry is screwed up. Your chemistry is screwed up because your thoughts are feeding that chemistry. If you continue to focus on your anger, you perpetuate the overdose of stress chemicals in your system and open the door to a thousand physical maladies. Don't wait for radical signs to do something about it.

I clearly remember a personally alarming incident regarding the effects of anger upon my body. I had to confront an employee who was engaging in some inappropriate behavior. I had warned him before, and now I had to give a stern and final admonition. I was so angry and stressed about this situation, that during the encounter I began to experience what I thought at the time was some sort of hallucination. The person I was talking to began to appear like he was far away from me. I couldn't figure out if he looked like he had shrunk or if he looked like he was a hundred yards away. At that moment, I thought I was losing my grip.

I later asked a doctor friend if he could explain this phenomenon to me. He informed me that all manners of strange events can occur when a body is overstressed. He informed me that what had happened to me was a buildup of abnormal pressure on my optic nerve, resulting in an optical illusion. I realized then and there that I needed to take responsibility for learning how to manage my anger so that I could prevent these emotions from overwhelming my system.

"YOU MAKE ME MAD!"

As long as we allow ourselves to blame someone else for how we feel, we will excuse our anger and deprecating actions. If, on the other hand, we "own" what goes on in inside of us and accept total responsibility for those feelings, we are then able to respond in new ways. We literally become "response-able." Great freedom comes when we are willing to own our own thoughts, feelings, words, and emotions. We become free to choose our own *actions* and *reactions.*

How many times have we played the "dumb and dumber" game? "You spoke rudely to me, so I'm going to show you what real rudeness looks like!" "I see your hostility and raise it by two units!" Our dumb and dumber reactions show that we are as guilty of a lack of control as the person we are angry with. It has been said that we are only as big as the thing or person that makes us angry. How then can we measure up? By taking responsibility for our reactions—no matter what sort of provocation may precede them. My actions are mine. Your actions are yours. I'll be responsible for my behavior.

"So and so makes me angry every time he opens his mouth." Does he? Or does "so and so" arouse the anger response in you, and you yield to it? The old lesson about using *I statements* to own your anger applies here. Not, "You make me mad," but, "I feel angry when I hear you say . . ." The bottom line is: *I allow you to make myself angry with you.* I own that reaction. If you struggle with that sort of emotional responsibility, then you are saying that, in your particular situation, anger is the only possible response. There is no situation where anger is the only possible response.

CANCELING DEMANDS

"Anger is the curse of interpersonal relations."

—HARRY STACK SULLIVAN

Author David Augsberger postulated, "Freedom from being dominated by anger begins by tracking down the demands made on others. Recognizing them, admitting them out loud, speeds up the process of owning the anger. One has the choice: (1) to negotiate the demands that matter or (2) to cancel the ones that don't."

If Augsberger is correct, then we can cancel out a large portion of the anger we carry by simply canceling out the demands we carry on others. Anger is a demand. I may "demand" that a client hear me, or respect me, or use my suggestions. I may "demand" that my boss see my worth or recognize my accomplishments. Simply cancel the demands, and the anger goes with them.

Emotionally intelligent individuals recognize that, although they cannot control their emotional systems' initial reactions, they can control and regulate subsequent reactions, thereby modulating their bodies' anger/chemistry system. Or, in other words, what they say will either cool the chemical effect or cause the pot to boil over.

THE VENTING MYTH

"In the midst of great joy, do not promise anyone anything. In the midst of great anger, do not answer anyone's letter."

—CHINESE PROVERB

"One day I was playing golf with a client, and he started stewing on the first tee box when he saw that we had a rather methodical-looking threesome playing in front of us, and we were a twosome in a cart. Sure enough, by the fourth hole we were waiting for them on every shot, and they didn't have the good sense to ask us to play through. Finally, my client could take no more and yelled, 'Could we please play through!' with his hostility barely concealed. They let us play through, and my partner was cursing them under his breath all the way up the fairway. After that he couldn't hit a shot to save his life, and the last five holes were a disaster." —Roy G., Bank Representative

In the 1970s, venting therapy was a fad of psychology. During that time, my family began having some problems. My parents brought us all into the psychologist's office where we were supposed to vent our real feelings—which we did—and we walked out hating each other's guts. Modern psychology eventually learned a lesson that venting (as a remedy) is a fallacy. The deception of venting, or telling someone how we really feel, comes from its seductive effect that it *does* make us feel better for the moment. However, venting only serves to heighten the agitated state and to increase the adrenal poisons already coursing through the system.

Researcher Diane Tice has found that ventilating anger is actually one of the worst ways to cool down. The outburst of rage pumps up the emotional brain's arousal, leaving people feeling more angry, not less. Tice found that venting anger typically prolonged the mood rather than ended it. She found that people were far more effective in confronting the offending party after they had a chance to cool down.

If we speak when our anger is heightened, we put much at risk. While we do succeed in "getting it off our chests," we redirect these poisons to the stomach, heart, muscles, and blood. The worst times for expression are when we feel extreme emotions like anger. If we were all given the opportunity to undo some of the words we've spoken, almost all would probably choose to undo words spoken in anger.

I once read a news story about a man who was challenged by a student while teaching an anger management course. An argument ensued and then a fight. The teacher of the course ended up killing the challenger in the fight. Amazing ironies result from misdirected emotions. William Arthur Ward advised, "It is wise to direct your anger toward problems, not people. To focus your energies on answers, not excuses."

THE RARE REACTION

"Those who fly into a rage always make a bad landing."

—ANONYMOUS

Anyone we allow to anger us can conquer us. So it was the client's fault. He did or said the wrong thing. Why should you or I let it ruin our day or week? Anger is the result of brain chemistry that we allow to enter, build, and eventually boil over. We have the ability to refuse anger when it knocks at the door. A friend offered this advice, "When you feel the slightest anger, count to ten slowly and then speak. If you're really angry count to a hundred slowly and then don't speak at all."

If we learn the *rare reaction*—the unexpected response—we can raze emotional molehills before they turn to mountains. At the very moment someone criticizes our work, points out our errors, or wrongly accuses us, we can choose a course of reaction that results in either hurt feelings, deepened misunderstanding, and soured relationships—or clearing the air and developing a new level of respect. The common response is to stand our ground and vent our feelings because "We have a right to be angry, don't we?" Yet how often has the exercise of that "right" to be angry brought us embarrassment and regret? We can all look back at our overreactions and blush.

The rare reaction is to not provide a fight when clients or coworkers expect one. They want a tug-of-war but find they are the only ones holding the rope. We have the chance to calmly answer, "Let me look into it," "I can see why you're upset," or, "Let me figure out what to do, and I'll get back to you." These responses give both ourselves and our critics time to diffuse the anger—and are guaranteed to catch our accusers and critics off guard.

Sometimes we win by losing. Martial arts expert and actor Chuck Norris tells the story of sitting in a small Texas bar and having a beer in a corner booth. A large man walked up and told him that this was his booth. Norris didn't like his tone or his implicit threat, but he said nothing and moved to another booth. The big fellow started coming toward Norris again. "Here it comes," Norris thought, "a local tough guy out to make a name for himself."

When the man arrived at the new booth, he said, "You're Chuck Norris." Norris nodded.

"You could have whipped me back there, why didn't you?" he asked.

"What would it have proved?" Norris asked.

The man thought it over for a moment and then offered his hand. "No hard feelings?" he asked.

"None," Norris replied, and shook his hand.

In his book, *The Secret Power Within,* Norris wrote, "Not only did I avoid a confrontation, I made a friend. I won by losing."—*The Daily Dose*

The chemistry of anger compels us to fight. The emotionally intelligent individual lets this chemistry subside until a more rational path of action can be chosen. If we feel competitive toward our adversaries or agitators, all the more reason to keep our cool and avoid the six seconds of sabotage. As football coach Lou Holtz put it, "You'll never get ahead of anyone as long as you try to get even with him."

SELLING WITH EQ

- Pay attention to your body's signals telling you that anger is gaining the upper hand.
- Own your reactions. Don't blame others for anger getting the best of you.
- Release the demands you are making on others that cause you to feel persistent anger.

CHAPTER EIGHT

THE VIRAL SPIRAL
OF EMOTION

*"Keeping our distressing emotions in check is
the key to emotional well-being."*

—DANIEL GOLEMAN

The Principles of Emotional Intelligence

- Once we express a negative emotion, it takes on a life of its own, over which we have no control.
- Anticipating the ramifications of negative emotions will hinder their expression.

TELL THEM HOW YOU REALLY FEEL

Trevor's index finger hung ambivalently over the send button. He sensed that this e-mail, once sent, could take on a life of its own. He felt that what he was saying needed to be said. He had turned down some pretty good offers to come to this company. He'd taken this job because the territory was close to home and he would be selling a product he had confidence he could sell. But things had changed in the two years since he'd arrived.

In his first year, he led the division in sales. He was promptly rewarded with a cut in pay! This grated on him every working day. The next year he persisted and had another very good year. His reward? They chopped up his territory and gave away some of his best accounts. By now, this situation was eating away at him like an emotional cancer.

His relationship with his boss was one of hide-and-seek. Trevor would try to seek him out to tell him how he felt about the situation, and his boss would find clandestine means of avoiding him. So Trevor decided to send an e-mail to air out his feelings. He told his boss how he felt the company had screwed him over and taken away his motivation. He talked about the great opportunities he had turned down elsewhere. He closed by saying he felt like things needed to change for him to be happy. He was confident the company needed him because of the great relationships he had built—that fact alone gave him permission, in his mind, to send this message.

He had been relishing the thought of writing and sending this e-mail for weeks. The very idea had become a reservoir of energy for him. He pounded the send button, leaned back in his chair, and almost immediately felt a sense of dread come over him. He had trouble sleeping all weekend and into the next week as he waited for some response—but none came.

Trevor's boss read the e-mail and then forwarded the e-mail to his boss, who promptly asked him to come in and talk about Trevor. He told Trevor's manager that he thought Trevor was a malcontent, a loose cannon, and an ingrate, seeing as he was making twice as much money now as he had before he came to this company. He instructed Trevor's boss to start looking for a replacement as he expected any day to find out that Trevor had gone to the competition. Thus, the snowball started rolling.

Within a month (of eerie silence for Trevor), his company came and offered him a "new" position with less pay and a different territory. They said that they were making changes with the sales structure in his division. By this time, the markets had started their meltdown, and other companies had put a freeze on hiring. Trevor eventually took a job for two-thirds the pay with another firm. End of story.

THE PRICE WE PAY

Trevor's situation indicates a lack of emotional intelligence (one to which we are all susceptible at times) that initiated a downward spiral of events.

- His lack of resilience within the context of changing conditions at his company caused him to get trapped in a bitter state of mind, in which all he could think about were the negatives of the situation.
- His need to vent his feelings made him an undesirable to his boss who worked hard to avoid him.

- Not knowing how to diffuse the negative emotions led to a volcanic eruption in the e-mail he sent. Leading up to that point, he had cherished the idea of airing it out, but once it was done, he sensed he had done the wrong thing.

What Trevor essentially created was a *viral spiral* of emotion. In Chapter 15, "Winning the Emotional Tugs-of-War," I discuss how to create a "contagion" of positive emotion (how a positive state literally infects others). First, we must deal with the negative side of this emotional principle—negative emotion, once expressed, spreads beyond our control like a virus. Emotions literally have a viral quality to them. Once people figure out that we possess emotional toxicity, they begin to avoid us for fear of infection.

Figure 8.1 shows the downward spiral effect that takes place with the expression of pent-up negativity.

First, we feel a particular *emotion*. This emotion may have been building up over time, and we may have considered a number of ways of expressing this emotion.

Next, the emotion is articulated in words or animated in *behavior*. We have let the proverbial cat out of the bag. And, like a trapped cat, the behavior that results is reminiscent of hissing and clawing.

Finally, the spiral descends toward the *impact* our words and actions have upon our audience and us.

THE "IRE" EXTINGUISHER

None of us wants to build a reputation as hostile, whining, negative, inappropriate, temperamental, complaining, pessimistic, abrasive, or any other low-EQ label. To avoid such labels requires that we find a way to turn down the heat *before* emotion reaches the boiling point. Clients can provide opportunities for us to feel anger and frustration when they:

- Look you in the eye and lie
- Insincerely play you against the competition
- Insult you by asking for too much
- Resist needed change because of their pride and ego

Your home office or support staff provides opportunities for you to feel anger and frustration when they:

- Fail to follow through in a timely manner, which makes you look bad
- Do sloppy work

FIGURE 8.1 The Viral Spiral of Emotions

A sense of self mastery, of being able to withstand the emotional storms. Individuals with restraint are those who are able to control their negative emotions, and not act or react inappropriately in situations. "Keeping our distressing emotions in check is the key to emotional well being."
(Goleman, Emotional Intelligence p. 36)

Impact on others

Behavior

Emotion

- Fail to grasp the importance of a particular task
- Say or do things that hurt good client relationships
- Fail to give you proper or timely information

When these annoyances are repeated, we are most tempted to blow up, air it out, or get it off our chest—or any other pseudonym we choose to mean *relinquish restraint*. These reactions rarely extinguish our ire but rather fan the flames of our wrath.

"Ire" extinguishers are especially effective for those times when you are hot under the collar. It is important to utilize your emotional fire-fighting equipment *before* your anger burns out of control. Anger researcher Dolf Zillman found that when your anger is stoked, there is a window of opportunity for de-escalating, when you can reappraise the situation, try to understand why the individual is acting the way he is, and choose not to retaliate. This is your window out of the burning building.

By ignoring this reappraisal, you stoke the anger within and quickly reach a point that Zillman refers to as "cognitive incapacitation"—where you literally can no longer think straight. We have all experienced this paralyzing effect on our rational senses when we allow our anger to build. At this point, the adrenal cortical chemicals are about to take us on a bad trip. Any mitigating information that tries to enter our thought processes at this stage is dismissed with cursing and logic such as, "That's just too damn bad. They asked for it!"

At times like these, it is most helpful to have a succinct thought or image that immediately dams the rising tide of stress hormones. For example, the image of a stoplight is used to teach middle-school students how to manage anger (simple enough for adults who are about to have a tantrum, as well). It goes like this.

- Red light   1. Stop, calm down, and think before you act.
- Yellow light 2. Say the problem out loud.
                 3. Set a positive goal.
                 4. Think of a number of solutions.
                 5. Think ahead to the consequences.
- Green light 6. Go ahead and try the best plan.

Simple, elementary-level thought and straightforward imagery like a stoplight are exactly what we need on the cusp of cognitive incapacitation.

When we develop a new matrix of thought that predicts the emotional injuries and offenses that stir us into action, we give ourselves reasons to practice restraint. The viral spiral is stopped before it ever gains momentum.

THINKING IT THROUGH

Emotionally competent individuals learn to diffuse the building negativity as well as attempt to predict the emotional outcomes of their potential words or actions. Typically, this contemplation will be enough to deter negative expression. Some individuals—and we all know a few—have developed a pattern for negative self-expression and subsequent self-loathing that they cannot seem to break. They lack the diffusion techniques and the rational matrix for predicting the outcome of their actions.

Walk yourself through the matrix (in Figure 8.2) of thought regarding an emotion that sometimes gets the better of you.

Typically, these behavior patterns will repeat themselves, until we give our brains a new way of processing the negative emotional information. Thinking through the relational/emotional consequences helps us to recognize the impact that spiraling emotions have upon our relationships.

The synapse system of the brain (the process of connecting one thought to another) will continue to drive us down the same negative response path, until we establish a new and better experience with that particular situation. Once we respond differently—and feel a new and better emotion—our synapse system will offer the new response the next time we face the same circumstances. When we say, "If you keep doing what you're doing, you'll keep getting what you're getting," we are referring, to a degree, to this emotional system and the habits we form in negative situations.

We can either blame our response on what happened, or we can choose to practice restraint and master our emotional environments. Once the emotional fog settles, we can walk through the rationale of:

- "What is this emotion I'm feeling?"
- "What am I tempted to do or say at this point?"
- "What will be the emotional impact on the other party?"
- "Do I really want that impact to take place?"
- "How will this negative expression affect my view of self?"

SELLING WITH EQ

- Count the costs before you tell anyone how you really feel.
- Recognize the viral effect of negative expression and protect your reputation as a positive influence.

FIGURE 8.2 The Viral Spiral—Thinking It Through

Directions: *Think of an emotion that often/frequently/at times gets the better of you.*

1. What type of situation causes you to feel this emotion?

2. How do you typically respond to this emotion?
   a. My tone becomes _____
   b. My body language is _____
   c. I say _____
   d. My behavior is to _____

3. What do you think the emotional impact is on . . .
   a. Those you are angry with?

   b. The spectators watching the situation?

   c. Yourself—three to four hours after the dust has settled?

CHAPTER NINE

HOW TO PREVENT AND CONTAIN NEGATIVE OUTBURSTS

The Principles of Emotional Intelligence

- Distraction and diffusion are keys to containing negative emotions.
- Learning to take emotional responsibility helps to de-escalate negative impulses.

"I've always had a problem with becoming sarcastic and condescending when I am upset with someone. I knew it was a negative pattern and destructive to relationships, but I couldn't seem to contain it in the heat of battle. One day I saw a mature colleague, who was being confronted in a tense situation, calmly put his hand to his chin, get up, and walk away saying, 'Hmmm, I need to think about this.'

"I observed this and thought, 'If that had been me, I would have torn into that ignoramus on the spot.' I later asked my colleague about it, and he said, 'Like you, I thought of some clever retorts and put-downs, but I've found that there isn't much percentage in speaking them out loud. I always put my hand on my chin because it reminds me to think—and I just walk away and tell myself to try to find the humor in the situation. Then, when I'm in a better state, I come back to sort things out.' After I heard this, I started mimicking his response . . . and you know, it works!" —Jack K., Sales Representative

In her book, *Living Your Best Life: Discover Your Life's Blueprint for Success*, Laura Berman Fortgang says that "Blowing your stack spells trouble, but that doesn't mean you have to be a doormat." She offers some tips for using your wrath to fuel positive changes.

- *Repress and respect yourself.* When you lose it, people lose respect. Count to 100, take some deep breaths, go for a walk, talk to a friend, write it down and throw it away, or go play a sport. Do whatever, but do not open your mouth.
- *Think of constructive feedback to give to the person who made you mad.* Mistakes and faults are the result of certain strains in their lives. Help people find solutions instead of rubbing their noses in problems. In this way, you are helping them build the strengths they lack.
- *Examine yourself.* Do an honest assessment of why you are angry. Was it something that the person did or said? Maybe it is not really about the person. Maybe you are angry with yourself, your situation, or someone or something unconnected to this person or situation.
- *Use a gentle tone.* A soft answer turns away wrath. The controlled, soothing tone works wonders in an emotionally charged atmosphere to calm the turbulent seas of anger.

CHILL TACTICS

A century-old discovery of anger research is that one of the best ways to cool off after our rage is triggered is to cool off physically by waiting out the adrenal surge in a setting where the rage will not experience further provocation. This is why a walk in nature is so effective. I built a waterfall in my backyard because I found that the sound of running water causes a lucidity of thought that helps me when I am writing. A side benefit I discovered was its calming effect when I am having a stress-induced or anger-induced adrenal surge. Ten to fifteen minutes in the presence of the sound of running water soothes the storm in my emotional brain.

Zillman's anger research also revealed that distraction is a powerful mood-altering device, because staying angry is hard when you start having a pleasant time. The challenge is to allow your anger to cool enough to be able to have a pleasant time. Just as distraction is the chief tool of the magician in fooling his audience, so it is your chief tool in fooling your emotional brain back into a state of calm.

We all should have a "designated driver"—a mechanism for calming down—when we are under the influence of an adrenal surge. How do we bring ourselves back to a state of calm? How long does it typically take? An hour? A day? We must discover this mechanism for ourselves and have a plan rehearsed, or we will end up driving off the road in some relationship that matters to us. As a side note, it is worth noting that a police officer friend informed me that the most dangerous drivers on the road are not the drunken ones but the angry ones. So, if your mechanism for cooling down is to take a drive, it is advisable to find an alternative. There are probably better ways to cool off than getting behind the wheel of a two-ton machine capable of going over 100 miles per hour.

Rehearse your de-escalation plan by filling out the Chill Chart in Figure 9.1.

I believe in preparing and rehearsing responses for challenging emotional situations for the simple reason that it is very difficult to do the rational thing in the heat of the moment. As our systems heat up, our logic can deteriorate quickly into a tit-for-tat mentality.

CULPABILITY CONTAGION

The other day, at a business meeting, I asked an associate about a matter that I thought I had asked her to resolve for us. She responded by saying, "No, you didn't!" and began telling me the facts as she saw them. Others were watching our conversation and waiting for what they thought would be the inevitable argument over who was supposed to do what.

I thought about her version of the story and realized that she was correct, so I said, "I'm sorry, I was wrong."

One observer in the office asked, "What did you just say?"

"I was wrong," I answered.

"Excuse my shock," she said, "but I don't hear too many people say those words."

"Well," I assured her, "I've had plenty of opportunity to practice, having been wrong so many times."

Why are the words, "I was wrong," so hard to speak? Are we afraid this will be news to anyone? The more easily we admit our wrongs, the quicker we will be at fixing the situation. The best way to make things right is to be at ease admitting, "I was wrong."

I have noted that anger commonly builds in a predicament where the blame game is being played. I don't know too many people who actually

FIGURE 9.1 Chill Chart

1. When I am at my angriest, I cool down by . . .
   _____ Taking a long walk
   _____ Exercising (type of exercise_____)
   _____ Writing down my thoughts and feelings
   _____ Talking to a friend
   _____ Engaging in a hobby (type of hobby_____)
   _____ Listening to music
   _____ Other (_____)

2. When my anger is peaking, it typically takes me _____
   (minutes/hours/days/weeks/other) to cool off (anger/danger ratio).

3. The first physical signs that alert me to an adrenal overflow are:
   _____
   _____

4. The individuals whose actions provoke this adrenal rush in my system are:
   _____
   _____

5. Thought(s) I can focus on to keep my system calm when encountering these individuals
   is (are) (write thought(s) that help you to better understand their behavior):
   _____
   _____
   _____
   _____

enjoy admitting they are wrong. Such an admission is challenging both to the emotions and intellect. A hallmark of emotionally intelligent individuals, however, is their ability to admit the slightest degrees of culpability in a problem as a means of starting a daisy chain of admission. I have witnessed this phenomenon again and again.

Typically, when there is a problem, people become defensive and mentally rehearse their rebuttals, which inevitably lead to arguments, disagreements, and anger. This chain of hostility is easily broken when an emotionally intelligent leader says, "Well, I know I have some responsibility here in that I should have . . ." This gesture then gives permission to others to do the same. Will everyone be a willing participant in this process (including the most culpable individual)? Probably not—especially those who desperately lack EQ. But in such a case, their culpability is readily demonstrated by their lack of participation in the culpability contagion.

Many of the issues that stir up anger are based on miscommunication. Communication implies that at least two individuals are involved—one person intended to send a message, and another intended to receive. It does not always go as planned. We are often distracted and hurried and do not clearly and patiently communicate or listen to the message. This is why culpability can often be legitimately shared in miscommunication. If someone fails to act on our message, we must first look at the clarity of the message we sent.

SEEING THE "SPECK"

Introspection—looking at ourselves before we judge others—is the cornerstone of awareness upon which restraint is founded. The famous Biblical metaphor, about taking the log out of your eye before removing the speck out of your brother's eye, speaks of this sort of awareness. We can prevent viral spirals of emotion in our lives and businesses by first asking what role we played in contributing to the problem and, secondly, by analyzing why we allowed ourselves to become so upset. While we cannot stop the angry thoughts from coming, we can keep them from taking up permanent residence. The mouth—and the discipline to focus on ameliorative thoughts—is the steering wheel that controls the brain's anger chemistry. As I heard a preacher put it, "You can't stop birds from flying overhead, but you can stop them from building nests in your hair."

In the next chapter, we begin to unravel the stress mess that each of us wrestles with on a daily basis.

SELLING WITH EQ

- Delay your response until you've found a constructive way to respond to a negative behavior or outburst.
- Refuse to play the blame game. Fix the problem—instead of the blame.

10

SOLVING THE STRESS MESS

*"Resolve to be thyself: and know that he
who finds himself, loses his misery."*

—HANS SELYE, MD, *The Stress of Life*

The Principles of Emotional Intelligence

- The first step toward avoiding stressed-out reactions is predicting the environments that chronically trigger stress.
- Our evaluations of events have more to do with personal stress than the events themselves.
- Certain personality types are more susceptible to experiencing and transferring high stress levels.

LOOKS LIKE TROUBLE

Stress is any type of action or situation that places conflicting or heavy demands upon a person. Stress is any situation that chronically irritates or upsets a person. Do these two definitions sound like a typical day at work to you? Or a typical day at home? Or both? If so, you may need to focus your emotional faculties on getting on top of the *stress mess.*

Author H. Norman Wright, in his book, *Helping People in Crisis and Stress*, writes that there are three elements in stress: the environment, the evaluation of the environment, and the reaction of emotional and physio-logical arousal.

All a person has to do to become stressed out is *believe* that negative con-sequences will result from a certain environment or situation. The *appraisal* of the environment or situation becomes a ramp for the physical and emo-tional arousal. Although we would like to blame the event, person, or envi-ronment for the stress we feel, we ultimately are forced to look within, at our own appraisal habits, to see the blueprint for stress in our lives.

The first principle for managing stress is to take personal responsibil-ity for the ways we appraise and react. This principle could be articulated as "*I* am the issue." The way I interpret negative situations. The way I re-spond to environments that don't please me. The way I manage to com-municate with individuals who provoke a stress response in my system.

Do you feel a constant sense of urgency and hurry? Is there an under-current of tension in your words? Are you often frustrated about getting things done? If the answer is yes, the reason is stress.

Despite the daily to-do lists, deeper, under-the-surface stressors could be causing us to live in a chronically tense state; we don't feel valued by our company or supervisor; we are continually given more responsibility but not necessarily more training or pay; and we often feel a sense of job insecurity. Add to this that many people are feeling stress at home because of financial issues, insufficient personal or couple time, and/or children's behavior.

These environments cause stressors to multiply at the rate of microbes. But our levels of stress depend on how we personally appraise our situa-tions and how we decide to respond emotionally and physically. While the stresses we face are common, our methods for dealing with these stresses vary from person to person.

PREPAID INTEREST

I once heard stress defined as "interest paid on trouble before it is due." Many people have trouble comprehending that by worrying and stressing, they are paying out emotionally for that which they do not owe. Stress, being rooted in worry and anxiety, often assumes the absolute worst outcome as a starting point for appraisal; as a result, their reaction is over the top emotionally.

My boss looked at me funny. Oh no, my numbers haven't been very good this month. Maybe he's going to tell me something. What if. . . ? Why did we buy this house . . . and car. . . ? I shouldn't have left my last job. What was I thinking? What if my wife gets fed up and leaves with the kids? What am I going to do?

This is the sort of stressed-out, anxiety-driven thought process we can go into all on account of a funny look from the boss who may have just been grimacing because of gas. This appraisal—a sort of domino drop to disaster—is what Daniel Goleman refers to as an "emotional, low-grade melodrama." This is the phenomenon where the worrying mind spins in an endless loop of low-grade melodrama—one set of concerns leading on to the next and back again.

Worry is simply a rehearsal of what could go wrong *before* it goes wrong. This sort of obviation is helpful to our survival. In this sense, worry attempts to come up with positive solutions by anticipating dangers before they arrive. It is, of course, possible to do this type of forward thinking without having tension in our bodies and a churning sensation in our guts. When we plan ahead—without stress in our bodies—we transform worry into strategic planning.

For many people, worry is a chronic and repetitive appraisal that only serves to take them deeper into the bowels of stress and anxiety. They never actually get any nearer to the solution. Eventually a steady pulse of anxiety fuels their system, and they do not know how to operate outside of this stressed and worried state. They get locked into a myopic view of a worrisome topic. These appraisal tendencies and amygdala hijackings can progress into full-fledged anxiety disorders, obsessions, phobias, panic attacks, and compulsive behaviors.

HEAL THYSELF

Americans are swallowing pills and medicines at an all-time record pace, yet millions are still nowhere near getting at what truly ails them. (Americans reportedly consume 100 million antianxiety prescriptions every single day.) People take medicine to lessen emotional reactions to the threat of pain or failure. Unfortunately, medication also interferes with our ability to tolerate stress. Until people learn to confront and manage their anxieties, these dependencies will continue to escalate. In the long run, we are far better off developing behavioral methods of coping than we are trying to dissolve anxieties with a pill.

Sometimes the pills of life are bitter and hard to swallow. But taking this medicine is what life and growth are all about—facing fears, wrestling with anxieties, and controlling our appraisals and reactions to stress. The longer we put off this emotional medicine, the longer the road is to self-confidence and restraint.

In *Stress and the Healthy Family*, author Dolores Curran writes about some simple ground rules for getting personal victory over personal stress:

- Expect stress
- Focus on our strengths
- Focus on the stress—not the symptoms
- Focus on what is controllable

These ground rules are concerned with how we view stress and where we focus during stressful predicaments. Stress goes with the territory of life and work. If we are not prepared, we will be knocked off course when the storms of stress blow in. We need to recognize the temporary nature of stress and avoid developing permanent attitudes based on stress.

It is important to focus on our strengths, because much of the stress we face is the fear that we do not have the personal resources necessary to overcome problems. We need to focus on the source of stress, not on the person who carried it. Developing a solution is more important than placing the blame. Finally, we need to focus on what is controllable, because nothing causes more stress than trying to change things that can never be changed.

Having a set of ground rules such as these for coping could be a predictor of your own health and longevity. Dr. George Valiant, in his book, *Adaptation to Life,* showed that stress management is the most important predictor of physical health. He studied Harvard alumni over a period of 30 years. He found that men with immature coping styles became ill four times more often than men who demonstrated more mature, hardier coping styles.

How we cope with stressful events is truly a matter of life or death, and of wellness or weakness. Medical science has made great strides in recent years in understanding the physical/mental relationship of stress and our hormones, neuropeptides, and central nervous systems—which, in turn, can affect every system in the body, from the immune to the cardiovascular.

SUSCEPTIBLE PERSONALITIES

What personalities are most at risk? According to one expert, pushy, domineering types ultimately succeed in pushing their way right to the front of the line—at the morgue. Psychologist Michael Babyak reports that this trait is as toxic to the heart as hostility. He says these types are easy to spot. They monopolize conversations, interrupt people, and are driven by insecurity to be on top.

These domineering types differ significantly from those who have a healthy drive to succeed—those who are spurred on by self-confidence and a desire for personal fulfillment. Babyak's study showed that the pushy types were 60 percent more likely to die of all causes and die younger from heart disease than their more reserved peers. One possible explanation is that they stay juiced on their own adrenaline, therefore keeping their arteries bathed in stress hormones.

On the other hand, individuals who were the most calm and thoughtful in their speech patterns were the least likely to die during this particular study. Behavior does have an influence on our health. Babyak suggests taking more time to reflect and finding ways to relax. Developing a more pensive, introspective style will help us outlive the problems and the problem people we face.

Are you a type-A personality? The answer is most likely yes if you've found your success by driving, pushing, confronting, and thriving on stress. Quite frankly, sales organizations do well with this personality type. Traits such as high energy, driven, overachieving, and "won't take no for an answer" are descriptions of President's Club members and, possibly, individuals with many failed relationships, problems with alcohol, compulsions, or worse. Living in this highly adrenalized state has a dark side. For one thing, how does an individual come down from that state and feel normal?

Alcoholism researchers speculate that people who abuse alcohol are trying to medicate some sort of brain abnormality. Alcohol temporarily quells the symptoms of this abnormality; however, when the effects wear off, the symptoms return—all the more heightened. To keep these symptoms under control, individuals continue to drink even greater amounts at more frequent intervals, until they become dependent.

Dr. C. Robert Cloninger of Washington University has proposed two fundamental personality types among alcoholics. The first is anxious, inhibited, eager to please, and rigid. The second resembles an action hero—confident, impulsive, and constantly seeking new experiences. The sales ranks are filled with these two personality types.

Perhaps these problems are better addressed at a preventative level—at the juncture of a stressful event. The manner in which we appraise and respond at that moment determines the flow of stress hormones that will be released into our systems. Once a destructive appraisal and reaction takes place, long-ingrained negative patterns and destructive habits gain power over us.

Remember that, even if you don't struggle with any serious issues because of a highly charged state, you still may be bringing stress into other people's lives by virtue of your perpetually adrenaline-charged state. As one executive assistant told me when I asked if her boss was stressed out, "No, but he's definitely a carrier!"

SELLING WITH EQ

- Predict the sales scenarios that trigger stress, and prepare plans for managing those scenarios.
- Focus your energies on factors within your control.
- Find healthy ways of working stress out of your system.

CHAPTER ELEVEN

FEELING HELPLESS OR TAKING CHARGE

"Motivation will get you started, but it
is habit that keeps you going."

—JIM RYAN

The Principles of Emotional Intelligence

- To get on top of stress, we must first carefully identify the common and recurring sources of stress in our lives.
- Stress can be reduced and managed through changes in physical, attitudinal, and behavioral habits.
- Longevity and successful aging are linked to stress management habits.
- A ready wit and sense of humor not only lower stress but also attract others to you.

Medical science is not yet sure about the effect our mind has on causing or preventing cancer, but they do know that stress activates the body's endocrine system, which messes with the immune function. Robyn Post, in an article on lowering cancer risk, reported that researchers at the University of Pennsylvania injected mice with tumor cells, then gave them electric shocks. The mice were divided into two groups—one was allowed to escape, the other wasn't. The mice that lacked an escape route developed tumors at a much higher rate. One theory states that feeling helpless lowers the immune response, even for a mouse.

I think the mouse-in-the-maze experiment serves as a good metaphor for people who feel their careers and/or reactions to stress are caught in a type of repetitious pattern. They eventually feel helpless—and stress gains mastery over their emotions and their lives. Dr. Joan Borysenko, in her book, *Minding the Body, Mending the Mind,* talks about a study on stress with business executives and lawyers. Researchers found that the rates of illness could be lowered with the employment of three significant attitudes of hardiness toward stress:

1. *Commitment.* An attitude of curiosity and involvement in whatever is happening. Its opposite is alienation, denial, or escapism.
2. *Control.* The belief that we can influence events, coupled with the willingness to act on that belief rather than become a victim of circumstances. Its opposite is an attitude of helplessness.
3. *Challenge.* The belief that life's changes stimulate personal growth rather than threatening the status quo.

DEFINING THE MESS

In the ARROW Program workshop, I take participants through an exercise to identify the stress valves in their daily routines. Before we can adjust our appraisals and reactions, we need a better awareness of when and where these incidents keep cropping up. This way we won't be caught off guard.

The Stress MESS Exercise helps to increase your awareness by identifying the moods, environments, and stressful situations where you are most susceptible. Following is my personal worksheet (see Figure 11.1) that helped raise my awareness of the times, places, and events that I needed to place my emotional border control on full alert.

The exercise in Figure 11.2 will help you identify the sources of your stress.

If we listed every situation and personality that causes us to feel stress, the list would be voluminous. For the purpose of awareness, it is helpful to list the triggers that happen most frequently or that cause the most radical response in our systems. Awareness leads to preparation. Once we are aware of the types of moods, environments, and stressful situations that trigger these responses, we can begin to prepare new, more positive responses to stressful stimuli.

The next exercise, "Preparing for Restraint" (Figure 11.3), walks you through a commonly recurring, stressful scenario so you can rethink your response.

FIGURE 11.1 Awareness Worksheet

Moods. (states where I am most susceptible to stress and anger)
- Tired
- Hungry
- Facing a deadline

Environments. (settings that immediately cause me to feel stress and discomfort)
- Messy, disheveled environment
- Crowded area
- Roads without adequate signage
- Loud, boisterous environments

Stressful Situations. (types of situations and people who historically have caused me to feel stressed)
- Disorganized situations
- Working with organizations that can't make decisions
- Working with defensive, argumentative types
- Dealing with individuals who slough off responsibility
- Working with those who don't care about quality of work
- Waiting a long time for an appointment
- Working with individuals who want to do little work yet reap a lot of credit
- Dealing with those who don't pay bills in a timely manner
- Dealing with control freaks

If you can apply this thought process toward the stressful scenarios, environments, and moods you wrestle with at home, in the field, or with the home office, you soon will find that you are no longer being blown about by the winds of stress and emotion but are, in fact, adjusting your sails and getting the most mileage possible from those winds.

AGELESS ATTITUDES

Can we learn anything from people who live to 100? Science believes so and has been, in recent years, paying close attention to both the physical and psychological habits of centenarians. One study conducted by Harvard Medical School tested subjects' intellectual abilities and personality patterns to see if a "centenarian personality" could be found. The study found these psychological patterns:

92

FIGURE 11.2 The Stress MESS Exercise

Moods. (states where I am most susceptible to stress and anger)

Environments. (settings that immediately cause me to feel stress and discomfort)

Stressful Situations. (types of situations and people who historically have caused me to feel stressed)

FIGURE 11.3 Preparing for Restraint

Reasons for this Skill:
- Stress is harmful to body, psyche, and relationships.
- Without preparation, stress hormones control our physical and emotional state.
- Preparation lays the ax to the root of stress.
- If tense and highly strung, you are a carrier of stress.

Identify a recurring stressful situation. _____

_____

_____

Describe your emotions and response in this situation. _____

_____

_____

What could you do to prevent this situation from recurring? _____

_____

_____

What communication needs to take place? _____

_____

_____

If you are unable to prevent this situation from recurring, how can you change your
response to experience less stress? _____

_____

_____

> *God grant me the serenity,*
>
> *To accept the things I cannot change,*
>
> *The courage to change the things I can,*
>
> *And the wisdom to know the difference.*

- Most of them knew about stress management before the term was ever invented.
- They rarely show anger.
- They tend not to fret.
- They have a good sense of humor.

Sounds an awful lot like emotional intelligence, doesn't it? Controlling stress, anger, and anxiety, and keeping a ready wit? Even though all of these subjects had suffered multiple losses of spouses, siblings, and/or friends, they somehow learned to work through these difficulties and forge ahead. Researcher Margery Silver noted that they seemed to be "low in neuroticism and high in conscientiousness" and most often "dependable at home and on the job."

Living long is about good habits and ageless attitudes. This is where you want to focus if you truly want to outlast your competition.

FIRED UP OR BURNED OUT

What is the difference between being fired up or burned out with the work you do?

According to a recent "Professional Work Force" survey by Peter McLaughlin Co., it could be one simple thing: whether or not you possess a good sense of humor. According to this survey, a sense of humor helps on the job in three specific ways:

1. People with a sense of humor are three times as likely to report top levels of energy than those who don't have a sense of humor.
2. Ninety percent of survey respondents believe that having a sense of humor helps them to perform better at work.
3. People with a sense of humor are half as likely to get anxious or frustrated fixing a problem and are twice as likely to be able to pull themselves out of a bad mood.

A ready wit holds some powerful personal keys to success:

- People who laugh often don't run out of fuel as quickly as the dead serious.
- People who can laugh at their mistakes are quicker to correct them and therefore perform better.
- People who laugh easily are in better control of their moods and attitudes.

A key to staying fired up is to laugh easily and laugh often.

SOMETHING HAS TO GIVE

Stress and laughter cannot exist in the same place at the same time. If you don't believe that, lift a 50-pound weight, have someone tell you a really funny joke, and see what gives. Stress and laughter fail to coexist not only in physical space but in psychological space as well. Laughter has a purging effect on stress hormones. Nurturing your sense of humor and keeping a ready wit are key weapons in your arsenal against the stress hormone rushes and potential amygdala hijacks.

A sense of humor helps to:

- Change your perspective in the situation (remember the importance of *appraisal* in triggering stress)
- Clear your thinking
- Attract other people to you

Almost every assessment or appraisal of a situation we face offers the opportunity to view that situation through a humorous lens. Like one mother commented, "Laughing at your problems is like changing a baby's dirty diaper. It doesn't change anything permanently but it does make things more livable for a while." If you want to transcend the stress mess in your own world, you'll have to form the habit of keeping your sense of humor by attempting to see a comedic lining in every cloud.

- When you find out your new company has a new job opening, but it's your job that opened . . . keep your sense of humor.
- When a client tells you that you and your company are so good they can no longer afford you . . . keep your sense of humor.
- When your spouse comes home from shopping and says he just saved $500 dollars . . . keep your sense of humor.
- When your teenager comes home and tells you the family lineage is not at risk . . . keep your sense of humor.
- When your spouse runs off with your best friend and you realize just how much you miss *your friend* . . . keep your sense of humor.
- When your ship finally comes in and you see that it's a garbage barge . . . keep your sense of humor.

Life can be sour without laughter.
The minutes go like hours.
Without laughter,
The days can be trying.
And in life there's no denying,
That the ones who are surviving,
Can be heard laughing.

Why does laughter work? Because laughter releases the endorphins in the brain that help rinse out the stress hormones. Little did we know that we had so much control over our brain chemistry—it is there to serve us, not to make us slaves. The opportunities to practice restraint and emotional intelligence confront us each day as we meet events and people that disturb our peace. Pay attention to your body's signals, reappraise the situation, and respond in a way that restores order to your system.

CLIMBING THE WALL

My final thought is a question based on a Steven Covey principle, "Is your ladder of success leaning against the wrong wall?" If you're doing everything you can to manage stress in your sales career but can't quite get on top of it, you might be climbing against the wrong wall. I have met many people who had a constant undercurrent of stress in their lives simply because they were either cut out for a different type of work or needed to work in a different environment.

Stress is not something to be downplayed. Conquer stress, or it will conquer you. While you will always experience a degree of stress in your life, you will find life much more manageable and fulfilling when you experience life doing something you love. Find a working scenario that brings your hands, head, and heart together.

SELLING WITH EQ

- Stay aware of the moods, events, and stressful situations where you are most vulnerable.
- Make stress awareness management a priority in your work and life.
- Use your sense of humor to keep yourself afloat in stressful times.

CHAPTER TWELVE

REDEFINING OPTIMISM

The Principles of Emotional Intelligence

- Optimism is grounded in a sense of hope and is the naturally intended state for the human psyche.
- Attitude is a matter of direction, not feeling.
- The leading predictor for personal productivity is your own level of personal expectations.

To begin this discussion on resilience and its relationship to outlook, complete the "Resilience Reactor" in Figure 12.1.

The difference between getting beat up or bouncing back is, more often than not, decided on how we process the events happening to us and around us. This processing at the emotional level eventually casts us in a mold of decided optimism, pessimism, or cynicism. Once this mold is cast, people have a hard time steering their thoughts and reactions in a new direction.

In this chapter, I discuss the importance of nurturing a resilient mindset and the role optimism plays in that process. Optimism is the lifeblood of great sales professionals, but like everyone else, even the great ones are tempted to give in and give up.

FIGURE 12.1 Resilience Reactor

Directions: *Read each statement and circle the number that best describes you.*

1. When I am rejected,

1	2	3	4	5
I retreat		I vacillate		I move on

2. When I fail,

1	2	3	4	5
I feel like giving up		I vacillate		I quickly change my approach

3. When I can't find an answer,

1	2	3	4	5
I resist help/counsel		I vacillate		I seek help/counsel

4. When I get a good idea,

1	2	3	4	5
I talk myself out of it		I vacillate		I forge ahead with conviction

5. When I don't meet my goals,

1	2	3	4	5
I search for excuses/rationalize	I vacillate			I take personal inventory

6. When confronted with a problem,

1	2	3	4	5
I complain and make excuses	I vacillate			I begin creating a plan

7. When circumstances conspire against me,

1	2	3	4	5
I feel unlucky/cursed		I vacillate		I salvage from the experience

8. My attitude toward each day . . .

1	2	3	4	5
I allow others to affect me		I vacillate		I set my emotional compass

9. When I do something stupid or embarrassing,

1	2	3	4	5
I beat myself up		I vacillate		I laugh it off

10. When confronted with a mistake,

1	2	3	4	5
I rationalize my actions		I vacillate		I quickly admit my error

Total [   ]

EVERYONE GETS TIRED

Norm was at an all-time low. He took the pile of pages (his manuscript and life's passion) and threw it in the garbage. That was it. Forty-plus rejections from 40 different publishers were quite enough. His hopes had been raised and dashed one too many times.

Norm's wife, Ruth, came into the room and was horrified to see his book in the garbage. She went to pull it out.

He said, "I forbid you to take that out. I've had enough."

Ruth was troubled. She didn't want to go against her husband's wishes, but neither did she want to see his life's work go to the landfill. He had been rejected so many times by so many people that he had finally run out of energy—even though he had always had so much energy.

She decided to follow his wishes—well, sort of. She left the manuscript in the garbage, wrapped it up, and sent it to one more publisher.

The publisher took notice. He'd never before received a manuscript in a garbage container. He read her explanatory note and then the manuscript. He decided to publish. Little did he realize it would become one of the top-sellers of all time.

The author? Norman Vincent Peale.

The book? *The Power of Positive Thinking.*

—Excerpt from *The Daily Dose*

Even the most optimistic of personalities is bound to suffer dejection and see his optimistic attitude wane in times of rejection, defeat, and adversity. If it happened to Norm, it's probably going to happen to you and me. Optimism is the lifeblood of anyone who hopes to succeed in the selling profession. Those who allow themselves to be seduced into pessimistic thinking patterns and cynical synapses poison their own lifeblood.

DEFAMATION BY USAGE

If you pay close attention to the way people use the word *optimist* and to the way people respond when you tell them that you are an *optimist,* you might find that not everyone has a high regard for the idea. The unnecessary baggage the word has picked up in its journey to modern usage disturbs me. Many have loaded their own personal baggage onto this word—which more than likely describes their former approach to matters before things went badly. To hear some people describe the optimist, you would think they were talking about a wide-eyed, naïve, country-bumpkin type that conjures up images of Gomer Pyle saying, "Why Gooollllyy, Sarge, ain't that great!"

I have heard the pseudo-intellectual describe the state of optimism as being in a place outside of the great circle of knowledge, as if the attitude of optimism could only be held by the uninformed. I have come to the conclusion that the words *optimism* and *pessimism* have evolved through usage to a place where many no longer have a clear comprehension of their meanings. The definitions of words do evolve over time—some for good and some for bad. For example, the word *adult* used to mean *mature,* and now it represents pornographic content. I think the same thing has happened to the word *optimism,* which for some has gained the undeserved connotation of "not being realistic." On the flip side, the word *pessimism* has garnered undeserved credibility.

To give clarity to both words, allow me to define them by their etymological root. The word *pessimistic* means to be *hopeless* and the word *optimistic* means to be *hopeful.* These two views are not about being "realistic about what is going to happen" vs. "looking at the situation through rose-colored glasses." These two views are about looking at any and every situation with an attitude of hope versus an attitude of despair or hopelessness.

Pessimism doesn't simply look at a glass of water as being half empty. It looks at a glass of water as being foul and declares, "It's surely contaminated and good for nothing." The optimist doesn't simply look at a glass of water as being half full but sees the potential in the water to nourish a plant, quench thirst, make ice, or produce hydrogen. The two words are nothing more than a dichotomous play on the word *hope.*

Skepticism is healthy but, when overused, can soon segue into a slippery slope that drains into a cesspool of cynicism. I have met more than a few rusty and crusty sales professionals who were careless about protecting their attitude and went down the slope from skepticism to pessimism to cynicism, failing to realize the impact on their selling relationships. These words warrant a glance into *Webster's Dictionary* to fully understand the footings of such attitudes.

- *Skep'tic.* One who habitually doubts matters generally accepted
- *Pess'i'mist.* The tendency always to expect the worst (secondary meaning—the belief that the evil in life outweighs the good)
- *Cyn'i'cal.* Denying the sincerity of people's motives and actions

And while we're at it, the original meaning of the word *sarcasm* sheds some light as well.

- *Sar'casm.* To bite the lips in rage

Notice the spiraling graduation of attitude that can easily infect a vulnerable emotional state. While the skeptic *doubts* or *suspects* the credibility of a situation or proposed solution, the pessimist takes it a step further and *expects* the worst to happen. By the time an individual degrades into this state of chronic cynicism, she now *believes* in insincerity to the point that she doesn't trust anyone's motives.

We are all at times, and with good reason, in a transitory state of skepticism, pessimism, or cynicism. Skepticism in and of itself is good. We don't want to take all matters at face value. It is essential to think through every situation, refine our approach, and critique conventional wisdom. We will, at times, be pulled into a cynical frame of mind when we are listening to those who have a track record of duplicity, spuriousness, and self-centeredness.

These responses are to be expected, but we must be on guard so that we do not allow these attitudes to become a permanent emotional state. This slippery slope to cynicism ultimately lowers our emotional intelligence and has a dangerous effect on relationships.

Furthermore, for the pessimists who cloak themselves in intellectual patter and call themselves realists, I have come to the belief that pessimism is little more than an exercise in intellectual laziness. Once pessimists declare that "It won't work," they are released from any cerebral, volitional, or imaginative responsibilities. Once you declare that failure is imminent, your work is over.

On the other hand, optimists, who are emotionally anchored in hope, declare, "We'll find a way to make this work!" and begin to utilize their full potential of rationality, imagination, and will.

EXPECTATIONS

Peter Brennan, who has been managing sales professionals for over two decades in the electronics industry, told me this.

"When I first started selling, I thought the word *attitude* was a bunch of motivational hot air used by my manager to get me to sell more. Back in those days, I figured it was all about ability and little else. But over time, my opinion has evolved full circle to the point that I think attitude is the single most important factor that determines success in the sales profession.

"Show me two people with equal ability and equal opportunity but with differing attitudes, and over time you will see two distinct productivity charts going in opposite directions. I have found that the optimistic attitude is inextricably tied to a tireless work ethic.

They keep going because they are convinced that the next great opportunity is just around the corner. The more rejection they face, the more anticipation they possess because they figure the law of averages is now in their favor."

When I asked him about an example of this phenomenon, he shared the following.

"We hired this kid who was sharp looking, well spoken, and understood our products and the industry—a real find, we all thought in the interview process. After a few months, this can't-miss talent hadn't sold enough to pay his per diem food bill, and I decided to ride along with him to figure out the problem. He went through all the selling procedures exactly as he was taught. When he surveyed the holes in the customers' inventory and presented his ideas, he was thorough and articulate. When the customer would hesitate and offer some rationale for not doing business with him, he would start nodding, repeat what he'd already said, and literally check out of the call.

"When the day was over, I asked him to review what was going on through his mind *before* he got to each of the stops we had made that day. He gave impressive and detailed accounts of what he knew about each client's business. He had done his homework.

"I asked him, 'Did you think you'd get the sale before you walked in the door?'

"He looked at me as if to say, 'Do you really want to know the truth?'

"I said, 'Tell me what you were expecting.'

"He said, 'I knew before I walked in there what they were going to say. I figured I was probably wasting my time but went through the motions anyway.'"

Brennan knew then and there that this young man had chosen the wrong career path. It is one thing to anticipate possible objections but an altogether different matter to expect no results.

Brennan summarized it this way.

"I learned a lot from that ride-along. I now tell new guys that optimism is the key to every conversation. I tell them the story of our talented wonder-boy and how the weight of a pessimistic attitude took him to the bottom. I tell them that those who carry pessimistic expectations are like the guy who walks in not knowing he's got a tomato stain on his tie. People are going to notice, and he's going to be baffled by their response to him. You can never surpass your expectations—and the pessimist is always looking for rationale for *not* succeeding."

THE ATTITUDE INSTRUMENT

My first (and only) flight lesson was an event I'll not soon forget. My instructor had a strange approach to teaching flying. He'd get you up to about 10,000 feet and then start hollering instructions. This teaching process tended to be a bit unnerving, especially on a first lesson.

Shortly into the flight, he began to yell, "Look at your attitude."

I replied, "What? I'm fine."

"No," he said. "Your attitude!"

"Why is he concerned with my mental approach?" I wondered.

He looked at me like I was an idiot, "Look at your attitude instrument."

"What's that?" I asked.

He pointed to an instrument that showed where the wings were in relationship to the horizon. It seemed my wings were a bit tilted. We were going to land all right, but not on the wheels. He then showed me how to level my wings or, in other words, how to straighten out my attitude. When we reached the ground, I realized that I had learned a good lesson from a poor teacher. —*The Daily Dose*

Whenever people talked about attitude, I thought they were talking about feeling positive emotions—which I thought was just a put-on. That day, I found that attitude is nothing more than keeping yourself headed toward your stated goals or keeping your wings pointed to your personal horizon. I also realized that those who have not defined a personal horizon quickly fall prey to dangerous attitudes.

If the winds of adversity and discouragement blow you off course, don't give up. Rather, make the necessary adjustments and keep moving toward your goal. Attitude is not a feeling; it is a mental adjustment we must make a hundred times a day or more, if we want to reach our horizons.

Attitude, in its literal form, is nothing more than adjusting to interfering winds and circumstances in pursuit of personal goals or horizons. Those winds may be blowing in from the home office, and the circumstance may be permanent, but the person who understands attitude and the need for optimism simply adjusts as often as necessary. Ultimately, our progress and performance depend on where we set those horizons. It is helpful to sit back every now and then and ask ourselves, "Am I setting my goals high enough to challenge my capabilities?"

MENTAL BARRIERS

A great story is told about farm boys recruited and trained to be pilots in the pilot shortage crisis during World War II.

With the sudden outbreak of World War II, the U.S. Air Force found themselves with a shortage of pilots. They recruited farm boys from the Midwest and gave them their wings. This group of men one day brought forth the ingenuity and design of the first supersonic jet.

This design team was not trained in the classical schools of aeronautical engineering like their predecessors. Had they been trained like the others, they would have been taught that flying past the speed of sound was impossible. In those days, the aeronautic engineering schools taught that supersonic flight was unattainable because:

- The weight of the fuel required would make the plane too slow and cumbersome.
- Reaching the speed of sound would cause spontaneous combustion, and the plane would blow up.

When questioned about how they had achieved such a remarkable feat, these men replied, "We did it because nobody told us we couldn't."

The barriers we cross in our lives may not be as dramatic as the sound barrier, but we too must overcome the scrutiny of "experts" or those who believe there is only one way of doing things. Remember, those who tell us "we can't" are usually those who "didn't." Barriers of achievement are meant to be broken—no matter what the "experts" teach. —*The Daily Dose*

SELF-SABOTEURS

My personal epiphany regarding a personal lack of resilience and weak expectations taught me a lasting lesson about shutting down the self-sabotaging voice that whispers when we embark on a new mission. I was driving home from a speech and listening to an audiotape from the *Chicken Soup for the Soul* series. It told a story about an 88-year-old lady who was asked about the regrets she had in life.

She said, "I have very few regrets about what I have done. But what I regret most are the things I didn't do. Ideas I wish I had acted on and the possibilities I never explored—all because of the foolish and flimsy excuse that I might fail. So what? So I failed. What would it have really mattered?"

Her answer stung me like a swarm of hornets.

A retrospective film began to play in my mind about the scores of ideas I had come up with, where an initial burst of enthusiasm had been popped by the first hint of disapproval from another. At that point, I would begin talking myself out of wasting my efforts by taking the idea any further. I now realize that this self-sabotaging mechanism was nothing more than a pessimistic monster that I kept alive by yielding to it. Pessimism becomes its own self-fulfilling prophecy as "I can't" evolves into "I won't."

After hearing this inspiring story, I vowed to myself and heaven that with my next idea, things would be different, and I would choose a more resilient and aggressive posture (and march right past the rejections and self-doubts). Ironically, I was tested in very short order.

Two days later, I received a phone call from the *Chicken Soup for the Soul* organization. Someone had heard a speech of mine and had suggested my name as a potential contributor for their next book. I agreed to put together a couple of stories for them. As I was looking at my short stories, something began stirring inside of me, but I couldn't clearly determine what it was.

That night at about 3:00 AM, I was awakened with a very clear picture of what I should do next. I saw the scripts in my head and the idea that came to me was to read those stories on the radio and to call them *The Daily Dose*. I was immediately excited about the idea and experienced my typical initial burst of enthusiasm.

The next morning I woke up and began to think through this idea. The self-sabotaging mechanism kicked in immediately. "Why would any radio station air a 90-second story? You don't know anyone to talk to, even at the local AM talk radio station," were the first rounds fired out of my own pessimistic artillery.

Remembering the promise to myself, I decided to call my father, a veteran of over 45 years in the radio business, for his opinion. My father is not one to hand out insincere flattery. I knew he would tell me the truth about my idea. I read two stories to him, and he was silent for a moment, then slowly uttered in his dramatic basso profundo, "Son, you've got something special there. Get on the phone and call your local station. Ask for someone in advertising. If they like it, they'll find someone to sponsor it."

I called the local station and talked to an account executive who told me I should record my stories and drop them off at the station. I dropped the tape off that day with a note saying the cost would be $200 per month and they would receive 20 stories each month. Two days later, I received a call saying the program director and account executive wanted to meet with me.

To open the meeting, the program director informed me that "They loved the show idea and wanted to play it in the morning and evening drive times." He then let the other shoe drop and said, "But we want you to know that the only programming we pay for is Rush Limbaugh and the Minnesota Twins baseball—and you are neither one of those." They then offered to trade the program for 40 seconds of advertising space that I could sell to a sponsor of my choosing. We shook hands and the show was launched locally.

One of my first sponsors was a new business enterprise that was expanding rapidly, and they decided to fund efforts to offer *The Daily Dose* to other stations. Within 9 months, the show was airing on over 160 stations around the country and is still going strong today with over 1 million listeners daily.

When I think of the number of people hearing these inspirational stories and ideas every day, I wipe my brow in relief that I did not succumb to my former pessimistic habits. My personal pessimism had been arrested— and the benefit was being felt by hundreds of thousands of people daily.

Adversity and difficulty are not the enemies to fear—pessimism is. Pessimism aborts ideas in the embryonic stage, ignores the possibilities, and complains about the noise opportunity makes when it knocks.

I've also observed this fact about pessimists: they live very predictable lives. I am an optimist, if for no other reason than a hopeful attitude keeps the doors of opportunity swinging and makes every day feel like an adventure.

Optimism is the state we were born for. If we have lost our optimism, we must recover hope in our emotional reactions to life's challenges. An optimistic attitude is not something we wait to feel; it is a direction we choose. We will never surpass the expectations we have for ourselves. Optimism is our greatest gift—as we follow its pulse, optimism opens up possibilities of personal achievement that we never dared dream possible. Hope knows no boundaries.

SELLING WITH EQ

- Keep pessimistic expectations in check. Your achievements must surpass your expectations.
- Make an attitude adjustment several times daily, especially when encountering negative people, discouraging reports, and disappointing results.
- Be on guard for self-sabotaging thoughts, speech, and behavior. Take your name off your enemy list.

CHAPTER THIRTEEN

SOURCES OF DISCOURAGEMENT

"Hope deferred makes the heart sick, but
when the desire comes, it is a tree of life."

—PROVERBS. 13:12

The Principles of Emotional Intelligence

- Discouragement can be traced to three sources. Recognizing the source is the first step in overcoming discouragement.
- We must develop a learning response to stay on top of failure, disappointment, and adversity.

Eric called and sounded downcast. He had taken a senior-level sales management position for a top financial firm that held high expectations for him. He had been successful at every turn except for the last job, which he had left after the market debacle of 2000–2001. His current employer was launching into new territory that Eric was familiar with, and they were banking heavily on his ability to get doors open. He told me he was discouraged with the pace of his progress. He was working at 150 percent but getting 75 percent results.

Mary was also discouraged. She loved her company and the industry (medical equipment) and felt she was well suited to the job. She told me her discouragement was so pervailing that she was nearing depression over her poor performance. Mary has a winsome personality, is intelligent, and carries herself with confidence. Her sales goals hinged disproportionately on the business she garnered from two major clinics. She had developed great relationships with the decision makers at both clinics; unfortunately, both decision makers had left for greener pastures in the last four months.

New decision makers had entered the picture with the predictable "need to prove that I know more than the last person" approach to the job. As luck would have it, both were defensive and highly sensitive personalities—mirror opposites of their predecessors. Both took the posture that all vendor relationships, no matter how long they had been established, should come under the scrutiny of due diligence usually reserved for new relationships. Consequently, Mary was facing a logjam, and she began beating herself up wondering where she was going wrong in her approach.

Brent was down in the dumps because he was seeing an abnormally high number of contract opportunities not being accepted in his consulting and training business. He was also getting cancellations on previously booked business. Financial pressures had created a barely perceptible tone of desperation in his voice. He admitted he was discouraged but was determined to stay positive. He blamed the economy, acquisitions and mergers, misunderstandings, and self-centered partners for his troubles. After a couple of conversations with Brent, it became apparent that he was not the most emotionally intelligent individual who ever walked the earth. He is assuming, in-your-face pushy, combative, and flippant.

Eric, Mary, and Brent are three sales professionals all suffering from what, on the surface, would appear to be the same malady—discouragement. But are they? When I finished conversing with these three individuals, I realized that, although they all gave themselves the same diagnosis, they were not suffering from the same affliction. No doubt they were all discouraged, but the causes of their personal discouragement emanated from three distinctly different sources.

When people become discouraged, they are often inclined to attach a sense of personal failure to their discouragement. "If I had done that, this might not have happened." While introspection is good in times of discouragement, beating ourselves up over circumstances beyond our control is not. The three cases cited above are perfect examples of the three distinctly different origins for discouragement.

In Brent's case, the discouragement is clearly brought on by his personal *failure* in the way he communicates with others and unawareness of his agitating behaviors. Mary's case is one of discouragement brought on by *disappointment* stirred up by the impeding and frustrating actions of others. Eric's air of discouragement is rooted in general *adversity*, in which circumstances have conspired to cause a dip in his productivity, despite his tireless efforts and willingness to rethink his approach to business. Failure, disappointment, and adversity are the chief bandits of optimism and encouragement; however, these three are easily muddled into a stewing sense of failure and pessimism.

An effective and liberating exercise is to examine our personal sources of discouragement (when we are feeling the weight of those emotions) to assess if we are unnecessarily being pulled into a quagmire of negative thought patterns. Let's start by offering facile definitions of these chief sources of discouragement.

- *Failure.* Where my actions are the chief cause of the situation
- *Disappointment.* Where others have caused these circumstances
- *Adversity.* Where circumstances have formed an obstacle

Far too often, the sales professional who carries disappointment concerning the actions (or inaction, as the case may be) of another internalizes the discouragement through a lens of personal failure. On the other side of the issue, there are those who blame others or adverse circumstances for their discouraged states, when they have failed to make the efforts necessary to succeed.

To assess your resilience in regards to these three separate sources of discouraging thought, take the short assessment in Figure 13.1. This self-assessment should help you to isolate your vulnerable areas.

THE LEARNING RESPONSE

Every time we encounter the three faces of discouragement—failure, disappointment, and adversity—we have the opportunity to respond either optimistically (with hope) or pessimistically (without hope). In studying the character traits of the most resilient sales professionals, one characteristic that quickly rises to the surface is the ability to maintain a hopeful attitude by means of employing the *learning response.* These individuals have trained themselves to respond to negative situations with the thought, "What can I learn from this situation that will make me better the next time I face it?"

In her book, *If Life Is a Game, These Are the Rules,* Cherie Carter Scott shares the following two fundamental rules of life.

1. Life is a series of lessons.
2. If you don't learn the first time, the lesson will be repeated until you do learn.

FIGURE 13.1 Sources of Discouragement

There are three sources from which discouragement develops in our minds. They are:

1. *Failure.* Where I am responsible for my situation
2. *Disappointment.* Where others have caused adverse circumstances
3. *Adversity.* Where circumstances have formed an obstacle

Rank yourself on these three areas and add up the total.

FAILURE

1	2	3	4	5

Beat myself up   Learn from it
Give up easily   Move on

DISAPPOINTMENT

1	2	3	4	5

Harbor bitterness   Understand human weakness
Fantasize about revenge   Forgive others

ADVERSITY

1	2	3	4	5

Feel like I have bad luck   Feel gratitude for what I have
Something always goes wrong   Look for growth opportunity

Total: [   ]

$3 - 6$ **Low Resilience**
$7 - 11$ **Up and Down**
$12 - 15$ **High Resilience**

These rules are fairly evident in the world of sales. Some people continue to make the same mistakes over and over and grow pessimistic and cynical because of a lack of results, yet fail to ask, "What is it about *me* that is causing this to happen repeatedly?" This fundamental lack of awareness segues easily to a lack of resilience.

Emotionally intelligent sales professionals, on the other hand, are in a mind-set of perpetual introspection and learning. When they fail, their hair-trigger emotion is not to fix the blame but to fix the problem—which could very likely be within them.

We all have stories to tell of responding both positively and negatively to negative stimuli in our careers. We have all experienced the harvests of negative and positive emotional reactions. In the case of failure, most of us can think of times when we embarked upon beating ourselves up and went into a dark spiral of discouragement, our enthusiasm zapped. On the other hand, we can probably also remember times where we failed and instead made a concerted mental effort to take notes and improve from each experience.

CARRY-ON BAGGAGE

In the case of disappointment, you can more than likely remember a time when someone treated you unjustly or thoughtlessly and you spent emotional energy in fantasizing revenge and harboring bitterness. On the emotionally intelligent side of disappointment, possibly you can remember a time where you chose to take a more understanding and forgiving approach—and moved on with your life. Arguments could be made from physiological, spiritual, and moral vantage points regarding the redeeming value of letting go of old injuries and moving forward with life. The deleterious effects of an embittered spirit are well documented in medical journals, which chronicle the declining effect upon one's physical health from holding on to old grudges. In this discussion, however, I want to focus on the emotional impact on others that results from hanging on to old baggage.

We all know people who are so devoid of trust that their suspicion and sensitivity become an unpleasant odor they carry into every relationship. Usually this emotional posturing can be traced back to a disappointing circumstance or experience they have experienced in their work histories. Those lacking resilience grow bitter and cynical when they get burned and consequently develop a lens of suspicion through which they filter every conversation and relationship. On the other hand, the emotionally resilient individual, who has a similar experience, grows wiser and more cautious but does not allow yesterday's toxins to pollute the air in today's dialogues.

Words and phrases such as *touchy, thin-skinned, chip on the shoulder, carrying too much baggage, oversensitive,* and *living in the past* describe the negative reactions people have to this unattractive, even repelling disposition.

If you personally struggle with bitterness, keep in mind that it is an emotional toxin that will find its way into relationships where it is not welcome. Others may be more aware than you are of your emotional competence in this area. My suggestion is to do whatever is necessary to remove these toxins from your emotional storehouse. Seek psychological or spiritual counsel if necessary, but do not fool yourself into thinking that this "virus" will not get in the way of your productivity. If you do not believe me, ask yourself a very simple question, "Do I know someone who has a hard and bitter edge, who is quick to go on a negative rant? How much do I enjoy talking to that individual?"

You cannot be in business and not incur some injuries in the process. The roadway is crowded and almost everyone is driving over the speed limit. The sales profession is a contact sport (think demolition derby). If you are not prepared for this and had hoped for something more akin to badminton, you will find yourself nursing some serious injuries the first time you take a blind-side hit. As one sales veteran put it, "You are going to get hit in this game, and how hurt you get depends on how prepared you are for the hit."

Perhaps you've seen those NFL film clips where a quarterback's career ended on one brutal sack from his blind side that he wasn't prepared for. To play the sales game with resilience, you have to be aware of the many sacks that will come in the form of disappointment. Clients will let you down. Stay alert, keep a positive disposition, and look downfield. When you get knocked down, dust yourself off, nurse the wound, and keep your eyes open. Resilience can be a little more challenging, however, when the hit comes from the home office.

Vince has been with the same company for over 25 years. He has been a star performer as an account executive, state manager, and regional manager in that time. He builds lasting relationships with his clients and his sales force. He is venerated by most of his troops as being the most loyal person they have ever known, which is a rare commodity in today's marketplace. Recently he told me about the most trying period of his career.

"A top-level position opened up, and he was the obvious choice for the job. For some inexplicable reason that could only be justified in the labyrinth of politics that is the home office, Vince was passed over, and the position was given to a person 15 years his junior with a production record that wasn't even half as good as Vince's record. This move dealt a serious blow to Vince's psyche. But the knockout punch was yet to come.

"The first thing this fellow did when he was promoted above Vince was to call him in and tell him he was moving him from the central region to the south. Vince had been in this region for 12 years and had developed an incalculable number of meaningful relationships with employees and clients. He was loved and respected as a leader. The hypocrisy of his company was almost more than he could bear. They preached that their business success hinged on building good relationships, yet they were pulling the footings out from under all the relationships he had built over a dozen years.

"The pain for Vince was profound. He told me, 'When they passed me over, they took out my heart, and when they took me away from all the people I cared about, they took away my soul.'"

But Vince is an emotionally intelligent individual. I saw him after the painful regional switch during his first meeting with his new people. There was never a word, tone, or nuance of speech to betray his injury. To hear him talk, you would think that he wanted nothing more than to spend his career helping this group become successful. He had confronted his disappointment, dealt with it, learned some difficult lessons, and moved forward with the sentiments that had helped him become successful in the first place— empathy for others, the desire to teach, and competitive instincts. As Vince learned, resilience is not about ignoring reality. It is about dealing with reality and dealing with it in a way that does not poison future relationships.

THIRD-PARTY OPPOSITION

The third source of a discouraged state of emotion is adversity. This is not trouble of our own or of another person's doing but a situation where circumstances beyond our control have conspired to form difficulty. We can adopt a learning response to adversity as well as to failure and disappointment. Some people draw pessimistic conclusions when they face adversity and basically decide that they are unlucky or that things just always seem to go bad. Soon they begin to work with the expectation that no matter how nice a sandcastle they build, the surf is going to come in and wipe it out. The more resilient individual has an altogether different way of processing adversity.

I asked a number of successful and seasoned sales professionals how they dealt with circumstances beyond their control that affected their success. Following are some of the notable phrases to come out of that discussion.

- "If it's hard times in the economy, then that means the weaker players are going to get shaken out. When the going gets tough . . ." (This is a time when survival skills are tested and survivors thrive.)

- "I figure my competition is in the same place I'm in. I'm simply going to attempt to show a better face than my competitors. I'm going to stay in touch with my clients even when they're not buying, because when the tide does turn, they'll remember how I treated them in downtimes."

- "The important thing is to not live at a level where you have to be earning the top potential dollar just to break even. If you put yourself in that position and tough times come, you'll suffer and start paying attention to the wrong things."

- "I was once in an industry that went south. I knew I had the stuff to bounce back, but I wasn't sure if the industry would bounce back. At times like that, you have to take a long, hard look at the industry you're in and decide if you want that challenging or that rough a ride."

All these statements reveal resilient mind-sets, which separate what is happening from personal feelings of worth. The person who internalizes every bad turn will be weighed down to the point of becoming lethargic. These resilient individuals had learned through experience to formulate thought processes and lifestyle processes that would help them weather tough times.

HAILING ON THE PARADE

My brother Mark sells insurance to car lots and implement dealers, and adversity is a predictable part of his business life. This adversity comes each spring in the form of hail. His company's compensation plan is tied to his loss ratio, which means that when it hails, he loses substantial income. Some years, he has just missed making the President's Club because of the hail. It is a circumstance beyond his control, but he pays an appreciable monetary and emotional price for it.

At first, he let the weather affect his resilience level, and he grew fearful and somewhat cynical as the season approached. He began to get angry with clients that he felt were taking advantage of his company in these circumstances. He soon learned that it would be necessary to prepare a mental approach that would buoy him for this eventuality.

"I decided that, other than saying a few Hail Marys, I didn't have much control over weather patterns and the damage they could cause to my clients' inventories or, subsequently, my paycheck. With my competitive nature, I decided that the only way I could stay positive was simply to set my goals high enough so that if hail did come, I would still meet the goals the company had for me."

This is a good example of the resilient response. Mark could have focused on the injustice of the compensation structure, he could have carried a hail-chip on his shoulder and let it poison his attitude, or he could have just given up. Many of his peers, facing the same challenge, chose those mental detours, and their productivity followed the negative emotional lead. Mark continues to produce at a high level for one basic reason—resilience.

Failure is a part of the game if you take any risks and try to stretch your capabilities. Deal with it. Bounce back.

Disappointment will be a part of the game, unless you can find a way to sell without working with others. Expect it, but be ready to bounce back.

Adversity comes in many forms. You cannot control when it will come, when it will leave, and what form it will take. Remember that others are being tested as you are. Some are passing the test, and others will need to repeat the exam. It is best to learn as much as you can this time around.

SELLING WITH EQ

- Identify the source of your discouragement—you, others, or circumstances. Don't blame yourself for factors beyond your control.
- Adopt the learning response to every setback. Find the takeaway that will benefit you later.

CHAPTER FOURTEEN

FINDING MOTIVATORS THAT LAST

"What lies before us and what lies behind us are but tiny matters compared to what lies within us."

—OLIVER WENDELL HOLMES

The Principles of Emotional Intelligence

- Successful individuals understand the need for intrinsic motivation.
- The most resilient individuals are continually guided by a sense of purpose.
- Extrinsic motivations, although alluring, have an emotional downside.

EXTRINSIC MOTIVATORS

"Money won't make you happy, but neither will poverty."

—ANONYMOUS

Most of us assume that if a sales professional is making a lot of money, this material factor is enough to assure career satisfaction. However, studies demonstrate that this may only be true with a minority of successful individuals. A study of highly successful financial advisors found that only about 20 percent of its subjects reflected any extrinsic emphasis when defining the question, "What does it mean to you to be successful?"*

The following quotes from the study typify the common attitude of high achievers.

- "It is enhancing other people's lives versus just selling a widget. It is helping others have a better quality of life."
- "To get acknowledgment from my clients that I have helped them accomplish their objectives. That they adopt the plan we worked on, and it makes a difference in their lives."

It is a fair assumption to conclude that most people will not enter any careers (sales careers included) without the prospect of furthering their material fortunes. But the paradox is that the extrinsic, material payoff loses its power to satisfy over time. This truth, of course, is most evident with those who have achieved notable degrees of material success—which usually leads the envious to declare, "Easy for them to say!"

"I've always liked money. I like making it, counting it, spending it, and making more. But the more money I've made, the more I realized that its power to move my pulse has diminished and has become secondary to other more powerful 'drugs,' if you will. For instance, I genuinely get more excited about putting together a deal that benefits everyone than I do over the check I get at the end. I get a huge rush out of overcoming obstacles. That's what makes me jump out of bed in the morning—not the prospect of owning a better luxury car. I'll tell this to a young guy starting out, and he'll say, 'Yeah right, easy for you to say, you've already got the prize.' I guess it's something you have to learn on your own. I've just seen too many people burn out whose every thought and breath was about the money."—Dale R., Computer Systems Representative

The question that cannot be avoided when discussing motivators is "If it's all about money, then isn't it all about me?" And how well can a client or customer be served with this attitude leading the parade? To quote the above-mentioned study, "We contend that even though monetary achievement is important to quality of life, satisfaction has less to do with money."

---

*Lauterbach et al., *The Attitudes and Behavioral Styles of Successful Advisors*. Wilmington: Capital Trust, 2001.

I bring up the topic of material motivation because it acts as a lightning rod—a perfect illustration for the discussion of *material motivation* vs. *lasting motivation*. Like the old scriptural teaching about building one's house either upon the sand or upon a rock, the motivations we choose to use in our careers may determine either an epilogue of joy or disaster. When the winds, rains, and storms of adversity come, foundations of sand wash away and years of work quickly erode. This is the inherent danger of placing too much emphasis on *extrinsic* motivators.

Webster's Dictionary defines extrinsic as something that is "not essential" or "not inherent." Three examples of popular motivators are *accumulation, recognition,* and *control.* It would be safe to say that all three of these extrinsic motivators are expected (to some degree) in any sales professional. Sales professionals are motivated to sell more in hopes of accumulating more for themselves and their companies. They are motivated to reach new heights in hopes of being acknowledged for their efforts as well as to control the factors that affect their success.

When these factors are out of sync, sales professionals lose balance and become emotionally dissatisfied. Here are some examples you might find in your own organization.

- *Accumulation.* Individuals so focused on making more that they begin "replacing their values with valuables."
- *Recognition.* Individuals who are so consumed with getting credit and recognition that they pirate credit, expend valuable energy fighting for recognition, and/or become deflated when they do not receive the recognition they feel they deserve.
- *Control.* Individuals who try to control people as well as processes end up transferring high degrees of stress as people and events elude their control. Relational fallout follows as others resent their need to control.

"Money hungry," "glory hound," and "control freak" are common characterizations given to those who are obsessed with one or more of the above extrinsic motivators. It might be argued that such personalities are drawn into the sales profession because of tantalizing promises to "Make as much money as you want to," or "Be a star in your field," or "Control your own destiny."

All of these promises are irresistible to the entrepreneurial, mover-and-shaker Enterpriser/Motivator personality. But we must be on guard that one or more of these extrinsic aspects do not dominate our personalities, causing us to fall into the trap of sacrificing relationships in pursuit of goals. If you've left a slew of damaged relationships and burned bridges in your wake, then chances are that one or more of the above three extrinsic motivators have gained the upper hand in your life.

The emotionally intelligent sales professional, however, avoids such pitfalls by applying a disciplined focus on safer and more powerful motivations known as *intrinsic* motivators. Think of it this way, we have a choice either to be guided by an inner compass or by an outer weather vane. Which is safer? Which is more reliable? Obviously, it is the compass—if it is tuned to true north.

WHAT MAKES YOU TICK?

For over a decade, I have been asking a simple question of sales professionals, "What motivates you to do what you do?" I have always been most interested in *why* people do what they do. Beyond the expected surface answers such as, "To make a good living" or "To take care of my family," exist layers of motivation that enable the sales pro to overcome adversity and supercede trying circumstances.

My question, "What motivates you to do what you do?" has been directed at discovering the intrinsic motivators that work best. Out of the hundreds of queries I have made, the answers seem to fill six psychological silos that prove to be a source of emotional sustenance to the seasoned sales pro—in spite of the perplexities and hindrances the career may offer. The six categories of lasting intrinsic motivation I have observed are:

 1. Competitive nature
 2. Desire for excellence
 3. Curiosity and the desire to grow
 4. An attitude of gratitude
 5. Desire for building relationships
 6. Noble purpose and goal

Competitive Nature

A competitive nature is the soil upon which the seeds of success are sown. It is the systolic rhythm of the high achiever. When I refer to competitive nature, I don't mean to simply imply the narrow definition of "I'm going to beat you at this game," although that is one common expression of the competitive nature. The competitive nature also expresses itself as:

- "I'm not going to let this thing beat me."
- "No one else has been successful in this territory, but I will be."
- "Every obstacle is just a challenge to measure the fight in me."

- "I will win them over. It may be by persuasion, persistence, or importunity—but I will win them over."
- "Records are made to be broken."
- "I know I can do this better than the next person."

At the risk of tripping up readers who have been quite successful in sales careers and feel they have not been intrinsically motivated by a competitive nature, I will say that you are few and far between. Anyone who is comfortable losing is a long shot for success in a sales-oriented professional. Why? Because the profession is filled with extremely competitive personalities who will take advantage of your every mistake, weakness, and oversight. Unless you have a distinct advantage in skill or networking, you are going to need a competitive nature to survive. I'm reminded of the riddle, "How do you beat Tiger Woods?" The answer, "Don't play him in golf." If you expect to survive in a world of skilled competitors, and you yourself cannot match their skill or competitiveness, then you'd better move to a field where your skill level is superior.

When you get down to truth of survival in a capitalist society, every person in every job must keep a competitive edge to survive—not just those in the sales profession. The tacit challenge of others who have their eye on your job or on your market share is always in the air, no matter what the profession.

The fact of a competitive foundation in a free-market society bothers many educators in our society who, lacking a competitive nature, are deeply disturbed by the reality that a competitive nature is critical to success. These individuals have done their best to sterilize learning and youth sports of the competitive spirit and have performed a disservice in the process. As an eighth grade basketball coach, I marveled at the inane policy of mandating equal playing time for all players, regardless of both skill level and work ethic. Players who didn't work in practice were rewarded and those who were skilled and worked harder than the rest were punished. This is hardly what one could call "career preparation."

When the competitive nature becomes destructive to relationships, however, it is harmful. Again, it is a matter of balance. Successful sales professionals have found proper and fitting expressions for their competitive drives.

The study referred to earlier in this chapter also noted that half of the sales professionals in financial services "traced back their individual success mentality to involvement with sports and athletics in their childhood." One interviewee put it this way, "I can't ever remember not wanting to succeed at something, delivering newspapers or magazine subscriptions, playing baseball, skipping rocks with my brother. I've always had a competitive streak."

If this statement does *not* describe your own approach to your profession, be assured that it most likely describes those competing *against* you.

Now, let's look at finding the noblest expressions for this competitive nature, which are tied to many other intrinsic motivators as well. "Curiosity and the desire to grow" is an expression of the competitive nature competing with one's own skill level. The "desire for excellence" is the competitive nature saying, "I can do this better than anyone else," and competing against one's own potential. A "noble purpose and goal" is the competitive nature taking on status quo, lack of progress, and injustice—and correcting them.

A good exercise for assessment of the competitive nature is Life Is a Test. This exercise is a highly constructive introspective means for channeling competitive drive. Try applying a trying situation you are experiencing to the exercise in Figure 14.1.

Desire for Excellence

It has been said that to become world class in an instrument or sport takes 10,000 hours of practice. At the core of such a disciplined schedule or rigorous routine is the desire to better one's own standards and the desire to supercede standards set by others. The most resilient sales professionals

FIGURE 14.1 Life Is a Test

Exercise: *Complete the following questions.*

1. Describe a negative situation. _____
   _____
   _____
   _____

2. What attributes of my character are being tested? _____
   _____
   _____
   _____

3. How will I pass the test? _____
   _____
   _____
   _____

---

possess standards for effort and achievement that surpass those set by their peers and corporations.

These resilient individuals are not in the business of avoiding high goals and standards and are, in fact, highly motivated by the idea of doing something better than everyone else does. They pay attention to both the big things and the little things because they know "God is in the details," and these details often spell the difference between mediocrity and excellence. In fact, the word *excellence* is often heard when they talk about their goals and business vision. They may have already outperformed their competition, but that fact does not cause any diffusion of energy, because they have not yet realized their goal of true excellence in their operation.

Curiosity and the Desire to Grow

Cynical people typically advertise a worn, "been there, done that" ambience toward their work. On the other end of the emotional spectrum are the curious with a "haven't been there, would like to do that" approach to life and work. They view learning as a lifelong process and see the connection between a desire to grow and life satisfaction. This desire to grow may cause them to leave the company of partners or organizations that are stuck and display no penchant for stretching and growth.

A memorable, inspiring moment in my life came on an airplane ride home from Australia. I found myself engaged in a long conversation with a man who, at the age of 77, was still teaching upper atmospheric physics at a major university. I asked why he hadn't retired, as was expected of a man his age. His answer was brilliant.

"I have been studying upper atmospheric physics for just over 50 years, just long enough to realize how much I don't know. I haven't quit because I have so much left to learn about the upper atmosphere."

"Doc," I said, "that makes two of us."

"Here was a man," I thought to myself, "who possesses more motivation at the age of 77 than most people 40 years his junior, and for one reason— he is intrinsically motivated by a desire to grow and learn. His curiosity is what keeps him young in spirit and mind and no doubt motivates him to keep his body in its best possible working condition."

An Attitude of Gratitude

Back in 2001, my friend Bobby Brooks was talking to me about all the people he knew (himself included) who were being hit hard by the market meltdown. Bobby, who is in a senior-level position at a major mutual fund company, told me of peers who were complaining and whining about their pay because they had overextended themselves in the good times and could hardly pay their tax bill in bad times. Bobby's take on the circumstances was different. He said:

> "I never let myself forget from whence I came. I never in my life thought I would see the kind of money I've seen. Years ago I worked for an appliance manufacturer. I was a young, energetic guy, and they took me from making $30,000 a year to over six figures. Then one day, they offered me the job as National Sales Manager. It was a tough decision, but I turned it down and went into the financial services industry, and I've been very blessed in my career. I try to think of it this way: even in a horrible year, I'm still doing better than I would have done if I had taken that National Sales Manager position."

It does not matter if the pay is $30,000 or $300,000, you can find plenty of people who are complaining and saying they deserve more. But you will not find this emotional posture in great achievers. In those individuals, you find grateful attitudes about the opportunities they have encountered, the people they have been fortunate enough to meet, and the material blessings they have received. This intrinsic motivation keeps them out of pity parties.

Desire for Building Friendships

John Wenzel, a sales professional, told me a story about retirement that I have shared with thousands of others because of the powerful lesson it teaches. His family owns a piano store where his mother worked her entire life. When she reached the age of 65, she retired just because it was expected. Six months into her retirement, John got a call from the family doctor.

"John, I'm going to shoot straight with you. If you guys don't put your mother back to work, I don't think she'll live out the year."

John and the rest of the family immediately responded, and John informs me that today his mother is 86 years old and shows up every day at the store to help sell pianos. This story illustrates the fact that alienation is one of the greatest psychological traumas of retiring. Here was an individual who was intrinsically motivated in her life by building friendships—and that motivator was stripped away. She missed talking to, selling to, and bonding with the lives of others.

Since I began telling this story, I have had numerous sales professionals approach me with similar sentiments and many who worried about retirement for this reason. Harry, an auto/home/life insurance salesman, put it this way: "I've spent years building a book of business made up of people I like. I may go to part-time but never leave permanently. Why should I leave just when it's gotten to where it's easy?" Harry's business had come to the point over the years where he felt like work was nothing more than sitting around talking with and helping friends.

On a final note, recent studies on successful aging confirm that maintaining multiple friendships is a key to aging well.

Noble Goal and Purpose

"The only ones among you who will be truly happy
are those who have sought and found how to serve."

—ALBERT SCHWEITZER

I have come to the belief that the most resilient souls on this planet are those who are guided by a sense of purpose in the work that they perform. In fact, when guided by a noble goal and purpose, these individuals can withstand great degrees of discouragement. To help you begin tapping into intrinsic motivators in your own life and career, complete the following Two-Minute Motivation Drill by answering the following questions:

- What would you do if you had unlimited time and resources?
- Describe the noble purpose you feel you are accomplishing with your work.

Steve sells estate planning. He is a top producer, and if you ask him why, he will tell you his success is because of conviction. He has seen financial misery added to grief to far too many lives because they didn't prepare.

Marsha sells homes. She is a top producer because she believes there is a difference between a house and a home. Her joy and mission is to help people find their home.

Edward sells psychiatric pharmaceuticals. He is a top producer because he has seen firsthand, in his own family, how people suffer with such maladies and what a difference some drugs can make.

Robin sells books. She is a top producer because she believes that the messages in these books have the power to transform and improve the quality of life for thousands. If she didn't believe this, she wouldn't show up for work in the morning.

In Chapter 22, "It's Not about You," I share stories of people who approach their work with a passion for serving and who do phenomenally well by doing good. For now, it will suffice to say that a central motivator for resilient individuals is knowing that their actions will make a difference in the lives of others. A noble goal is a goal with a healthy dose of idealism. It is a goal that reaches beyond your own satisfaction or accumulation. This goal can be measured by its ability to profit and improve the quality of life for others. Those who lack this sense of purpose are both easily distracted and discouraged.

THE EMOTIONAL FOUNDATION

Extrinsic motivators—external rewards, attention, recognition, and control—have a vaporous power to motivate us. They are but a sandy foundation for emotional success. The first waves of discouragement and adversity can wash them away, and shoring up the sandy foundation causes constant stress.

Intrinsic motivators are different. They are bedrock solid. They can take beating and abuse, look adversity in the eye, and say, "That's fine, but I've got my own reasons for doing this." These motivators are the cornerstones of resilience in sales. Resilience is the earmark of the sales professionals with whom you will one day do business because, although you can knock them down, you cannot keep them down.

SELLING WITH EQ

- Know that the *why* of your work is as or more important than *what* you do.
- Take inventory of your inner life to find sustaining motivation.
- Make sure you gain more than clients—gain friends.

CHAPTER FIFTEEN

WINNING THE EMOTIONAL TUGS-OF-WAR
The Power of Positive Intent

"The harder the conflict, the more glorious the triumph. What we obtain too cheap, we esteem too lightly. I love the man that can smile in trouble, that can gather strength from distress, and grow brave by reflection. 'Tis the business of little minds to shrink, but he whose heart is firm and whose conscience approves his conduct, will pursue his principles unto death."

—THOMAS PAINE

The Principles of Emotional Intelligence

- In every situation, you transfer an emotional state.
- You can intentionally and positively influence the emotional state of others.
- Effective and positive responses exist to all manner of negative emotional states.

In his book, *Emotional Intelligence,* Daniel Goleman tells the amazing story of an American troop in the midst of a firefight in a rice paddy in Vietnam. During the battle, six monks started walking directly toward the fire of one of the elevated berms that separates the paddies. One of the soldiers in the battle gave this account.

"They didn't look left and they didn't look right, they walked straight through. It was strange because nobody shot at them. And after they walked over the berm suddenly all the fight was out of me. I just didn't feel like I wanted to do this anymore, at least not this day. It must have been that way for everybody, because everybody quit. We just stopped fighting."

This story depicts in dramatic fashion an emotional phenomenon that takes place in everyday life. The dominance of one emotional state over another is the result of *intentionality*. Intentionality is the tug-of-war that takes place when two emotional states confront one another and one state wins out. This is a component of the *emotional contagion* discussed in Chapter 8, "The Viral Spiral of Emotion." The resilience component I wish to dissect here is how to dominate negative environments and situations with the power of positive intent.

THE MOOD DANCE

A study of mood transfer (reported by Ellin Sullins, *Personality and Social Psychology Bulletin,* April 1991) reported on the subtleties of transferring one's emotional state to another.* The study conducted an experiment in which two volunteers filled out a checklist about their moods at the moment. After the volunteers completed their checklists, they were left to sit and face one another silently for a two-minute period. After the two minutes, they were given a mood checklist again. What the volunteers did not know was that they were paired on the basis of their degree of expressiveness. One volunteer was highly expressive while the other was deadpan. In each case, the emotional state of the expressive individual was transferred to the more passive individual.

This emotional transfer has been explained by some as an "unconscious imitation of the emotions we see displayed in someone else." Swedish researcher Ulf Dimberg found that when people view a smiling or angry face, their own faces show evidence (visible through electronic sensors) of changing toward that mood.

Think of it as a "mood dance"—a synchrony and transmission of emotional states—that takes place in every conversation. At the end of each conversation, this synchrony of mood becomes the measuring stick of whether we felt the meeting went well or not.

---

*Ellin Sullins, "Emotional Contagion Revisited: Effects of Social Comparison and Expressive Style on Mood Convergence," *Personality and Social Psychology Bulletin* 17 (1991): 166–174.

DOMINATING THE PAINT

Great NBA centers feel a sense of ownership and jealousy toward the center lane of the basketball hoop they defend. This lane is their territory. By their imposing stature and occasionally blocking and misdirecting a shot of an opponent, these players send the message that they "own the paint." They intend to dominate that territory with their presence. Those who are skilled in the social skill of building rapport have also learned to establish and jealously guard their spheres of influence in a positive, graceful manner that makes a profound impression on those they interact with.

Intentionality could be described as that emotionally resolved state of being that is firmly settled on bringing a domination of positive emotions to interactions. Intentionality is also being determined not to be tricked or provoked into hair-trigger, negative responses. This feature is a hallmark of those skilled in building social rapport. These individuals are convinced that no good can come by lowering themselves to the lowest common emotional denominator, and they proceed as emotional leaders in their conversations.

In *Emotional Intelligence,* Goleman writes about the research of John Cacioppo of Ohio State University, who has studied the subtleties of emotional exchange. Cacioppo postulates that one major determinate of interpersonal effectiveness is how deftly a person carries out this emotional exchange. Those who are adept at tuning in to the mood of others, and bringing those moods into sway with their own positive state, have much more successful interactions at the emotional level. Contrarily, he notes that people who are poor at receiving and sending emotions are much more prone to relationship problems; people often feel uncomfortable with them yet have trouble articulating why.

Goleman states, "Setting the emotional tone of an interaction is, in a sense, a sign of dominance at a deep and intimate level: it means driving the emotional state of the other person. When it comes to personal encounters, the person who has the more forceful expression—or the most power—is typically the one whose emotions entrain the other." To exercise emotional dominance does not require that we dominate the conversation, just the quality of that conversation. The definition Goleman offers in his text for intentionality is "the wish and capacity to have an impact, and to act upon that with persistence."

Those who are interpersonally effective and competent seem to have mastered this particular emotional competency. You are exercising intentionality when you determine to be a dominating emotional force in your territory of influence. This is sort of like the difference between being a sail that is blown by every emotional wind and being the wind itself.

MAKING THE MOST OF GARBAGE

Garbage dumps give off dangerous gases, the most notorious of which are carbon dioxide and methane. Methane is the chief atmospheric criminal, contributing to the famed greenhouse effect that scientists say threatens the earth's atmosphere. Some innovative scientific minds in Quebec felt that this highly vilified environmental enemy could actually be a friend in disguise. This idea led them to invent a system for capturing, storing, and converting the gas into energy. They have now stored enough methane to supply electrical energy for over 35,000 homes.

How do you go about converting the emotional methane given off by the negative personas you interact with? Can I, with intentionality, turn the tide on arrogance, curtness, impatience, defensiveness, and the various other gases contributing to the emotional greenhouse effect? We have three basic choices when entering a polluted atmosphere.

1. Breathe it in.
2. Take offense and heighten the toxicity.
3. Convert the poison with positive intentionality.

A key for understanding negative behavior is understanding that an area of emotional lack undergirds every negative word or action. To practice intentionality, you must avoid responding to the emotion on the surface and attempt to read the underlying emotion. Once you have read the situation, you can work to satisfy or pacify that need rather than react to the tone on the surface. This skill requires maturity, patience and, most important, an educated view of the emotional landscape.

When confronted with a negative or stressed tone by a client, before you react or respond, ask yourself, "What is the *emotional need* here?" When confronted with arrogance, rather than taking immediate offense because of your own emotional need to be treated with respect, ask yourself what this individual lacks that causes her to communicate with arrogance. Is this individual's arrogance really chocolate-covered insecurity that causes her to feel a constant need for recognition and to be right? Quite possibly.

For example, Stuart was perplexed that Marie met the business solution he offered to present to her company with defensiveness. This solution was clearly what her business needed. What Stuart later realized was that her resistance was undergirded by an emotional need to be seen as the strategist in the organization. The solution didn't bother her—the fact that Stuart wanted to be the hero by doing the presentation bothered her a lot.

If you respond to arrogant statements based on the speaker's needs rather than on their arrogant tones, you stand a much better chance of connecting and building social rapport. Although you may not necessarily feel any genuine affection for an individual, you have built an interpersonal bridge where most people would walk away. I originally developed the chart in Figure 15.1 to help customer service representatives respond to clients who called with issues or complaints. Many sales professionals have found these prescribed responses quite valuable when dealing with negative clients who are spewing poisonous gases.

Rehearse some of these responses so that the next time you are confronted with cynicism, arrogance, attacking, etc., you are not caught off guard. You will be amazed at the level of rapport that can be established in negative situations with intentionality. Remember, intentionality is about the wish and capacity to have an impact and to act upon that wish with persistence. The difference is in your intent.

You can take offense, which is akin to breathing in the poison, or you can convert the poison into energy by reading and responding to the underlying need. Of course, if you face clients who are so notoriously negative that it requires a gas mask to sit in their presence, you may want to question how hard you want to have work at the emotional level to keep such clients.

MAKING PAR FROM HERE

> "My buddies and I play a golf game every week. One aspect of the game we reward is making par after a terrible tee shot. We call it the 'all-American par,' and we treat it with great respect, because you have to keep your head to make it happen. I try to take this same approach to mistakes I make in work and life. When I goof up, which I inevitably do, I just tell myself, 'I can make par from here.'" —Jerry A., Sales Representative

One of the most difficult times to keep your emotions in check is when you have just made a costly interpersonal mistake and you are attempting to recover it. Either you get discouraged, or you try to justify the mistake—and both will sink you.

Anthony sold parts and had been working for a long time to grab a key account from his competition. It looked like his opportunity had finally arrived, and he was scheduled to come in and make his proposal. Just before his meeting, Anthony was informed by someone inside the company that they were entertaining his proposal just to be able to go back to their current supplier, drive their costs down, and push the service level up.

FIGURE 15.1 Changing a Negative Climate

Negative Climate	Prescribed Response	Example of Prescribed Response
Arrogance	Give strokes.	"You're right. I see what you are saying."
Attacking	Calmly take ownership of problem.	"What would be the best way to improve this situation?"
Curtness	Listen and take note of details.	"Let me take some notes here on how to resolve this situation."
Cynicism	Use candor and sincerity.	"I'm not going to promise what I can't deliver. You'll be the ultimate judge of my performance."
Defensiveness	Accept input and take servicing approach.	"I can see why you're saying that. How would you like me to help?"
Demands	Give realistic expectations.	"So we can avoid any disappointment or misconceptions, I'm going to paint a realistic picture of what might and might not happen."
Skepticism	Provide facts.	"Let me pull out some data on this topic."
Evasiveness	Use leading questions.	"Let me ask you a series of questions that are designed to ensure that our services match your needs."
Frustration	Be empathetic and come up with a simple game plan.	"I would be frustrated too in your circumstance. To resolve it, how about if we do the following?"
Struggle for words	Write down reflective statement and proposed direction.	"Let me get this down, you want me to first . . . and then put together a plan that will do the following."
Confusion	Provide guidance with brevity and clarity.	"Here's a clear and simple way to solve these issues."
Impatience	Give *immediate* plan of action.	"Today, I'm going to do . . . and call you to confirm it. Then, I will do . . . and immediately confirm that in a letter."
Oversensitive/ volatile temperament	Lead by asking permission; do not give orders.	"So would you like me to do A, B, and C or just A? All right, with your OK, I'll get started on that."
Disorganized presentation of thoughts	Organize thoughts and create a plan.	"Let's make a plan of action here and define the steps each of us needs to take."

Being upset with this news, he called the decision maker to see if he had a real chance at landing the account. This individual said, "Why do you ask?" Now, Anthony was trapped. He either had to say he doubted the sincerity of their intentions or that someone in the company had tipped him off. He chose to say the latter. This angered the other party, and he told him not to even bother because he would look elsewhere. Anthony had hit his tee ball into the water.

If Anthony had been focused on positive intentionality in this situation rather than on the negative emotion of being used, he would have created an entirely different path of conduct. With intentionality, Anthony would have been happy to take advantage of the face time before the client to impress him with the sheer emotional force of his personality. Lacking such confidence and intentionality led him to become defensive and send the interaction down the wrong path. Fortunately, Anthony's boss understood this particular emotional dynamic and helped him to recover.

Anthony went to his sales manager and told him his mistake. His manager advised him to allow this gentleman time to cool off and to then show up personally, offer his apologies, and reaffirm how much he wanted to do business with him. He assured Anthony that this fellow would appreciate such a good demonstration of character.

Anthony followed through and received a second chance to offer a proposal. As he expected, he didn't get the business. But a year or so later, when some problems developed with the current vendor, Anthony was the first to get a call and eventually landed the account.

Many sales professionals would have reacted differently than in the manner prescribed by Anthony's sales manager. Many would have become discouraged with this misstep, beaten themselves up, and written off all possibility of redemption. Others would have told themselves that it really didn't matter anyway and moved on. Both reactions would be like taking a double bogey regarding the account in play.

Mistakes are as much a part of the game in sales as they are in golf. Just as you must pay close attention to your grip, posture, and approach in golf, you must do the same with all prospects. Inevitably you will hit some bad ones. Make sure you have a game plan for making par when:

- You say the wrong thing to a prospect.
- You miss a time line or deadline.
- Your product or service fails to perform as promised.
- You fail to consult a key person in the decision chain.
- You must deliver news of rising costs.

Sales professionals who have the emotional strength and social agility to navigate through such difficulties have much greater rapport with clients than those who avoid dealing with the situation or try to minimize the matter. Intentionality is bringing a positive or calming emotion to negative interactions with clients, and it is an axiomatic skill for survival in the sales world. As one client stated, "I would much rather have my account representative deal bad news to me personally than to find out on my own or get it from a third party. Then I feel like they don't have enough regard for me to warn me."

SMOKE IN THE EYES

A man named Duane Pearsall was testing an electronic device that controls static electricity, when he noticed that smoke from a technician's cigarette caused the meter in the device to go bad. At first, he was irritated because he had to stop the experiment and install another meter. Later, he realized that the reaction of the meter to the smoke might prove to be a valuable bit of information. This brief irritation proved to be a great opportunity, because it led to the invention of the smoke alarm—now a standard part of every home.

As a sales professional, you will experience a constant stream of irritations. Some annoyances come from the field, and others come from the home office. How you react to those irritations will determine your emotional state, level of resilience, and, ultimately, the quality of interpersonal relationships—which are critical to your success.

If you are easily rattled or thrown off your emotional game by small annoyances, offenses, and irritations, your troubles can be attributed in part to a lack of intentionality—not settled on being a dominatingly positive interpersonal force. If so, you may not yet have constructed an emotional agenda that you want to bring to the table. Take a moment and answer the questions in Figure 15.2 to help organize your emotional intent with others.

Decide to be a force of nature, not a reed blowing in the wind. This is intentionality and, as such, will build rapport when others do not believe it is possible. If six monks can possess enough calm to walk into a firestorm of bullets and cause everyone to lay down their guns, you can walk into any situation and dominate it with a resolutely positive emotional agenda.

FIGURE 15.2 The Emotional Agenda

1. When I'm around others, I try to make them feel: _____

_____

2. Key emotional words I try to focus on each day are: _____

_____

3. Others would describe my emotional presence as:_____

_____

4. Key characteristics about me that contribute to rapport with others include:

_____

_____

5. When things aren't going my way, I tell myself: _____

_____

SELLING WITH EQ

- Settle on the kind of emotional force you want to be. Decide how you want others to feel after they have been in your presence.
- Decide how you will set your emotional sails in times of conflict and adversity.
- Understand that good results only come from bad situations because of positive intentionality.

CHAPTER SIXTEEN

RISKING REJECTION
Getting Past No

"Every problem introduces you to yourself. It shows
how you think and what you're made of."

—GEORGE MATTHEW ADAMS

The Principles of Emotional Intelligence

- Resilience is a matter of both nature and nurture.
- Some other form of fear underlies the fear of rejection.
- Emotionally intelligent individuals can separate themselves from the *no*.
- Self-consciousness will limit your sales success.

THE RESILIENT PERSPECTIVE

A young boy went out into his yard to play baseball, all alone. This young fellow had big dreams. This week, he would try out for a position on the local Little League squad.

He picked up the bat and a ball and prepared himself. He announced, "Ladies and gentlemen, coming to bat is the greatest baseball player in the world."

He tossed the ball into the air, took a swing and missed.

"Strike one on the greatest baseball player in the world!"

He tossed the ball into the air a second time, took a mighty swing and missed again.

"Strike two on the greatest baseball player in the world!"

With a look of dogged determination, he threw the ball into the air one last time, swung ferociously, and caught nothing but air.

"Ladies and gentlemen," he announced, "the greatest baseball player in the world has just struck out—to the greatest pitcher of all time." —*The Daily Dose*

THE ROOTS OF FEAR

If you tend to beat yourself up, you are going to struggle in sales. If you dream up reasons the client will say no before you even make a presentation, you will find selling difficult. If you have a morbid fear of rejection, you will probably starve in sales. The fear of rejection is one of the great emotional hurdles a sales professional must learn to conquer. This is not a one-time hurdle but an every-time hurdle. You must keep yourself in excellent emotional shape, or you will find yourself tripped up—with skinned knees and a bruised ego.

The fear of rejection can be traced to many quarters in the psyche. First, look to your personality and temperament. I have made the observation in the TEAM Dynamics personality classes that two of the four personality types (Togetherness/Analyzer) struggle with rejection more than the other two (Enterpriser/Motivator). The fear of rejection can also be a matter of post-traumatic stress syndrome, in which the memory of a rejection earlier in life sends you diving under the table like a war vet at the sound of a pop-gun. The fear of rejection can also be rooted in various other fears such as the fear of failure, fear of success, fear of humiliation, fear of not being liked, or the fear of financial disaster. Or your fear of rejection could be a lethal cocktail of all of the above in varying measures. Awareness of where your fear takes root will go a long way toward overcoming it.

PULLING AT THE ROOTS

Azriela Jaffe, author of *Starting from "No," 10 Strategies to Overcome Your Fear of Rejection and Succeed in Business*, alleges that a number of underlying fears form the soil for the fear of rejection to flourish in. These fears include:

- *Fear of failure.* Individuals fail to attempt selling in situations where they do not feel safe. These individuals choose the path of least resistance.

This fear can result from having unrealistic definitions of success or having a "beat yourself up" personality.

- *Fear of success.* Individuals feel undeserving of the success they think they want and sabotage their progress with foolish decisions and conflicted lifestyles.
- *Fear of humiliation.* Every decline is taken as a personal rejection. This fear is often rooted in memories of rejection/humiliation in earlier life or childhood. The sales rejection stirs up this negative spin cycle, and the individual prematurely exits the sales process to avoid these feelings of humiliation.
- *Fear of not being liked.* This is common to the people pleasers. They spend most of their time with people who like them. They avoid unpleasant tasks and difficult bargaining conversations. They are also known for spending money and buying gifts as a way of ingratiating themselves to clients.
- *Fear of financial disaster.* Individuals with this fear can be dangerous to others and themselves. They will often push too hard to expedite results and may rationalize questionable selling scruples out of desperation for a payday. They are also vulnerable to placing their own interests above those both of clients and of peers within their own firms.

The excuses for rejection in selling scenarios are many, and sales professionals must have thick skin and ample emotional resilience to withstand the chorus of nos that they will hear on the way to yes.

POST-TRAUMATIC SALES SYNDROME

We have all heard stories about the war vet who goes ballistic with the least bit of provocation and instinctively dives under the table at the sound of a muffler backfiring. This condition is known as post-traumatic stress syndrome and is suffered by people who have encountered any sort of life-altering trauma. Victims of crime, abuse, and catastrophic events also fight the impulse toward radically defensive responses toward everyday stimuli. The equivalent to this malady in the sales profession is the prospect or client who has been burned by a competitor or associate.

Jimmy was a fresh-faced neophyte walking into a lion's den of discontentment when he made the first sales call of his career. His company had gone through six different reps in five years in this territory. His manager told him to buck up for rejection, as prospects and clients would be in a state of justifiable skepticism. *Skepticism* was too sterile a term for what he would encounter on this first call.

The business owner looked down at Jimmy's business card and spouted, "I'll tell you what you can do, why don't you and your company go and @#*&% yourself."

Jimmy, knowing he was not responsible for previous battle scars and not being one to take himself too seriously, retorted, "Sir, if I could have done that I would never have left home this morning."

The business owner looked up with a stunned smirk on his face, knowing he had failed to chase this kid away, and said, "You know your company has made some real screwups here."

"I've been told," Jimmy replied, "and though I have no right to ask it, I would like the opportunity to rectify past mistakes and show you a better face for my firm."

"You're all right, kid. I've got your card. I'll give you a call when we start taking quotes again. Keep in touch."

Jimmy eventually heard the stories of previous grievances and within two years recovered the business for his firm. He accomplished it by virtue of playing psychologist and mediator. If you sense a tone of animosity or agitation in their rejections, some old war injuries may be behind the dismissal. If you have the desire to listen and the skill to inquire, they will tell you stories about:

- Your company
- Your product category
- Your industry
- Previous reps

You can begin to rebuild trust with these clients by listening to their stories, and by reading between the lines, about the values they want to see in a vendor. Hopefully, you are confident in the character of the firm and the integrity of the product you represent, because it is that integrity and character alone that can win back a client suffering from post-traumatic sales syndrome.

ANALYZING NO

"If someone chooses not to buy from me, I am not afraid to ask why. Some people will give me lame reasons, but others who are more straightforward have helped me to improve my presentation. I have found that a certain percentage of rejections I get are based on perceptions that I helped to create or failed to create. I would have never known this had I not asked." —Paul F., Communication Systems Consultant

While every good sales professional knows why a prospect would say yes to their offerings, it may be of equal or greater importance to know why they are saying no. If you ask, enough people will be straightforward that you can gain valuable insight into their decision-making logic. A high percentage of the answers you hear will fall into the following categories.

- Price
- Satisfied with current product
- Features—not the right fit
- Not ready to change
- Lack of confidence in product or company
- Bad experience with company or similar company

After you have performed careful rejection analysis, you will intuitively alter your presentation to answer these objections and, most important, do a better job of uncovering areas of dissatisfaction first. People buy to solve problems, and selling is difficult without knowing what the problems are. If your rate of nos is higher than it should be, it could be attributable to the lack of discovery of the prospects' world and challenges they face.

TOO MUCH MONEY

If your nos are based primarily on price, then you may need to work on how well you demonstrate value. Price is an issue most often when sufficient value is not perceived. Economic logic will always be the source of the majority of nos, simply because most people tend to value price (to you it's the price, to them it is the cost) over benefit. If you are certain that the product you offer is worth the price premium, then you must find ways to communicate that value. The following creative story comes to mind.

J. J. looked at his watch and asked his prospect what time he had. The prospect told him, "Quarter past ten."

J. J. said, "That's the same time I have, but I can't help but notice the fine watch you're wearing. Is that a Rolex?"

"Yes it is," the prospect replied.

"I would guess that my watch probably cost less than one-tenth of what your watch cost, yet it just gave the exact time that your watch gave. Why do you suppose your watch is worth so much more money?"

The prospect explained the fine workmanship that the Rolex name represents.

J. J. replied, "The similarities are only on the surface. I would offer that as an analogy of my product vs. the competitor's product. They may sound like they are telling you the same time as we are, but when you look below the surface, you will find that we are the Rolex of this industry."

When people reject your proposals on the basis of price, very often they do not understand the value of what you offer. We have all learned the lesson of "you get what you pay for." We pay ahead of time for value. We pay later for the lack of value.

DEALING WITH CHANGE

A certain percentage of your nos will be based on this principle—many people struggle with change, and shifting their business to you means they have to engage in change. This is an emotional issue that emotionally intelligent individuals will address with gentle persistence and by exposing their own personalities, until the prospect becomes comfortable enough to trust them.

Individuals may be comfortable with the product they are using, even though it comes up short. They may be comfortable with the person or people they are currently dealing with, because they have invested in that relationship. They may abhor the prospect of rearranging systems and retraining people. Some individuals just hate the idea of anything that threatens their routines.

Strangely, people are often resistant to and threatened by what they need most—new and fresh approaches. Clarke's Law of Revolutionary Ideas states that every revolutionary idea in science, politics, art, or any other realm evokes three stages of reaction, summed up by these three phrases.

1. It is impossible. Don't waste my time.
2. It's possible, but it's not worth doing.
3. I said it was a good idea all along.

Clarke's Law will apply to you if you are selling a product or idea that forces a paradigm adjustment or a new way of doing things. Rather than filing the no in the rejection bin, consider that some rebuffs are indicative of the struggle to change and invite persistence until the client is duly acclimated to the idea.

LANGUAGE THAT FITS YOU

Will described to me the difficulty he was having with the close his company told him to use. I asked him to use the close with me as if I was a potential client. I couldn't help but notice the discomfort in his eyes and body language as he asked me to "get started." His words were aggressively moving forward and his body language was backing up in apology for the aggressive words. I told him he didn't look or sound convincing with the close, and he admitted he wasn't. The baseline problem was that his personality (Togetherness) is not aggressive by nature. He wants to make sure the other person feels comfortable before moving forward. We worked on scripting a close that was synchronous with his personality—he positioned himself as a partner and teammate with the client. When he used this approach, he felt no emotional awkwardness, and, consequently, expressed no apology in his eyes.

Each personality style can succeed in sales only so long as his or her natural temperament matches:

- The product/services being sold
- The method in which the product is sold (e.g., cold calling vs. following up on inquiries)
- The script the company prescribes

Operating outside of these comfort zones will only increase the fear of rejection.

A PRODUCT OF NATURE

I often have been amazed at the number of people who enter sales careers without making an honest assessment of their own resilience levels. A fellow approached me after a speech and said, "I can't stand when people don't like me. Consequently, I tell them what they want to hear and overpromise, and they end up not liking me because of it." Another sales professional told me, "I went into sales because I wanted to make more money, but I'm a perfectionist and I hate getting rejected. I honestly prefer working by myself. My wife, on the other hand, makes huge money in sales, because she is made of Teflon when it comes to being rejected. I'm going to have to get out before I drive myself crazy."

You can learn many interesting lessons from watching children make their first selling steps, be it selling lemonade at a stand, selling pizzas door-to-door for the hockey team, or selling boxes of Girl Scout cookies. I have made notes on the personality types of my older children and their natural responses to selling. Here is what I've seen.

- *Nate (high T personality—easygoing, sensitive nature).* He made one effort to sell assertively and never returned. He could not stand the embarrassment of hearing no. He did start a successful lawn service by placing fliers in mailboxes and waiting for customers to call him.
- *Nic (high M personality—outgoing, energetic, uses charm to advantage).* He led his entire school in a booster club campaign selling wearable accessories. When I questioned him on his strategy, he said he started with the police officer that led the DARE campaign who initially said, "No," to which Nic responded, "Well, I know you want to promote school spirit." The officer bought. He then went to trendsetters and leaders in the student population and sold to them, etc. As a parent, I know all too well his penchant for refusing to take no for an answer.
- *Sophia (high E personality—thinks out of the box, not afraid of being unusual).* She painted rocks and sold them door-to-door for $1 each. She holds periodic lemonade/garage sales with a kid emphasis. She promoted a $1.50 car wash throughout the neighborhood. She likes to develop unusual concepts like "lost pet recovery service."
- *Alec (high A personality—at age seven, Alec has absolutely no interest in selling, but is happy to share in the proceeds).* He is possible future sales management material.

I am convinced that any personality type can be successful in a sales career, as I have seen each type flourish and prosper. No doubt, however, two types (Enterprisers and Motivators) display natural resiliency toward the rejection inherent in sales. You must find an approach synchronous with your personality.

THE NUMBERS GAME

I have made this observation about the most resilient sales professionals in every industry: they understand the ratio of rejection inherent in their industry, and they create emotional separation from those rejections by treating the business as a numbers game.

"There is no way to totally detach yourself emotionally from the selling process. You will feel elated and disappointed. But you can't get caught up in either or the ride is too manic. It always seems to come back to the law of averages. You have some prospects who look and sound so promising, but they don't pan out. You have others that look like it will never happen, yet it does." —Louise T., Sales Professional

Theresa sells advertising and knows that, in a good economy, one out of twenty prospects are likely to buy her product. Her product has a rejection ratio of 95 percent. Until she had a firm grip on the rejection ratio inherent to her product, she felt like a failure every day. Now she knows the numbers game, and even though she goes through streaks where the ratio is higher or lower, she expects to close at least 5 percent over time.

Mitch sells retirement plans. He told me that when he first started, he would go through an emotional ebb every time he was rejected—until he realized that it was a numbers game. Some people needed what he had to offer, some were satisfied with what they had, and some were habitual procrastinators. Once he realized that his rejection ratio was going to be 60 to 70 percent, he decided he had to see more people every week to achieve success.

He is now obsessively organized in scheduling as many prospects as he can fit into a week's schedule. He led the nation for his company in the number of new accounts signed up in his first year. He signed up over 900 new accounts. Most were small and medium accounts, but he knew they would grow with time. Mitch never lets a day go by without seeing at least four or five prospects. He works hard at utilizing referrals and keeping on top of scheduling. He understands how the numbers work.

Less resilient sales professionals focus too much on the emotional aspect of the sales rejection and too little on the law of averages. What sales professionals have is not for everyone, and even if it is, not everyone will understand it. To be successful in sales, individuals must study their industry, calculate the success ratio of the top-level achievers, mimic their habits, and try to avoid getting caught emotionally by rejections.

KEEP FISHING

Robert Louis Stevenson wrote, "To travel hopefully is better than to arrive." To fear rejection is not what one could call "traveling hopefully." Paul Quinnet, in his book *Pavlov's Trout,* wrote, "It is better to fish hopefully than to catch fish. Fishing is hope experienced. To be optimistic in a slow bite is to thrive on hope alone. When asked, 'How can you fish all day without a bite?' the true fisherman replies, 'HOLD IT! I think I felt something.' If the line goes slack, he says, 'He'll be back!' When it comes to the human spirit, hope is all. Without hope, there is no yearning, no desire for a better tomorrow, and no belief that the next cast will bring the big strike."

The sales game is best played with a focus on the bites, strikes, and catches—not on the fish that swim by, or those that look and swim away, or those that ignore you altogether. Embrace rejection as an integral part of the game. Try new lures, work on your casting skills, remain quiet enough to not scare the big fish away, and, most of all, make sure you are fishing in the right pond.

SELLING WITH EQ

- Take time to figure out why people are saying no.
- Don't take no as a personal rejection.
- Work hard at finding out what a client needs to feel comfortable enough to buy.

CHAPTER SEVENTEEN

THE FACE YOU SEE
The Face You Show

"When the eyes say one thing and the tongue another, the practiced man relies on the language of the first."

—RALPH WALDO EMERSON

"Women speak two languages, one of which is verbal."

—STEVE RUBENSTEIN

The Principles of Emotional Intelligence

- Facial and body language are more reliable forms of communication than the words people speak.
- People who are skilled in reading nonverbal signals are more popular and successful in all social aspects of life.
- People help others to feel more comfortable in their presence by paying closer attention to the signals they send.

The above quote about women speaking two languages is only half true. All people speak two languages, one of which is verbal. The reason women receive more notoriety for mastery of the unspoken language is because they naturally are more attuned to the sending and receiving of nonverbal signals. Women literally have superior "wiring" in their brains in terms of the communication that takes place between the rational functions (left side) and the sensing, intuitive functions (right side).

Split-brain research has revealed that in the bundle of nerves (corpus callosum) that connects the two sides of the brain, women literally have 15 percent more nerves. This is analogous to having a cable modem vs. a phone modem. Not only do women get a clearer signal, they get it quicker. This would explain why the following scenario happens. Two couples are out to dinner. One wife kicks her husband under the table as he is saying something. He stops and says incredulously, "What?" Then, suddenly, comprehension registers on his face, and he says, "Ooh . . ." He got the tacit clue about six seconds after his wife.

Just because a woman has superior wiring, however, does not mean intuition is her exclusive domain. Intuition is not a mystical, ineffable phenomenon possessed only by psychics and mothers. Intuition is literally the language of the right side of the brain as it reports on observations about a person's tone, body language, movements, and manner. We, as members of a society that has always prized scientific reasoning above all else, have never been trained to listen to the "logic" of the emotional, sensing side of our brains—intuition.

Research has also demonstrated that this side of our brain takes about 1/24th of a second to receive, process, and report a nonverbal signal. However, depending on how well developed their empathy skills are, many people take 24 hours or more before "the coin drops" and the intuitive message can work its way through the rational clutter that drowns it out.

The link between what the emotions are feeling and what the face and body are advertising is so quick that much of it falls beyond a person's control. The facial reactions are almost automatic and, consequently, are highly reliable indicators of a particular emotion. The Latin word *motere*, from which we derive the word *emotion*, means *to move*—suggesting that emotion in the brain sets the body into motion. Different emotions trigger the body for different responses. Here are some examples.

- If we feel angry, we experience an adrenaline rush, our heart rate increases, and blood flows to our hands preparing us for battle. Our faces tense and lock into an intimidating posture, and we clench our fists.
- If, on the other hand, we feel happy, activity increases in the part of our brains that inhibits negative feelings, quiets anxieties, and increases our energy levels. The body goes into a state of rest and calm, enabling us to recover more quickly from upset. The face and eyes reveal this blissful condition with a hakuna matata (no worries) demeanor, which indicates that nothing, at this point, can upset us.

Jo-Ellan Dimitrius, Ph.D., is a leading expert on jury selection and has been a consultant in many high-profile trials, including the O. J. Simpson and Rodney King cases. In her book, *Reading People,* she writes:

"Most of our body language is beyond our control. . . . Few people are aware of all their physical reactions to the world around them, and fewer still can always control those actions, even if they want to. Manners and poise may be consciously learned, but facial expressions, eye blinking, leg crossing, and nervous tapping are difficult to consistently repress. I've seen enough people on the witness stand to know that it's nearly impossible to control body language, even if one's fate depends upon it."

EMOTIONAL ADVERTISEMENTS

Because physiological chemical reactions shift into gear as emotions are felt, the symptoms or signals of this brain/body reaction are instantly advertised on the face and body. When making a presentation to a client, it is important to be aware and highly attuned to this fact. People don't have time to think about sending signals; it just happens. The emotions they feel trigger an automatic motor response. When we are angry, we tense our lips. When we are doubtful, we raise our eyebrows. When we are disgusted, we wrinkle our noses. When we sense a lack of credibility, we roll our eyes.

We must be conscious of unspoken signals at two levels—those we see and those we send. The reason we should think about the signals we send is because signals easily can be misinterpreted. For example, I noticed that my wife and children would often ask me, "Are you mad?" because of my habit of pursing my lips and narrowing my eyes when I'm concentrating. Their brains were telling them that I was displaying the facial language of anger, which actually is my facial language displaying intense thought.

Just as the cerebral calculator in our brains can deliver faulty logic or a wrong number, so the intuitive calculator can deliver the right interpretation in the wrong context. Once my children became aware of the context (paper and pen or book in hand), they no longer asked me if I was angry when they saw that look on my face. This is why it is dangerous to believe that body language doesn't lie—because of the fallibility of our interpretations.

I have heard people teach how to read body language in a manner that suggests, "Every time you see this, it means this. . . ." This sort of thinking is naïve and only serves to narrow our interpretation of the context of the situation and to shut down our empathy capabilities. My intention here is to raise awareness of body language, not to narrow that awareness. A more reliable interpretation of body language signals is "When you see this, it usually or quite often indicates this. . . ." A less dogmatic view will keep your emotional radar from jamming.

For instance, I have heard it taught that every time clients move forward in their chairs, it means they want you to close the deal—they are ready to buy. What happens if you dogmatically act on this teaching and begin closing the sale only to find out that the individual moved forward in his chair because he had to go to the rest room? As a rule of thumb, I suggest paying more attention to what the face and body are saying—with a caution to pay equal attention to both context and one's own capacity for jumping to the wrong conclusion. You could be reading some false advertising.

BODY LANGUAGE CHECKPOINTS

Successful sales professionals would not think of going into an important presentation without first rehearsing their content. Yet studies show that people are more influenced by tone and body language than they are by content. Go through a quick rehearsal of your body language as well. Study your face in the mirror when experiencing specific emotions. For example, think about being surprised and watch the reaction on your face. Think of someone lying to you and watch that reaction register. Think of being ready to purchase something and see how it affects your countenance. Think of hearing a price that you think is out of line and observe the facial signals. Think of saying something when you do not intend to follow through and watch for the indicators on your face and in your eyes. This technique is a simple method for schooling your powers of observation to be sharp and attuned with your clients.

It is important to be aware of the signals you are sending as well as the signals your client is sending. Following are two short checklists (Figures 17.1 and 17.2) for your mental file before you walk into a presentation:

FIGURE 17.1 Check Yourself

☐ *Your eyes.* Are your eyes open, receptive, and inviting, or questioning, intense, and scrutinizing?

☐ *Your facial muscles.* Are your facial muscles tense (communicating disapproval, stress) or are they relaxed? Can you smile easily with your teeth and eyes?

☐ *Hands.* Are your hands closed? Are you pointing? Are your hands open (communicating generosity, helpfulness, and open-mindedness) and your gestures smooth and gentle?

☐ *Posture.* Are you looking down your nose? Are you too far or too close? Is your posture open or closed?

FIGURE 17.2 Check Your Client: Warning Signs

- ☐ *The raised eyebrow.* Needs validation, shows pessimism.
- ☐ *Scrunched-up nose.* Lacks credibility, foolish.
- ☐ *Narrowed eyes.* Uncertain, skeptical.
- ☐ *Rolling eyes and/or pursed lips.* Shows disapproval, disgust.
- ☐ *Frozen smile.* Afraid to express true feelings of disapproval or disagreement.
- ☐ *Nervous gestures.* Anxious about topic at hand or just a constant nervous habit (e.g., tapping fingers, shuffling objects).
- ☐ *Darting/fidgeting eyes.* Bored; feels pace too slow or material irrelevant.
- ☐ *Hand to forehead.* Confused or stressed.
- ☐ *Hand to chin.* Processing the information.
- ☐ *Looking away.* Avoiding topic or conflict.
- ☐ *Looking up.* Thinking through topic.
- ☐ *Head on desk; loud snoring sound.* Presentation so good you put them in a dream state!

FACING YOUR CLIENT

Bill Acheson is a Professor of Communications at the University of Pittsburgh and a highly popular speaker on the topic of reading body language in a selling situation. He believes that facial expression is the most common tool by which we gather information about other people. He states, "We not only use the face to identify others, we use it to determine their initial emotional state and any changes that might occur during the communication process." Acheson believes that facial expression is more emotionally revealing and more accurate than the spoken word.

"In sales," Acheson writes, "facial expression is the primary feedback tool that guides you through the selling process. It provides valuable feedback about how the selling process is progressing. Level of interest, desire, and indication of honesty or deception can be identified by changes in facial expression. Sales professionals not only react to facial responses to reinforce points that are important to the prospect but also identify and deal with objections before they become stumbling blocks."

How important is facial expression? Another way to answer that question is to ask why each year sales professionals log millions of miles to get face-to-face with their prospects and clients. It is rather pointless to log all those miles if we are not going to practice extreme vigilance in regards to body language. Why make the drive if not to capitalize on the face-to-face opportunity to become a better observer? When we face the prospect or client, we can witness the subtle indications of heightened awareness suggestive of positive feedback as well as signs of tacit disapproval. Both are critical for initial sales success and for maintaining long-term professional relationships.

Communication researchers have determined as many as 38,000 different combinations of facial expressions involve over 20 muscles. And yet, despite this wide range of possibilities and the impact of cultural influences, facial expressions are not only readily identifiable, they are surprisingly reliable indicators of emotional responses.

Researchers Paul Ekman and Wallace Friesen have identified six universal facial expressions: surprise, happiness, fear, anger, disgust, and sadness. Of all possible emotional states, only these six expressions are displayed similarly throughout the world. Researchers also find that these expressions are typically identified with very high levels of accuracy.

FACIAL LITERACY

Acheson warns that although facial expression is the primary means by which we transmit information about our emotional state to others, it has some potentially limiting factors. Following are some key points to consider regarding body language.

Facial expressions may be consciously controlled. Ekman points to three basic rules in the social consensus about which feelings can be shown and when they can be shown. Three common displays are minimizing, exaggerating, and substituting. Individuals can choose to withhold information by minimizing their facial expressions, projecting an emotional response where none is actually present, or project a false emotional state. Each of these choices can greatly impact the quality of communications in a professional setting. In many scenarios, you can gain a distinct advantage by restricting emotional expression. Feigned interest is an unstated goal of the sophisticated buyer.

Facial expressions are notoriously short in duration. Although we tend to display a general emotional state to those around us, a genuine facial response is short-lived, usually less than several seconds. The expression of shock has the longest duration, lasting over three seconds. To achieve an accurate assessment of facial expression in a sales situation, one must focus on the face as information is shared. Otherwise the actual response is easy to miss, or it may be consciously manipulated either to conceal or mislead the sales professional to maintain some degree of negotiating power.

A relatively new term, *microexpression,* describes a facial expression typically lasting a microsecond. Microexpressions are highly accurate emotional responses, which often indicate a socially unacceptable response or may reveal a highly charged emotional state that is best concealed, thus their short duration. In research, even when observers are coached to look for microexpressions, they actually identify them less than 30 percent of the time. Yet microexpressions are extremely accurate and revealing. In sales, a particularly high price might reveal a prospect's naïveté, which she may immediately attempt to conceal behind a veneer of indifference (literally "lack of emotion"). The discovery of the microexpression is due to advanced film technology. With more sophisticated tools, greater precision is possible in assessing facial expression.

Facial blending is the term used to describe the fact that, very often, we express more than one emotion at a time. This notion is critical to the sophisticated sales professional. Given the propensity to minimize facial expressions (much more common to males than females) in a sales meeting or negotiation session, subtle cues indicating positive or negative responses become even more valuable. Enlarged pupils, chin stroking, or a combination of pursing of the lips and slightly nodding the head are favorable indicators. Breaking eye contact, furrowing eyebrows, or shaking the head side to side indicate negative responses.

Bilateral symmetry indicates level of intensity and possible deception. If you draw an imaginary line down the center of a person's face and then compare or, more likely, contrast the facial responses on both halves of the face, you will often gather revealing information. With very few exceptions (my own estimate is less than 2 percent), the left side of the face is more emotionally honest. If someone gives you a half smile by raising the right cheek and turning up the right corner of the lips, the expression is literally halfhearted. Simply stated, the right side of the body is controlled by the left hemisphere of the brain—the conscious or logical side—and the left side of the body is controlled by the right hemisphere of the brain—the subconscious or emotional side. By assessing the level of involvement of each half of the face, you can pretty accurately read how genuine the response is. In a sales situation, a full, balanced response is the most desirable response, in that it indicates a higher level of involvement and commitment. A predominantly right-sided response indicates a potential lack of emotional commitment. And a left-sided response suggests some level of internal conflict that may need to be resolved before reaching a satisfactory conclusion.

There are three identifiable smiles. The upper smile exposes only the upper teeth and is the most socially acceptable smile showing a balance of response and control simultaneously. The full smile indicates both upper and lower teeth and in a professional setting is most likely to be perceived as inappropriate. In a group, when only one individual smiles to this extent, that person is typically perceived to be out of control or inappropriate. The simple or "self" smile shows the upper lip turned up (without showing the teeth) and indicates smugness.

FACE THE MUSIC

Most of us tend to give substantially more weight to the face than other channels of nonverbal communication such as posture, gesture, or eye contact. This emphasis probably stems from our belief that facial language reveals much about personality and character. This emphasis on the face can become problematic when we ignore the signals coming from gesture, posture, or the eyes. Have you ever seen a prospect smiling and nodding approval, yet leaning toward the door? All signals should be taken in balance to become nonverbally literate.

KEY TO POPULARITY AND SOCIAL SUCCESS

Empathetic acuity—the ability to read the feelings of others—has been correlated in studies with popularity, better adjusted emotional lives, and, not surprisingly, better love lives. Robert Rosenthal, a Harvard psychologist, learned this by developing a test of nonverbal sensitivity that he has conducted with over 7,000 adults in 18 different countries.

In a test he developed for children, Rosenthal found that those who showed an aptitude for reading feelings nonverbally were among the most popular in their schools, were among the most emotionally stable, and were better performers in the classroom—even though their IQs were not higher on average than those who were not empathetically literate.

The implications of this finding are profound. The only ways to explain this superior performance, not dependent on IQ, are:

- Empathetic ability smoothes the way for classroom effectiveness.
- Empathetic ability causes students to be better liked by their teachers and results in some degree of favor.

Here again, we are faced with evidence of success hinging on EQ as much or more than it does on IQ. The empathetic children in the classroom are a perfect analogy for the effective sales professional in the field.

Those skilled at reading nonverbal messages and responding appropriately are more popular, more emotionally stable, and more effective in their jobs. They know what to look for in the faces they see, and they know what to display in the faces they show.

A common trademark in top performers in the sales profession is that the best of the best are great observers of people around them. They study. They listen. They watch. They've learned that the real work of sales gets done by what they see, not by what they say. It is by your powers of observation alone that you can discern whether your client "gets it" by truly understanding and feeling the need for the product you sell.

SELLING WITH EQ

- Pay as much attention to clients' reactions as you do to your presentations.
- Don't talk past "buying signals."
- Display a face that advertises friendliness, openness, and flexibility.

DEVELOPING
EMOTIONAL RADAR
The Powers of Observation

"Don't watch the cards while they are being dealt; watch the faces

of the players watching the cards being dealt. You can check

your hand later. It's not going anywhere. Just see if anybody

flinches or blinks or smiles or even looks away."

—ANDY BELLIN, *Poker Nation*

The Principles of Emotional Intelligence

- Your powers of persuasion are wasted if not matched by equal powers of observation.
- Each personality type is given away by idiosyncratic body language clues.
- The clients' tones and word choices are clear indicators of how they want to be approached.

I recently gave a presentation to the board of a large international bank. I was there at the invitation of a senior-level executive who had risen to a lofty position at a very young age. During my presentation, I couldn't help but notice that he was paying very little attention to me, or so it seemed, until I realized that he was reading the room like a great poker player.

This gentleman had "skin in the game." He had asked me to present to this powerful group of independent thinkers in hopes that they would adopt my ideas. When I delivered critical points in my presentation, he was gauging the expressions in the eyes, faces, and postures of all 12 board members. He wasn't reading the cards; he was reading their reactions. I had no doubt that his observational artistry had something to do with his precocious rise to the top.

BECOME A BETTER OBSERVER

To master the emotional intelligence competency of empathy requires learning how to improve observational skills. An impeding factor that prevents many from succeeding with people and building strong relationships is an inability or unwillingness to observe clients skillfully. If we are the ones doing most of the talking, it is much more difficult to observe the client. We rarely learn anything while our mouths are moving. Those who win are the people who master the art of observing. The reason many do not observe is simply because they don't know what to look for. In this chapter, we will focus specifically on the "tells" of personality.

To improve your observational skills, you must learn how to recognize quickly the personality style of your clients and prospective clients. This skill is really quite simple. Although it may sound complicated, after you learn the signals and begin observing those around you, you will be shaking your head at how obvious and predictable most people are. The natural follow-up is learning how to apply these skills in a selling situation, which is what the following chapter, "Shifting Gears—Four Critical Selling Adjustments," is about—customizing your sales presentation for each personality type.

One organic problem in a typical sales organization is that those doing the selling are typically passionate people. While their passion contributes toward making them interesting and engaging, this passion also leads many of them to believe erroneously that "selling is in the telling." In actuality, we can only sell after we've properly *read* the client. It is more important to be able to read a tell than to do the telling. Telling before listening or observing is like throwing random seeds prior to checking the suitability of the soil and climate. Being passionate will not help you overcome the soil and climate. Oranges won't grow in North Dakota, no matter how convinced the sower is that they will.

Following, I will give you the visual and audio clues or tells of each of the four personality styles. You will become a better player by first becoming a more skilled observer. Commit these personality tells to memory and begin to look for them in your next conversation.

First, let's review the core of each of the four personality styles. Your empathetic radar must be alert to pick up on the personality needs of each client. Every personality has a receiver and an antenna that is tuned to pick up on specific signals. Ask yourself what the receiver of each personality style is looking for.

When individuals of the Togetherness personality walk into the room, their receivers are tuned for *feelings* and *respect*. Their main concerns are sensitivity—how something is going to play out to other people and the degree of respect you demonstrate.

An Enterpriser's receiver is tuned for *results* and *competency*. "Are you going to help me get results?" "Are you competent enough to get the job done?"

If you are working with Analyzers, their receivers are tuned towards *accuracy* and *predictability*. "Is this going to be right?" "Can I count on you to follow through in a predictable fashion?"

The Motivator's receiver looks for *friendliness* and *energy*. "Are you going to be easy or difficult to work with?" "How much energy can you bring to the table?" "How positive a person are you?"

RECOGNITION TOOLS

Ultimately, the goal is for you to make these radar observations intuitively. You want to be able to walk up to anyone, enter into a conversation, observe the way they talk, observe the way they look, make mental notes, and start adjusting your communication to connect with their core personalities. As a ramp to this automatic and intuitive skill level, I've designed a tool called the Client Conversation Profile. You can use this profile to gauge a prospective client's personality style. After a conversation with a client on the phone or in person, fill out the profile based on that conversation, and you'll have a strong indication of what that individual's personality likes and dislikes are.

Take a moment right now and think of a client with whom you are trying to build a relationship. Think about the last conversation you had with this individual, and then go ahead and fill out the Client Conversation Profile in Figure 18.1. When you're finished, tally up the letters the same way you would on a TEAM Dynamics personality quiz. Tally up the number of *T*s, *E*s, *A*s, and *M*s. The totals will give you an indication of their leading and villain roles.

The Client Conversation Profile is a quick and easy way for you to start assessing the personality style that drives each client. The reason this assessment works so well is because personality is "automatic." By this, I mean that personality inclinations are blueprinted in the DNA of our psyche. Our personality style is animated by our eyes, demeanor, faces, vocal patterns/pace, and conversation—as well as the style of questions we ask. Our core personality simply sends automatic signals through our mannerisms.

FIGURE 18.1 Client Conversation Profile

Directions: *In the following groups, circle one attribute that is most true about your client. Total each letter at the bottom of the sheet. The highest scoring category is a strong indicator of your client's leading role.*

Demeanor	MOST	Conversational Flow	MOST
• friendly, even keel, calm, passive	T	• respectful, responsive, nods	T
		• interrupts, confrontational, abrupt	E
• candid, confident	E		
• reserved, meticulous	A	• deliberate, focused, hesitant	A
• free-flowing, animated, playful	M	• flexible, random flow, fidgety	M

Eyes	MOST	Style of Questioning	MOST
• soft, caring, appreciative	T	• role questions	T
• laser-direct, busy	E	• time questions	E
• scrutinizing, scanning, squinting	A	• detail questions	A
• happy, dancing, wide open	M	• networking and potential questions	M

Face/Physical Style	MOST	Vocal Patterns and Pace	MOST
• nonthreatening, mirrors mannerisms	T	• limited range, slow and steady	T
		• punches certain words, fast, punctuated	E
• smirk, uplifted chin, poised for action	E		
		• precise, sometimes monotone, slow	A
• poker face, rigid posture	A		
• easy smile, energetic	M	• full range	M

Add totals of each letter.

_____ T _____ E _____ A _____ M

I have interviewed hundreds of clients from each personality group and scores of them on camera. After watching the tapes of those interviewed, one would almost be inclined to believe that the people were scripted, because the individuals from each personality group gave the same types of answers in the same types of tones. However, the individuals were not scripted—the answers they gave were their natural responses. I asked questions such as what qualities they were looking for in a sales professional and the types of people they liked and disliked working with. As they answered those questions, one could clearly observe their personality styles. I have developed a training exercise on this skill set, where I show this video to sales professionals and they can observe firsthand how clear personality signals are.

Start observing right away. As soon as you set this book down, turn on your observational skills. Start looking for signals in the following categories: demeanor, eyes, face, physical style, conversational flow, style of questioning, and vocal patterns. Rather than just meandering through conversations, make mental notes—observe! These signals are fascinating and make every conversation much more interesting.

The Togetherness Personality

Let's begin with the visual clues the individuals of the Togetherness personality will transmit. Here is what you will see.

- Their demeanor is friendly but not effervescent.
- They are calm and passive.
- Their eyes are soft, caring, and approachable.
- Their physical style is nonthreatening, and they typically allow others to take the lead.
- They tend to mirror other's mannerisms.

One visual clue to look for in identifying a Togetherness personality is the nod. Individuals of the Togetherness personality unconsciously nod as a way of affirming the person speaking.

During camera interviews with scores of clients from each personality group, I also observed another visual clue for identifying the Togetherness personality. After answering a question, they would look at the interviewer with a questioning look, as if to say, "Was my answer OK?" Instead of punctuating with an exclamation, they punctuated with a question mark. Their need for approval, as well as their nods to provide approval, are automatic features of the Togetherness nature, which they cannot easily hold back.

Next, let's examine the auditory signals of the Togetherness personality. The conversational flow of the Togetherness personality is responsive, respectful, and cooperative. Observe the types of questions you are asked by the Togetherness personality. You will hear role-oriented questions such as "What is expected of me?" or "What will you need from me?" or "How will you support me?" These are what we might call "hand-holding" questions.

Listen also for the voice patterns of your clients. If you were to segregate people by personality, audiotape their conversations, and then watch an audiometer, you would be able to see patterns that correspond with each personality style. The Togetherness pattern, as illustrated in Figure 18.2, is slow and steady, like gently rolling waves—never too demonstrative, and neither too high or too low.

FIGURE 18.2 Conversational Clues: The Togetherness Personality

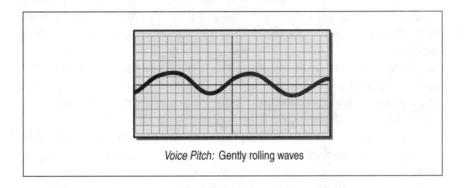

Voice Pitch: Gently rolling waves

The Enterpriser Personality

With the Enterpriser personality, their confidence level comes through loud and clear. In the business world, Enterprisers are the ones doing a great deal of the controlling. For a great rule of thumb to win over the Enterpriser personality, I will paraphrase Mark Twain's quote about public speaking: "You have to walk the fine line between flattering and abusing your audience."

Enterprisers have little or no respect for people who tell them what they think they want to hear. On the other hand, there needs to be some flattery, because Enterprisers tend to believe they are God's gift to the world—there is no shortage of ego with this personality. Yet Enterprisers respect those who have earned the power to abuse them now and then. But do not make the mistake of abusing Enterprisers too early in the process.

The visual clues Enterprisers will give you are as follows.

- Their carriage demonstrates confidence and control.
- Their eyes are laser-direct and busy.
- They will often smirk and hold their head high.
- Their chin will be uplifted.

To help you identify the Enterpriser personality, think of the looks you see at an amateur poker table when the players want to give the impression that they have really good cards. Enterprisers like to give the impression that they have cards they have not played yet. Even when they don't have the cards, they attempt to give you the impression that they do.

Enterprisers are restless and poised for action. Think of a viper—ready to strike at any minute. In conversations, you'll primarily hear them pushing for the bottom line. This obsession with the bottom line is their most obvious tell. Enterprisers cannot help themselves because they are impatient by nature. Enterprisers are also notorious for their frequent interruptions—to move the conversation along at a faster pace and insert their forceful opinions.

Enterprisers are confrontational. For them, it's not about tact and diplomacy; it's about getting to the point of resolution *quickly*. They tend to be abrupt in their speech and often ask questions about time and results, such as, "Where's this headed?" or "How long will it take?"

In conversation, differentiating between the body language and auditory signals of Enterprisers and Analyzers can sometimes be confusing, because both personality styles are good at exhibiting a poker face. Yet we know there's a huge difference in our approach with Enterprisers and Analyzers. The most significant difference between the two personality styles is their preference between *quick* and *right*. Enterprisers will push toward *speedy* results and Analyzers will push toward *accurate* results. Their differing pace is what sets them apart.

Another way to differentiate between Enterprisers and Analyzers is their voice patterns. The voice pattern of the Analyzer personality style is controlled. The voice pattern of Enterprisers is also controlled, but just when you think they've settled into an even pattern, they'll punch a word for effect (see Figure 18.3).

FIGURE 18.3 Conversational Clues: The Enterpriser Personality

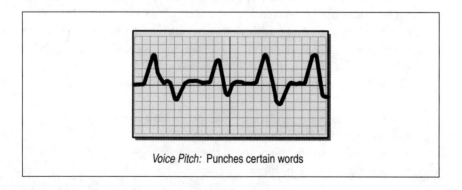

Voice Pitch: Punches certain words

The Analyzer Personality

Here are some visual clues for identifying your Analyzer clients.

- Their demeanor is reserved, meticulous, and nervous.
- Their eyes are scrutinizing, scanning, and squinting.
- Their face is controlled and unemotional—a poker face.
- Their posture is rigid.

Eyes provide important clues for identifying the Analyzer personality. Their eyes are serious and intense, almost as if you can see question marks in their eyes. Their eyes seem to ask, "What are you talking about here?" Their eyes seem to be begging for clarity. They have the look that says, "Explain that one more time."

There are also many auditory clues for identifying Analyzers. The conversational flow of Analyzers is deliberate and intensely focused. Take notice of the hesitation in their speech and choice of words. While Enterprisers impatiently want to finish sentences for others, Analyzers meticulously look for the perfect word to express what they're thinking. Analyzers also will ask more questions than any other personality style. They like to ask detail questions and begin their questions with who, what, when, where, and why. Keep in mind, though, that all their questions are really about one big question: "Is this the right thing to do?" This is why the words *right* and *caution* have a comforting effect with Analyzers.

You can see in Figure 18.4 that the voice pattern of Analyzers is precise, sometimes monotone, slow, and deliberate—and always controlled. Remember, Analyzers strive to be in control of their own emotions, and, consequently, are resistant towards the attempts made by others to persuade them.

FIGURE 18.4 Conversational Clues: The Analyzer Personality

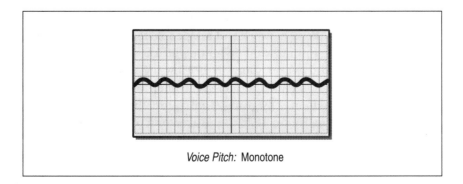

Voice Pitch: Monotone

The Motivator Personality

Here are visual clues you will observe with the Motivator personality.

- Their demeanor is free-flowing, playful, and animated.
- Their eyes are happy, dancing, and wide open.
- Their face and physical style is warm and energetic.

With the Motivator personality style, life and business are about having fun and enjoying the process. You will observe a great deal of motion in their body language. A conversation with Motivators is like dancing—a lot of lingual moves are going on. From many Motivators' points of view, work is just something that gets in the way of having fun. For the Motivator personality, it is almost like getting a result or signing a contract or making a deal is just an aside. "Why were we here again?" they might ask, and then suddenly remember and say, "Oh yeah, let's do it."

Here is what you will hear with Motivators. The Motivator's conversational flow is flexible and random. It is hilarious to watch Analyzers and Motivators in a meeting (that is, if you're not involved). Analyzers deal with everything in a linear fashion: A, B, C, and *then* D. Motivators, on the other hand, hardly know how to spell *linear*. Their conversations jump all over the map. A good talk to Motivators is like a pinball game. Motivators can also be fidgety because they possess such high energy levels.

Motivators use the power of personality to get things done. They rely on their charm. Because of that, Analyzers and Motivators can literally hate each other, especially in the selling process. To better understand the difference between the two personality styles, remember that they have different routes to achieve results. Analyzers achieve results through processes; they define a clear process to get the result—and stick to it. Motivators, on the other hand, do not believe in processes as much as they believe in the power of personality to get things done. Motivators know that if they are engaging and charismatic, they will win people over. So who is right? They both are—they've just got to learn to deal with each other.

Motivators also like to network and ask people-focused questions like, "Who are you working with?" and "Who do you know?" They also like to focus on potential and ask questions like, "How big is this thing going to be?" Because Motivators look and feel great when they're telling a good story, you can win them over by giving them a story they can tell to others.

As you can see in Figure 18.5, the Motivator's vocal pattern is like a roller coaster—a wide range of ups and downs.

FIGURE 18.5 Conversational Clues: The Motivator Personality

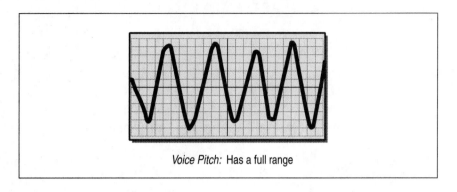

Voice Pitch: Has a full range

To be a great player in the game of sales, you must begin by learning to read others. Start with the eyes, which truly are the gateway to the soul. Core personality shines through the eyes. An individual's core personality also manifests itself in posture, facial expression, and tone and pace of speech. You will find it intriguing to become a keen observer of these mannerisms. You will be both informed and entertained by the predictable signals that have been opened up to your awareness. Once your emotional radar has picked up on "who they are," you're better prepared to deliver a laser-specific presentation. The next chapter will show you how.

SELLING WITH EQ

- Fine-tune your skills of observation to be on target with the core personality of each client.
- Remember that body language signals are automatic and present themselves in conversation and through the discovery process.
- Pay attention to the tone of voice and word choices of clients. They are telltale signals on how they want to be approached.

CHAPTER NINETEEN

SHIFTING GEARS
Four Critical Selling Adjustments

*"Politeness is better than logic. You can often
persuade when you cannot convince."*

—JOSH BILLINGS

The Principles of Emotional Intelligence

- Success in communication hinges on our ability to "flex" to the style preferred by the client.
- Each personality style possesses a unique agenda for likes and dislikes in communication.
- The emotional impact of our presentation is more important than the rational impact.

"I'm at this car dealership telling the salesman that I want all the 'bells and whistles,' and he keeps talking to me about practical and performance-type vehicles. After trying to steer the conversation to the kind of car I wanted—and him not getting it—I finally said, 'Look, you're not hearing me. I want bells and whistles, not the kind of car that's right for you.' I then pulled my personality profile (TEAM Dynamics) out of my briefcase and said, 'Look, I'm a motivator. I want a car that's fun!'"—Gary K., Mutual Fund Wholesaler

Gary is right. Some salespeople just do not get it. They persist in imposing their style and preference instead of observing the style of the client and shifting gears to fit that style.

This chapter addresses emotionally intelligent methods of communicating with each personality to optimize persuasion opportunities and to minimize confusion, conflict, and misunderstanding. This is accomplished by learning to view scenarios through the clients' perspectives. Too often, sellers are perceived to have placed their own interests above those of their clients. Through the personality sensitive TEAM Dynamics approach, clients are assured that their core needs and comfort levels are understood. This approach assures the improvement of existing relationships and a sound footing for developing new relationships.

At the very center of a client's actions and reactions is the *core personality* that drives behavior and communication. Once you have discovered the personality orientation of your client, you can choose a communication path that leads to clarity, understanding, and teamwork.

The classic mistake that many sales professionals make is to assume that every client will automatically plug in to their style of communication. They won't. This leads to communication breakdown and the disintegration of trust, which is at the heart of the buyer/seller relationship.

In this chapter, we explore the subtle adjustments that are necessary with each personality style to improve the quality of our communication with clients. Think of it as personality politeness—learning to use words or phrases that fit the emotional comfort zone of the client.

Each personality style is profiled regarding the communication approach they are most comfortable with, including the type of presentation they prefer. Also profiled are the likes, dislikes, risk tolerance, and challenges of communicating with each personality.

My organization has surveyed hundreds of members of each personality group and asked the question, "When in a sales situation, how do you like to be approached?" Their varied answers on the following pages reveal in insightful detail the diversity of persuasion needs for each personality style. A strong correlation exists between a client's personality style and the appropriate sales approach. For example, two of the personalities are risk-averse by nature—Togetherness and Analyzer—and two are comfortable with risk—Enterpriser and Motivator.

The changes you make in your communication approach, though simple in nature, will be profound in effect, because they will help your clients to be comfortable with the information and ideas you are sharing. Some readers find that they have already been making these adjustments with people on an intuitive level, and the following information will affirm those communication strategies.

CRITICAL SELLING ADJUSTMENTS

Let's take a look at some of the critical selling adjustments (in Figure 19.1) you want to make with the Togetherness style. Remember to go slowly

FIGURE 19.1 Shifting into *T:* The Togetherness Personality

- Demonstrate respect by paying close attention when they talk.
- Demonstrate sincerity. They want to like you before they work with you.
- Demonstrate a concern and caring for people.
- Go slowly. Wait until they trust you.
- Ask about their feelings regarding your product or services and its applicability.
- Do not force them into a buying decision. Avoid pressure tactics.
- Tread lightly because it is easy to offend the Togetherness personality.
- Allow them time to think things through.
- Refer to your satisfied clients.
- Use statements of commitment and seek a commitment.
- Identify specific steps and time frames.

and pay close attention when they talk. If you don't pay close attention when individuals of the Togetherness style are talking, you turn them off right away. If you are distracted while they are speaking, you may have jeopardized the whole deal. If you're a multitasker—Enterpriser—or have "professional level ADD" (Attention Deficit Disorder)—Motivator—be careful not to offend this personality.

Demonstrate the concern you have for your other clients. The stories you tell should illustrate this concern. Remember to use statements of commitment. And remember to ask how they feel about your product.

Close with specific steps and time frames. Do not paint your close with a broad-brush stroke; paint it with specifics. "So what we're going to do is this: one, two, and three, and then the time frame for number one will be this, and the time frame for number two will be this. . . ."

Do not force a buying decision. One of the things members of the Togetherness personality have told us is that they will let you know when they're ready to be closed. They lean forward, start nodding, and say something to let you know that they are ready for you to hold their hand through the process. If you try to close them before all their issues are dealt with, it is not going to work. One of the problems with the Togetherness style is their inability to say no, so they will say yes but not mean it. That will cause endless frustration for both seller and pseudobuyer.

Brent S., an account executive who fits the Togetherness personality style, tells about going shopping for a mattress and how the salesperson pushed all the wrong buttons with his personality.

"We walked into a store and asked for a specific type of mattress and what their best price would be. The salesman gave us a price and assured us that this was the best they could do. I told him I could get the same mattress across town for $200 less. He said, 'Don't leave, let me talk to my manager about this.' So, he comes back and tells us that he can now beat their competitor's price. I said, 'No thanks,' and walked out. I didn't feel like he was being sincere with me the first time and that he was going to take us for an extra $200 if he had the opportunity."

This story typifies the Togetherness approach. This personality style has its antennae up for honesty, integrity, sincerity, and respect. They are quickly turned off by those who fail to demonstrate those abilities.

Here is an overview of what the Togetherness personality wants in dealing with others.

I want:	• A reliable, stable relationship
I don't want:	• To be coerced or pushed into a decision (has trouble saying no)
	• People to be upset with me (has trouble when others are not pleased or approving of them)
You must convince me:	• How your product or service will bring simplicity and security into my life.
	• That you will be there to support me when I have questions or problems.

Is word choice significant when working with the different personality types? Absolutely. My organization has conducted research by asking individuals from each of the personality types to tell us which words made them feel *comfortable* or *nervous*. If our job is to make our clients feel good about who we are so that they'll do business with us, we certainly don't want a vernacular that is going to make them nervous.

The following chart reveals the words that appealed most to the Togetherness group. If you're selling to a Togetherness person, make a note of a couple of these words that will help you, particularly as you open a discussion with them.

Words that fit the Togetherness personality comfort zone:

- We/let's   • Commitment
- Concern   • Security

- Sensitivity - Step by step
- Teamwork - Long term

The word *we* is particularly significant to the Togetherness personality. When you use *I* with them, their response is typically to assume that you are ego driven. If you say *you* too much, they may feel like you are putting too much pressure on them. *We* is also very important to the Togetherness personality, because it connotes partnership and collaboration. And, remember, if you're an Enterpriser, the Togetherness personality style is most likely your villain role, so it will be even more important for you to start using these words.

CRITICAL SELLING ADJUSTMENTS

Time Is of the Essence

The magic bullets for dealing with Enterprisers (see Figure 19.2) are speed and efficiency. Enterprisers want to know ahead of time how much of their time you want. To win their undivided attention, tell them up front, "I need ten minutes of your time," and then stick to it—unless *they* prolong the conversation. If you do not tell them up front how much time you

FIGURE 19.2 Shifting into *E:* The Enterpriser Personality

- Don't talk about your company before you ask what they want (concisely).
- Uncover their top concern/priority.
- Stress bottom-line benefits.
- Establish context up front. Start with the end result and work back.
- Don't waste time with small talk.
- Paint a broad-brush stroke. Enterprisers will make decisions with a small amount of information.
- Ask for their opinion and affirm it without sounding like you are pandering.
- Do not persuade Enterprisers with long stories or with overly enthusiastic presentations. They see this as contrived and phony.
- Prepare for a quick decision based on facts.
- Allow them a way to win.
- Give options and possibilities and let them decide.
- Don't contradict unless you have information and the confidence to back it up.
- Appeal to the ego.
- Allow them to talk themselves out of a position rather than to be talked out of it.

need, they will check their watch every 30 seconds and begin extrapolating the length of your presentation by the pace of your voice and the number of pages in front of you. At this point, they have mentally checked out of your presentation.

If you want to sell to an Enterpriser, walk into the room and, instead of making a presentation, say something like, "Let me give you a brief overview of what we are talking about." What this telegraphs to the Enterpriser is, "If we agree on the fundamentals, we might have something to talk about, and if we don't, let's not waste your time or my time." They will immediately voice agreement or disagreement. They may add an addendum to your overview, but as soon as they buy into your business philosophy, it is downhill from there.

Pick up the pace, don't be a slave to your script, and paint with a broad-brush stroke (remember to allow them a way to win). You also better be able to pinpoint when the deal is going to get done and then follow through quickly. Show them that you mean it.

Another key to establishing your competence with Enterprisers is to look the part. If you think there is even a chance that you do not project a look of confidence when you walk into a room, then fake it. Get your chin up in the air, look directly into people's eyes, and put some force into your words. If you don't, the Enterpriser will look right past you. Enterprisers demand competence.

Inquire about their achievements—it *is* all about them. Put an Enterpriser behind the wheel. You should always give Enterprisers the feeling that they are controlling the whole deal—they're in charge.

Suzanne B., a sales professional who fits the Enterpriser personality style, tells the following story about a neighbor who tried to sell her on some nutritional supplements.

> "This neighbor of mine belongs to one of those multilevel marketing things that sells vitamins and such. So, he comes to me and says he wants to tell me about this opportunity that he's sure I would be just great at. He's a nice guy and everything, but he gave the worst stumbling, bumbling presentation I have ever witnessed. He goes on and on and can't string together a coherent thought process. The whole time I'm thinking, 'This guy is so weak! I wouldn't buy Girl Scout cookies from him.' The funny part of it is, his products were actually something I could probably use, but there was no way I was going to buy from this bozo!"

Suzanne's comments reveal several key aspects of the Enterpriser personality. The Enterpriser looks for both competence and confidence in the people they work with and buy from. They smell weakness like a shark smells blood. Act the least bit unsure of yourself, and they will be gone in a flash. It is also quite apparent in Suzanne's story that Enterprisers want you to tell your story well and get to the point fast.

Here is an overview of what the Enterpriser personality wants in dealing with others.

I want:
- To be in control
- Quick results
- The bottom line

I don't want:
- To be taken advantage of
- To be slowed down

You must convince me:
- On what your product will do for me
- Of your competence

Words that fit the Enterpriser comfort zone:

- Results
- Customized solution
- Innovative
- Efficient
- Highly competitive
- Research
- Unique
- Expedite

An important word in presenting to an Enterpriser is *you*. "I want to know what you think." "What has been your experience?" Even when Enterprisers know that their egos are getting stroked, they still like to hear it. Enterprisers like those individuals who are "smart enough" to recognize how brilliant they are.

They want to hear the word *results*. They want to hear that you will "get it done." They like customization. Enterprisers don't want a boilerplate plan. Their point of view is, "I have my own specific situation, so customize it for me." They like the words *innovative, efficient,* and *highly competitive.*

CRITICAL SELLING ADJUSTMENTS

With Analyzers, it is all about facts (see Figure 19.3). Analyzers are a tough group to sell to because they have a natural aversion to "selling." Slow your pace and listen intently when working with an Analyzer. Always lead with facts, or Analyzer clients will quickly shut you down. And never go into a meeting with an Analyzer without having a pad of paper and a pen. Analyzers are impressed to see you taking copious notes while they are talking. This way you will find out the facts *they* want.

FIGURE 19.3 Shifting into *A:* The Analyzer Personality

- Slow your pace—listen intently.
- Be accurate. Don't approximate or round off numbers.
- Do your homework. Be prepared to give every detail about your products or services.
- Set the stage for trust by using data.
- Explore their interests (the latest technologies, etc.).
- Support each feature/benefit statements with logic and rationality.
- Never hurry them with tone or body language.
- Summarize your presentation carefully.
- Detail how you'll follow through.
- Never say, "I know you'll like this" or "You're going to love this!"
- Avoid hyperbole and animated presentations.
- Allow time for decisions.

Do your homework. How may deals have we not closed because we failed to have one or two critical facts about a client? We found out later what the client really wanted to know. We make our final presentation, and we get back a letter saying, "Thanks, but no thanks, because . . ." And that "because . . ." is often something that we could have found out if we had done our homework. The research we did not do and questions we did not ask prevented us from winning the Analyzer account.

I met one sales executive who always asks the CFO (Analyzer), "What are the important issues for you—the issues that you need to be sure are addressed?" He does that because he doesn't want to have to find that information out later on—in a rejection letter.

Avoid exaggeration, emotion, and overpromising. Analyzers are turned off when a salesperson becomes passionate and animated. I have heard many Analyzers say, "I read enthusiasm as a replacement for a lack of information or training." (Conversely with Motivators, if you do not display enthusiasm, they won't give you the time of day.) Also, don't be derailed when an Analyzer seems unenthusiastic about your presentation, because Analyzers are famous for their poker faces.

Summarize your presentation carefully. Use those notes that you took to summarize exactly what you heard during the meeting: the main concerns, the direction you discussed, and the time line. It telegraphs to Analyzers that you paid attention. And remember to give them time—do not try to close the deal too soon.

Andrew S., a sales executive who fits the Analyzer description, tells this story about dealing with a car salesman.

"I went into a car lot because I was pretty well set on buying a model they had on their showroom floor. A salesman comes over to me—he's all smiles and handshakes—and starts telling me how great this model is. I'm annoyed immediately, because I already know this is a good model. Right away he says, 'Why don't you take it for a drive?' I decline and say, 'Well, I have a few questions first.' So I sit in the car, and he sits with me. I see a couple of buttons on the dashboard that I'm unfamiliar with and ask what they are for. He says he doesn't know and why don't I just look at the owner's manual after I take it for a drive. This guy is trying to sell me a $35,000 product and doesn't know a damn thing about it! No matter what I asked him, he didn't have the answer. Finally, about the fourth time he suggested I take a test-drive, I gathered my information pieces and left."

Andrew's response is very characteristic of the Analyzer personality in a selling situation. He wanted information, not emotion. He wanted his many questions answered before he got behind the wheel. He did not like dealing with someone who was unprepared, uneducated—and who kept pushing to a close.

Here is an overview of what the Analyzer personality wants in dealing with others.

I want:	• Accuracy, assurances, and proof
I don't want:	• To be criticized
	• To be hurried
You must convince me:	• On the logic of investing in your product
	• On your track record

Words in the Analyzer's comfort zone:

- Caution
- Logical
- Research
- Analysis
- Projections
- Thorough
- Proof
- High standards

Here are some of the magic words to soothe the Analyzer's highly charged nervous system: *the facts show . . .* and *research*. Particularly if you're a Motivator, and if Analyzers are your villain role, start using words such as *analysis, thorough,* and *high standards*. Remember that Analyzers have very high standards for themselves, and it is difficult for them to deal with people who don't have high standards for themselves. Use the word *consistent*.

Analyzers detest processes and people that are whimsical or "here today, gone tomorrow." This is what they worry about. They want to hear about consistency.

The biggest concern that Analyzers have is doing the right thing. This is why they ask so many questions. Your job is to help them find the right products for them and assure them that they are right.

CRITICAL SELLING ADJUSTMENTS

Start with a smile. Motivators need to see friendliness (see Figure 19.4). Try to be somewhat informal or a little playful about what you are doing, even if it is not easy for you. Lightening up signals to them that you will be enjoyable to work with.

Ask about their histories, their victories, and their goals. Motivators love to tell their stories. When selling, lead with passion, and follow with features and proof. Motivators require the opposite of Analyzers. The approaches Analyzers hate are the ones Motivators love—and vice versa.

Use stories, anecdotes, and metaphors. Motivators love a good metaphor, illustration, anecdote, or analogy. These more colorful forms of communication resonate with the Motivator style, because they bring dry facts to life.

Avoid small print and thick presentations. When you put small print in front of Motivators, they back up and become tense. Their nervous system gets rattled when they have to look at small print or a thick presentation. They are thinking, "Oh no, we're not going to do all that." Neither does this sort of presentation play well to the Motivator's short attention span.

FIGURE 19.4 Shifting to *M:* The Motivator Personality

- Pick up your pace and energy.
- Talk about the potential of your product and services.
- Describe your benefits and program with passion.
- Use storytelling, illustrations, anecdotes, metaphors, and true life experiences.
- Be prepared to respond to a quick decision.
- Ask lots of questions about your client—their histories, their victories.
- Provide an opportunity for your clients to vocalize their goals.
- Remember, they are sold more on your enthusiasm and convictions than they are on features and proof.
- Use an informal and sociable approach.
- Avoid small print and thick presentation.
- Focus on payoffs for them (recognition, excitement, income).

Never write a detailed letter to a Motivator. In written correspondence, use bullet points for the Enterpriser and Motivator personality styles, and use details for the Togetherness and Analyzer personality styles.

Emphasize the payoff for the Motivator. The Motivator's antenna is up for, "What's my payoff here?" and "How is this going to be good for me . . . or make me look good?"

Remember, negativity is a deal killer. Don't walk into a Motivator's office complaining. Don't exercise your cynicism in front of Motivators. They want to know that you are a positive person. They want to deal with optimistic people who are going to get the job done—not with people who are habitually whining and complaining.

Jacqueline T. is a sales professional who fits the Motivator personality style. She told us the story of how a peer tried to sell her on working for his firm.

> "I was at a point in my career where I felt I needed a change, so I accepted an invitation for an interview with another firm. What a total turnoff that was! The guy who interviewed me never smiled or laughed—he took himself so seriously. He just talked about expectations, guidelines, and the competitive advantage he felt his firm had. I remember thinking to myself, 'I wonder if everyone in this place is as boring as you.' I couldn't imagine working for or with someone who took himself so seriously. I mean, the money would have been better, but I think I would have hated every minute."

Jacqueline, like other Motivator personalities, has her radar up for friendliness, flexibility, and optimism. Motivators are more concerned about people than they are about processes. They want to know that they will enjoy and look forward to working with you. Motivators seem to be looking for positive energy in others that they can connect with. They want to squeeze all the enjoyment out of life that they possibly can.

Here is an overview of what the Motivator personality wants in dealing with others.

I want:	• To be noticed
	• To have fun
	• To persuade and influence others
I don't want:	• To be rejected or ignored
	• To get boxed in with detail
You must convince me:	• On whom is using your product
	• On how I can promote it to others

Words in the Motivator comfort zone:

- Quick
- Easy
- Innovative
- Fun
- Big/huge (adjectives about potential)

- Cutting edge
- Competitive
- Possibilities
- Fluid/flexible
- Opportunity

The first magic word for Motivators is *great*. Walk into an office and listen, and wherever you hear "Great!", that's where your Motivators are. *Easy* is also a magic word for Motivators. They also like the words *innovative, creative, big,* and *exponential*. Get a thesaurus and search for synonyms for big and exponential. Motivators like statements like, "This is going to be large!" When presenting your ideas to Motivators, let them know that if they change their mind, "It's not a problem," or "This whole idea is very fluid," or "We're flexible," or "We can move this and move that out." These statements make motivators feel comfortable, because they don't want to get locked in.

Another magic word for Motivators is *opportunity*. Motivators by nature are optimistic people, and they want to believe that there's something bigger and better that they can do. They love to hear motivational speeches about doing the impossible. They want to reach the goal that's never been reached, so talk in terms of opportunity and achievement.

Remember, at the core of everyone you meet is a personality blueprint or personality DNA that drives their perspectives, communication, and responses (including their response to you). Master persuaders learn to adjust their communication intuitively to their clients' comfort levels. Start using these personality persuasion insights, and see the difference in how clients respond to you.

SELLING WITH EQ

- Adjust your presentation style to the personality style of the client.
- Memorize the agenda of each personality style.
- Use a pace and tone of voice that lends comfort to each personality style.

CHAPTER TWENTY

THE POWER OF CURIOSITY
Overcoming the Narcissistic Urge

*"The first step toward improving empathy is
learning to suspend the narcissistic urge."*

—MITCH ANTHONY

The Principles of Emotional Intelligence

- Your interest level in others is the emotional foundation for relational success.
- Many sales approaches pay only lip service to inquiry and consequently raise the defenses of the client.
- Listening skills must be mastered through a disciplined approach toward conversations.

Two men, one of whom was a zoologist, were walking down a crowded urban sidewalk. In midstride, the zoologist remarked, "Listen to the lovely sound of that cricket!"

His companion, amazed that he could distinguish the sound of a cricket amidst the clattering and honking of traffic, asked, "How in the world can you hear a cricket amongst this cacophony of noises?"

The zoologist, rather than answering, took a coin from his pocket and let it fall to the sidewalk. Twenty people stopped in their tracks and looked around for the money. "We hear," the zoologist said, "what we are looking for."

JUST CURIOUS

It was the second year in a row that I was delivering a keynote speech for this company's President's Club banquet. When the awards were handed out, I noticed that the same gentleman (John) had finished number one last year. I also noted that the distance between number one and number two (for both years) was like the distance between first and second at the 2000 golfing U.S. Open (15 strokes between Tiger Woods and Ernie Els). John had again lapped the field.

I asked someone next to me if John did this every year, and he said, "Every year that I can remember."

This aroused my interest in learning what made this guy tick. I approached John after the banquet and asked if he would be willing to have dinner with me the next evening—to which he agreed. I then asked him to do a homework assignment before we met again. I asked him to try to distill his success into a solitary word.

The next evening, John informed me that he found the answer to my question. He thanked me for asking, as he had never before attempted to condense his success into a single principle. The word he chose was basically a description of his nature. If I were to pause here and allow you, the reader, to try and guess what this word was, chances are that you would not get it on your first 20 guesses. In fact, I have performed such an exercise in sales trainings, and John's key word rarely comes up in the first 30 guesses. Here is the word he gave me—*curiosity*.

John explained it this way. "I thought of all the other words that others attribute to sales success: hard work, goal oriented, people skills, etc. But I decided that the one feature people notice about me is that I am naturally a very curious person. I love learning about people. They all have unique stories to tell, unique paths that they have taken, and unique hopes for the future. I like hearing about my clients, their children, and their grandchildren. I think clients like this about me, so they tell their friends about me."

"ENOUGH OF ME TALKING ABOUT ME . . ."

John's compelling success is due to his curious nature, which in turn holds at bay his own inner rumblings for attention, glory, and credit. These inner rumblings, reflected in our conversations and behaviors, are what I refer to as the *narcissistic urge*. My favorite example of this urge is the guy in Hollywood who said to his friend, "Enough of me talking about me, how about you talk about me for a while?" Overinflated egos and personal insecurities are just two of the forces at work contributing to this obsessive self-centeredness. Ultimately, this narcissistic urge provides emotional discomfort for others, who either avoid the narcissist or stop taking them seriously.

How prevalent is this narcissistic urge? To answer, first ask yourself about the last time you were in a conversation where the person you were talking to could not ask enough about you. Do you remember such a conversation? Of course you do—if such a conversation has ever taken place. Selflessness is in short supply, a fact that is strikingly obvious at any cocktail party. What is not in short supply, however, is one-upmanship, or egotism, or megalomania, or self-promotion, or what I like to call the "Clark Kent conversation pattern" (stories designed to make you look like Superman).

In the next ten conversations you have, make mental notes on the polarity or central focus of these conversations. Is the other party trying to create a polarity around you or herself? Or is the individual trying to create equal polarities? As you observe these polarity patterns, you may feel admiration for some people, disgust for others, but most of all, you will move to a higher level of awareness about the polarities you are creating. Beyond the socially acceptable but supercilious greeting, "How are you?", the majority of people you meet either do not know how or do not care to make further inquiry. A clear but negative example is the jaded (and narcissistic) salesman who said to me, "I'll tell you the people I can't handle—the ones who, when you ask, 'How are you doing?', think you actually want to hear the answer." Obviously this man's sales career has not been anchored in empathy.

Self-centeredness and self-absorption are common (in varying degrees) to all people. Narcissism can be described as the cancer of the human psyche and personal relationships. It prevents the development of empathy. Many sales professionals do not have good inquiry skills, because they simply are not interested in others.

Victor Frankl, the famed psychiatrist and philosopher, who survived imprisonment at Auschwitz, stated that one of the most elevated states humans can rise to is that of "self-transcendence," which in succinct terms means, "finding meaning by putting the concerns of others above your own."

In my workshops I ask, "How does it make you feel when you are trapped with a person who dominates the conversation?" One participant quickly replied, "Married!" On a more serious side, the answers I most often hear are *bored, angry,* and *frustrated,* and eventually the word *unimportant* comes to the surface. When you peel away the layers of the emotional onion, you find the conversational monopolist—much like the onion—causes discomfort.

THE SIGN AROUND EVERY PERSON'S NECK

Early in my career, a wise mentor, who was especially skilled with people, instructed me on how to make profound connections. He said, "From this day forward, remember this one fact about every person you meet—everyone is wearing signs around their necks that very few people know how to read. The sign has only four words on it, but 95 percent of those competing with you do not have a clue as to what it says. The four words are *Help me feel important.*

I do not believe I've ever received more important instruction than those four words. Everyone wears that sign, and yet so few know how to read it. I am conscious of the sign around my own neck, and I love to talk to those who know how to read it. I also am highly conscious of the signs around the necks of those I meet. This desire to feel important is in our very nature. In a competitive society, where self-promotion is as common as the air we breathe, you will have little competition at making this empathetic connection once you recognize this sign. These individuals are typically in corporate cultures that do little to tell them how important they are. Many carry doubts and insecurity about themselves. Anything you can do to help people feel more significant will be welcome.

THE SELF-CENTERED SELF-DELUSION

A feature article in a recent sales industry magazine talked about a study conducted on the communication skills of sales professionals (in this case, investment advisors).[*] The findings, if nothing else, confirmed that most sales professionals overestimate their empathy skills. What they found, in a nutshell, was this: 71 percent of respondents said they believed that their clients were content with their communication skills, yet 57 percent of the clients stated that their representative was falling short of their expectations in communication. This tidbit of research is the tip of the empathetic iceberg that threatens every sales professional—believing you are a good communicator when you are not. One may be the greatest presenter in the company yet the worst listener. It is probably not too difficult to think of any examples. As the relationship progresses, the client is much

---

[*]Kathleen Gurney and Mel Srybnik, "Listen Up," *Investment Advisor* (December 2001): 36.

more impressed with listening skills than with presentation skills (one study found that one out of four high net worth investors were thinking of leaving their advisors—and the number one reason was communication).

THEY JUST DON'T GET IT

"He just doesn't listen!" were Nancy's words, as she explained why she had just changed vendors for her company. "I would look this guy in the eye and tell him what I wanted and needed, and he would just continue to push on his own agenda. Obviously this was not about us for him, so we switched. And, truthfully, he probably has the superior line, but I can't deal with him anymore."

It would hardly be possible to quantify how much money is lost and left on the table because of poor listening skills, but I'm sure it would be in the billions. The question to ask yourself is "How much money is it costing me?" Is it possible that some of your clients—who you assume are satisfied with the way you communicate—would say they are not satisfied? The safest premise we can operate from is this: I can always do a better job of listening. This premise will safeguard us from smugness, arrogance, and the sort of hubris that causes important accounts to flee.

Those who possess excellent inquiry skills are curious and genuinely interested in others by nature. Yet they have also learned that this skill must be purposefully developed to become habitual.

THE EMPATHY SELF-ASSESSMENT

If your most important client contacts were allowed to fill out a listening skills report on you (see Figure 20.1), how well do you think you would score?

We are all guilty at times of being poor listeners. Some personalities, however, are more susceptible than others. One irony of the sales profession is that the field naturally attracts the enterprising and motivated individuals, who, by nature of personality, have short attention spans and are given to impatience. Ironically, their success hinges on their ability to tune into others. Because neither feature—distractibility or impatience—aids in the development of better listening skills, sales professionals must constantly check their psychological impulses (picture a hockey check here) when talking to clients.

We are not all great listeners by nature; however, that does not mean we cannot become great listeners and observers of others. If we approach

FIGURE 20.1 The Empathy Self-Assessment

1. _____ (your name)	gives undivided attention when I am talking.	A	B	C	D	F
2. _____ (your name)	is tuned into me rather than thinking of his or her own response.	A	B	C	D	F
3. _____ (your name)	answers in a way that reflects my major concerns.	A	B	C	D	F
4. _____ (your name)	keeps the conversation polarized on my needs, issues, and concerns.	A	B	C	D	F
5. _____ (your name)	gives a summary of what I have said.	A	B	C	D	F

listening as a discipline and a habit, we eventually can conquer our impulses. We can develop a pattern that we will feel at home with when engaging in conversation. We simply need a clear agenda for the behaviors that constitute good listening skills.

Poor listeners are those individuals who:

- Are thinking of their own response rather than tuning into the speaker
- Are looking to the statements of others as a springboard to their own agenda (the chief temptation for sales professionals—jumping too early into presentation)
- Are grandstanding with witty comments, stories, and opinions at the expense of the client's story and opinions
- Focus more on facts than on feelings
- Are obsessed with details, so they miss the point or the big picture of what the speaker is trying to say
- Are not in control of nervous or uptight body language signals
- Hint at disapproval and impatience with tone and body language

Who doesn't occasionally trespass across these boundaries of poor listening? Tight schedules, demanding goals, and trying clients can combine to take us off of our best listening game, unless we are vigilant regarding our listening behavior. Ultimately, our discipline in these little matters helps to define our destiny.

We need not possess a psychologist's listening aptitude by nature to develop these skills. If, however, we do not possess a natural aptitude for listening, we will have to work that much harder at developing the skill. In Figure 20.2 is a short assessment that, if you are honest with it, will help you to gauge your natural aptitude for empathy. Don't be dismayed if you do not have a high natural aptitude for empathy, as we have discovered that many high-achieving sales professionals who are naturally high in resilience are also naturally lower in empathy.

IS SELLING IN THE TELLING?

Two patterns in sales training courses concern me.

1. Overweighted emphasis on presenting, and token attention to development of discovery skills
2. Teaching that questions and listening are forms of manipulating clients

The top salespeople know that, more important than having a shoe to sell, is that they have an accurate measurement of the client's foot, the type of walking the client does, and the particular stresses the client experiences. In other words, they are not distracted by the fact that they have a nice product to sell. Much discovery work needs to be accomplished to be sure the client will be happy with the product. True selling is not in the telling; it is in the gathering of information regarding the client.

When I was introduced to Larry, I had been told by the introducing party that he was legendary in his sales ability. He had led the nation in sales for his company for seven consecutive years until he was promoted to national headquarters. I was invited to tag along on an important sales call. In my mind, I was prepared to meet a polished, eloquent presenter. What I witnessed left a lasting impression about the powers of empathy or emotional radar.

I never saw or heard Larry sell anything, but I knew that the client was sold by the time the meeting was over. Larry sat back and asked well-thought-out and incisive questions about the client's business operations and concerns. By asking questions, he cajoled the client into revealing frustrations and annoyances he had experienced with competitors and his own company. Larry was able to coax out the compromises the client was willing to make to get a deal done. The exchange was all nonthreatening in nature. The conversation was clearly focused on the client's concerns.

FIGURE 20.2 The Empathy Rubic

Directions: *Read each of the following statements and rank yourself on the continuum.*

I inquire into the ideas, opinions, and feelings of others . . .

1	2	3	4	5
Not much at all				Quite often

When others are talking to me . . .

1	2	3	4	5
My mind is racing ahead			I'm trying to absorb their thoughts	

When someone gets hurt or is suffering, I . . .

1	2	3	4	5
Tell them to get up or get over it				Sympathize with them

When someone is expressing their feelings to me, I . . .

1	2	3	4	5
Get easily annoyed				Seek to understand

When it comes to body language, I . . .

1	2	3	4	5
Get confused				Can easily interpret

When I sense an agitated tone, I . . .

1	2	3	4	5
Quickly move on			Seek to understand the source of agitation	

When responding to others, I . . .

1	2	3	4	5
Address facts only			Address facts and emotional undercurrent	

When someone expresses a view I disagree with, I . . .

1	2	3	4	5
Correct them				Inquire further

When I encounter views I strongly disagree with, I . . .

1	2	3	4	5
Confront and / or disassociate myself				Try to disagree agreeably

When someone is angry or condescending with me, I . . .

1	2	3	4	5
Fight fire with fire			Seek to know source of frustration	

Add your total score [＿＿＿＿＿＿]　　　　**Place yourself on the Empathy Continuum**

10	20	30	40	50
Uninterested				Empathetic

Larry's close—if you could call it that—was to say something like, "You might want to take some time to weigh out the extra peace of mind we can provide you against the premium we're going to charge to provide it. Why don't I give you a call in a week or so." Larry did not have to wait a week, though. Most of the time, the client would call back the next day and say, "Let's do it."

I left that meeting with a new appreciation for what selling is all about. Larry demonstrated an uncanny sense of emotional radar. Through years of discipline in asking the right questions, listening closely, and reading between the lines, he was able to pick out what mattered most to each client. An emotional need must be met in the sales process, and Larry has demonstrated his ability to discern that need. In Larry's words, "It's hard to find out what the client really wants—while your mouth is moving."

Now that I'm convinced I need to put the spotlight of conversation on the client and suppress my own narcissistic urges, what do I ask? Glad you asked. The next chapter will reveal the approach that will help you move from a vendor to a partner in the eyes of your clients.

SELLING WITH EQ

- Check your narcissistic tendencies at the door.
- Help every client feel important.
- Listen for the messages behind the message. Practice reading between the lines.

CHAPTER TWENTY-ONE

EMOTIONAL ARCHEOLOGY
Mastering the Art of the Irresistible Question

"Questions are the creative acts of intelligence."

—FRANK KING

The Principles of Emotional Intelligence

- The common logic for sales presentations raises a client's emotional defenses.
- Asking the right questions unlocks the emotional motives of the client.
- Skilled inquirers do less selling but make more sales.

Experienced archeologists ignore nothing in their digs. They establish boundaries, form grids, and pan through every inch of dirt. They know that each small and seemingly insignificant piece that is brought to the surface could be connected to a much larger artifact lying below the surface—one that could be of monumental historical significance.

The greatest mistake sales professionals make is neglecting to learn more about the customer before making the presentation. Commonly, sales professionals are so passionate and enthused about their product story, they fail to hear their customers' stories. No factor has more influence on productivity than the simple process of asking the right questions. The following story illustrates the consequences of failing to ask the right questions—of failing to dig a little deeper—before presenting a product.

An insurance agent sat down with my wife and me to talk about buying a life insurance/savings product that, in his opinion, would be a great tool for saving for our children's college education. There was just one problem with his presentation: he did not bother to ask us how we felt about paying for our children's college education.

Had he bothered to ask, we would have told him our story and opinions. My wife had worked her way through eight years of college, and I had worked my way through four years. Neither of us had received any help from our parents (who couldn't afford to help). We had both observed classmates who were on what we called the "Budweiser scholarship" from Mom and Dad. Consequently, we came to the conclusion that the development of work ethic would be as high or higher a priority than pedigree with our children.

We had developed a college funding plan with our children in which we would match every dollar they saved with a dollar of our own. This also included matching funds on scholarships they earned. The result? When my oldest son went to college, he had three years of college expenses saved and in the bank. Because this agent didn't ask and pressed on with his assumption, we didn't tell him—and he didn't get the sale.

The next agent that came to our home was brilliant in regards to asking the right questions. First, he asked me how my wife and I met (I remember wondering how he knew to ask such a question of us). In my home, this is the magic question, because my wife and I have a *Sleepless in Seattle* kind of story. We met on a blind date and were married 13 days later. I always tell people, "I could have married her in five days but you can't rush these things!" My wife loves when I tell this story to strangers.

Next, he asked my wife what she was doing before we met (he couldn't have asked a more important question). She proceeded to tell the story of how her first husband had died from lung cancer—which was discovered three months into their marriage and which killed him three months after that. She also told him how, in the course of dying, her first husband had neglected to sign a beneficiary transfer form that would assign his life insurance benefit to her. As a result, the benefit went directly to his parents, who somehow reasoned that their dead son would want to leave his young widow bereaved and broke.

Regarding this second agent's approach, my question is this: "At this point in the conversation, can I possibly buy enough life insurance to make my wife feel secure?" This agent had not said a word about his company or a product, but the sale was over in two questions. He learned everything he needed to know about our lives and the emotional reasons we would have for owning his product. He left with the sale of a million-dollar policy.

LOGJAMMED LOGIC

There is a fundamental error in the rationale offered by most schools of selling. Figure 21.1 illustrates the common logic that sales professionals learn.

Sales presenters typically go into the following logic pattern.

- A = **Ask** a few questions to get to know the client.
- B = Talk about why people **buy** their product(s).
- C = Begin to make **closing** statements.
- D = Ask for a **decision.**

After the first two steps of asking a couple of cursory questions and offering reasons to buy, a strange psychological phenomenon begins taking place. The customer begins to raise a wall of objections. Why would a potential customer be objecting? Possibly because you have not yet uncovered or addressed their emotional reasons for needing or wanting your product.

There is a chance that they do not need or want your product, and you are just assuming they do. Whatever the case may be, this wall of objections is emotional in nature and cannot be circumvented with closing logic. The error is in not doing more discovery work up front to discover their emotional motives for the purchase. We have failed to dig below the surface. The client's emotional agenda is *the* issue. It does not matter how brilliant your company or your product features might be, because if you are not meeting their emotional agenda, you are wasting your breath. It is foolish to present a single fact without the assurance that you understand their emotional agenda regarding your product or service.

Resist the temptation to promote your product, until you have asked enough questions to understand the emotional agenda that will lead to a decision. As illustrated in the case with the two insurance agents, the one

FIGURE 21.1 Linear Sales Process

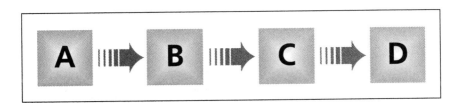

who asks the right questions gets the decision—not the one who tries to dazzle with features and benefits. How many times have you seen a client nodding but not signing? What you are witnessing is the "distance between agreement and action." When people nod in agreement, it means that their intellectual or rational agendas have been met. When they sign their names, it means that their emotional agendas have been met.

Remember that the distance between agreement and action is exactly 18 inches—the distance between the head and the heart.

GETTING YOUR CLIENT'S STORY

"Every man is, in certain respects, (A) like all men,
(B) like some other men, (C) like no other man."

—C. CLUCKHOM AND H. MURRAY

Intelligent inquiry, or *emotional archeology,* is like mining. We explore the recesses of the clients' memory banks and emotional storehouses, looking for veins with which we can legitimately connect. Classic sales training breaks the sales process into three categories: discovery, presentation, and closing. For some reason, whether because of impatience or imprudence, many sales professionals pay token observance to the discovery process and, instead, put all their chips on their ability to wow the customer with their presentation.

The payoffs of intelligent inquiry go far beyond discovering why clients might buy our products and services. There are far-reaching relational dividends that we experience by asking the uncommon question and digging deeper into the thoughts and opinions of clients.

THANKS FOR ASKING

- People like being asked.
- People like to talk about their opinions, ideas, and lives.
- People respect you for asking.
- People feel more important because you asked.

One sales professional told me that she asks questions of her clients until she can find something to "respect and admire" about that client. At this point, she feels she makes a personal connection.

I believe another reason for the dearth of discovery is that many sincere sales professionals do not know what to ask. They lack a model for emotionally intelligent inquiry. For this reason I have developed the q1 and q2 models of discovery (see Figures 21.2 and 21.3). The questions clients typically get asked by sales professionals are quantitative in nature. "What are the features of what you currently have?" "How much are you paying now?" "What features and benefits are you looking for?" "What is the budget you are working with?" Occasionally the seller makes a foray into the qualitative by inquiring into the goals of the client or the client's current satisfaction level, but the qualitative aspects typically get short shrift. In the end, what we don't know about our clients comes back to haunt us.

"It takes reason to answer a question well;

it takes imagination to ask it well."

—ANONYMOUS

GOING TO *Q* SCHOOL

In the q1 (quantitative) side of discovery, the factual landscape is covered by an inquiry into price/costs/budgets (numbers), necessary features and benefits (needs), people involved in the sales cycle (names), and settling on a solution and on a price (negotiation).

Remember that, although these inquiries are quantitative in nature, emotional land mines are attached if you do not tread with empathy (emotional radar) in your approach. Following are some examples of how salespeople offend clients in the quantitative discovery process (in the words of some clients).

Numbers (price/costs/budgets). "Some salespeople ask far too much information, and it feels like an invasion of privacy."

Needs (necessary features and benefits). "There have been times when I was describing a product I had purchased, and the salesperson got this condescending look on her face, like, 'You bought *that?*'—not realizing that I was the person who made that purchasing decision and they were insulting me. It made me feel stupid!"

Names (people involved in the sales cycle). "I do a lot of due diligence for purchases the company makes, yet I can tell some sales reps are just trying to use me to get to the boss. They want to deal with the decision maker

FiGURE 21.2 q1 Inquiry (quantitative)

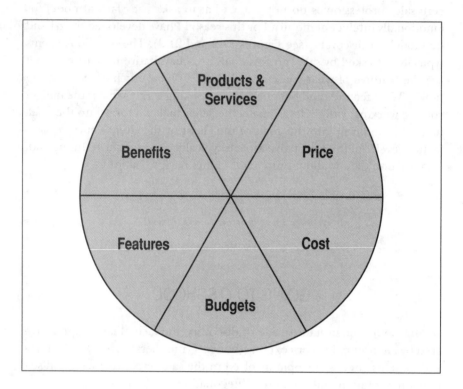

and view me only as a stepping-stone. They do not realize that, come decision time, the boss is going to give a lot of weight to my opinion of both product and representative. When they take that approach, it makes me feel like they don't appreciate my role in the organization."

Negotiations (settling on a solution and on a price). "This is the point where we see some of people's worst colors surface. You can pick it up in their tone and negotiating style. Some are controlling egomaniacs, some are whiny, some are overly rigid, some are overly sensitive, while some are promising much more than they can deliver (lying). Ideally, negotiating can be like a tennis match where you battle it out but enjoy the other player's competitiveness and game in the process."

Moving to *q2*

In the q2 approach (see Figure 21.3) to discovery, sufficient weight is given to the quantitative but is preceded in importance by the qualitative

FIGURE 21.3 q2 Inquiry (qualitative)

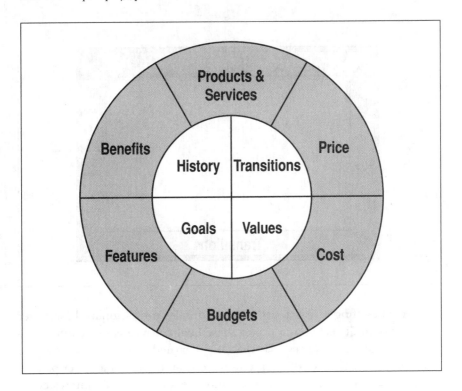

discovery process. The q2 school of thought assumes that you are building a long-term relationship with the client and are not in it for a one-year fling. In this school of thought, the emotionally intelligent sales professional begins the excavation process intent on uncovering four critical areas of qualitative discovery.

- History (where they've been and how they got to where they are)
- Goals (where they are headed and their plans for getting there)
- Transitions (the problems, challenges, and growing pains they are currently experiencing and anticipate in the near future)
- Values (the principles upon which they have centered their life and business)

If you want to get a more accurate portrait of who your client is and how he or she operates at the emotional level, these four areas of inquiry will tell you what you need to know. Picture the four areas of inquiry as the four boards that, when put together, form a frame around the portrait of who the client is (see Figure 21.4).

FIGURE 21.4 Framing the Picture

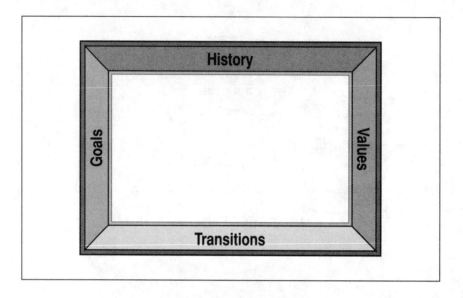

In conducting research with successful sales professionals, I have met many who intuitively inquired into these qualitative categories and attribute much of their success to what they learned from these questions. Following are examples of q2 questions you can use to get a better picture of who your clients are. Remember, most vendors are only interested in "what their clients have" and not in "who they are." You stand out like a beacon when you master the qualitative side of the discovery process. You are doing business with people, not entities. The q2 approach is a quantum leap toward personalizing every business relationship.

Questions about History:

- Where are you from?
- How did you get started in this business?
- What other kinds of work have you done?
- How did you get from "there" to "here?"

Questions about Goals:

- What are your personal goals?
- What do you want to be when you grow up?
- Where would you like to see this business in five years?
- Where would you like to see yourself in five years?

Questions about Transitions:

- How do you see your business changing?
- What are your biggest issues right now? (Where do you need the most help?)
- What stage of the life cycle is your business currently in?
- What concerns do you see on the horizon for your business?

Questions about Values:

- What values have you focused on in building your business?
- Why did you go into this business?
- What do you love most about your work?
- What do you like least about your work?
- What do you like most/least about your current vendor?
- How do you feel about _____ (our company, our product, our people, our proposal, etc.)?

BECOMING BETTER BIOGRAPHERS

Inquiring into your clients' histories enables you to read between the lines of where they came from, how they got started, and the paths they have followed—which helps you to understand your clients more clearly.

I met one sales professional who placed a major emphasis on finding out where his clients were from. He had a map of the United States on his back wall with pins on it signifying where all his clients came from. It soon became the central conversation piece as clients commented on individuals they knew from some of those places—and sometimes they discovered they had a common connection. By asking where they were from, he was simply reducing the degrees of separation between himself and the prospect. Remember the six degrees of separation from Kevin Bacon? (Someone you know, knows someone, who knows someone, who knows someone, who knows Kevin Bacon.) The connections exist—and the good archeologist will uncover them.

Your inquiry into the clients' goals can tie the products and services you offer to their hopes and aspirations. If you have a product or service that can help your clients reach their goals at a faster pace, then you have found a legitimate reason for doing business. Many have discovered that by asking clients about their dreams and goals, they have been able to make strategic introductions tying their products to their goals. The very worst that can happen by inquiring into their goals is that you have learned something about them that most competitors will never bother to learn.

The transition inquiry is about finding the sore spots, the immediate needs, and the annoyances that are taking the fun out of the business for the client. Every business has problems that need to be solved. Even if your product cannot solve these problems, you are in a much better position, because you see the big picture in regards to the challenges of the client's particular business.

Understanding the values of your client is the linchpin to empathy. Too often, vendors cross lines of conversation and behavior that trespass on values that the client holds dear. The specific values that each of your clients have followed in building their businesses will give you a psychological and moral portrait of the person you are building a relationship with. It is paramount in importance to know the clients' likes and dislikes so that you can stay on the credit side of their emotional ledgers.

I once read a study of the conversation patterns of sales professionals and their clients, where a clock measured who did most of the talking. It may come as no surprise that the seller talked 49 out of every 60 seconds. I have to pause at such a statistic and ask, "What can you possibly learn while your mouth is moving?" You do not discover treasures by looking at a map and talking—you discover by digging. Rouse your curiosity, use your imagination, and ask *irresistible* questions. Once your clients start talking, they will tell you all you need to know to succeed—with them.

SELLING WITH EQ

- Spend more time listening than you do talking.
- Ask irresistible questions.
- Focus on your clients' needs and goals.

CHAPTER TWENTY-TWO

IT'S NOT ABOUT YOU

"Human nature will not easily find a helper better than love."

—SOCRATES

Principles of Emotional Intelligence

- A serving mind-set is key to building long-term loyalty.
- Inexhaustible persistence is rooted in empathy for the plight of the client.
- Great sales professionals do not allow opportunism to short-circuit long-term opportunity.
- Personalizing your story demonstrates empathy and delivers greater impact.

In the mid-1980s, I moved my young family to a new city where I barely knew a soul. I asked my lone acquaintance in this city whom he would recommend as a real estate agent. He said he had the perfect person and would be glad to make the introduction. His recommendation would become a life-altering event.

He introduced us to the sweet, petite, gray-haired Beulah, who had an angelic face and who commenced a conversation more typical of a grandmother than a real estate agent. She asked us questions such as "Why are you moving here?", "Where did you live before, and what were you doing there?", "What about your children, how old are they?", and "And aren't children wonderful?" Soon enough she segued into the discussion of housing. "What kind of house did you move from?" "How big a mortgage do you feel you can afford?"

At the time, we felt we could afford a $50,000 mortgage. We had no equity from our previous home, and we would have to borrow some money from our parents for a down payment. She was candid and told us that our choices were limited at that price, but she would do her best to find us the best home possible within our means.

As she drove us from home to home and we saw what $50,000 would buy, we found she had prepared us for reality. Coming from a small town in Iowa, we were accustomed to more house for this price. After a long and disappointing day, Beulah informed us that she had one other house she wanted us to see. Although she thought the home would be perfect for us, she said it was a bit out of our price range. This house was about to be listed for over $70,000 by some close friends of hers who were in the same line of work as us. As she had predicted, we fell in love with the beautifully kept, blue, one-and-a-half story home but feared we would not be able to raise enough down payment to make it work.

Beulah offered to do the following: She would introduce us to a banker who might work with us (I was self-employed with a sporadic income stream), and she would reduce her commission for selling the house and talk to her friends to see what might work for them. She told us we should go to our parents to see how much money they might be able to lend us toward the down payment.

We visited with each set of parents, and they lent us what they could, which gave us a total of $7,000 to use as a down payment. A few days later, we reconvened. The sellers had agreed to a price of $67,000, which we offered to pay contingent on funding. We drove with Beulah to talk with the banker. The banker told us he could lend us the money only if we could put 20 percent down toward the purchase. This meant we needed an additional $7,000, which we did not have and had no way of getting. The banker might as well have asked for an additional $70,000. Beulah seemed as deflated as we were by the news.

As we got into Beulah's car, she turned to us and said, "I just can't help but feel that this house is supposed to be your house. There must be a way to make this work out for you."

I thanked her for her sentiments but confirmed the fact that there was simply no more money available anywhere for us to borrow.

"Well," she said, "don't you give up just yet. Let me think about it and call you tomorrow."

The next day, Beulah called and said, "I just know you're supposed to be in this house, and I have decided that I am going to personally lend you the additional $7,000 you need, and I won't take no for an answer."

We were speechless. All we could say was, "We can't ask you to do this!"

She replied, "You didn't ask me. I offered it and that's that." She lent us the $7,000 and gave us five years to pay back the sum—so "we wouldn't have too much pressure." Beulah passed away just days after we paid her the last payment on that note.

When I think of the greatest salesperson I ever met, I think of Beulah. Here was a woman, a commissioned salesperson, who was utterly selfless in the process and whose generosity was a gift from heaven. Obviously, this woman didn't go around every day waiving her commissions and making personal loans to virtual strangers, but the fact that she did this time indicated that her job was about more than selling houses. It was about helping people get to the place they belonged and being able to turn a house into a home.

IT'S ABOUT LIFE

Mark had reviewed Sam's insurance coverages and was concerned that Sam, in his early 60s, had neglected to give serious attention to his level of life insurance. At the current level of coverage, his untimely death would cause certain hardship for his family-owned business. Mark emphatically stated this in Sam's review and watched as Sam dismissively waved him off, "Yeah, yeah, I'm fine."

That night, Mark tossed and turned thinking about Sam. Not that he had a premonition, but he felt Sam needed to understand the serious threat to his estate. He went back to see Sam the next day and rearticulated his concerns.

Sam said, "I'll think about it," which Mark knew from experience meant no.

Three days later, Mark stopped in again. Sam greeted him with, "Now whaddya want?"

Mark said, "I'm not leaving here until you sign this application and get this situation where it needs to be for your wife and family."

Sam finally acceded, saying, "I will, if you promise to get off my back."

A few weeks later, while driving down a country road, Mark happened upon a one-car accident that had just taken place. The Lincoln Continental was turned over. Mark thought the Lincoln Continental looked vaguely familiar, so he jumped out of his car to see if he could be of any help. When he looked in the overturned vehicle, he saw Sam, dead of a heart attack.

The very fact that you get paid for providing the service or products you provide will always leave open the door of cynicism in the client's mind. Sam thought Mark was just trying to make a sale, but Mark persisted because he knew his motives transcended Sam's opinion of his motives. Genuine, sincere motives such as those possessed by Beulah and Mark fuel an inexhaustible supply of persistence.

People will wonder why you are so persistent. Clarity will come by virtue of the fact that you will not go away. Opportunity comes by way of impor-tunity—persistently pursuing what you want. But that importunity must be sincere in its desire to help the client.

One member of my seasoned sales pro roundtable offered the follow-ing metaphor regarding the role that empathy-motivated persistence has played in his career.

> "I often think of the story I heard about teaching new tricks to a old dog. There was this owner that put up an invisible defense that zaps the dog in order to control the dog while he was at work. The dog overcame the zapper defense by moving just close enough to it to set it off, but not close enough to get the full charge. Even-tually the dog wore down the battery and walked right out of the yard. Many potential clients have such defenses. I wear down their batteries by my persistence in demonstrating that I'm here for their good."

Stephen Halperin, president of a leading, professional static-control service, told me a great sales story that contains an instructive subplot on identifying and empathizing with the client's need. Stephen's father, who started the firm, invented a solution that, when applied to carpets, would eliminate static electricity for one year. His father, being a natural-born salesperson, would walk into corporate office suites on the top floor of high-rises where, apparently, static electricity would be at its worst, and announce to the receptionist, "I'm here about the static electricity."

The receptionist, accustomed to seeing customers receive a shock when touching her counter after walking across the carpet would declare, "Oh, thank God, it's about time!"

Mr. Halperin would then ask, "Who should I see?" and go about mak-ing his sale.

We would all agree that this sales ploy was very clever, but we should also pause long enough to ask *why* it was so clever. The reason his approach worked so well was that he understood their problem, empathized with them, and had a solution in tow.

Before you open your mouth about your product or service, be sure you know what problem you are there to solve.

SHORTSIGHTED LONG SHOTS

Nate B., a telephone systems consultant, says that one way a sales professional can convince clients of their genuine desire to help (and not exploit) is by declining to sell that which you know will be counterproductive to your client. He told me:

> "I had a client who had a growing business, and he wanted state-of-the-art everything in it. After I installed his first phone system, he told me he was ready to move up to something better. He told me about a friend who had recently purchased a high-end system for his business and mentioned some of the bells and whistles he found attractive. Although I stood to make more money by selling him what he thought he wanted, I informed him that I thought that the system he was looking at was a poor match for his type of business—and in the long run might prove problematic. I proposed a less expensive system that had the capabilities to handle the growth he expected in the next three years.
>
> "Some time later, he called to tell me how happy he was that I put his interests ahead of mine. His friend who had once called bragging about his system now was complaining about the mess this system had caused in his business. I get more referral business from this client than anybody else. He tells every business owner he knows about how I treated him."

In interviews with successful sales professionals, I have heard commentary over and over again on keeping the long-term relationship with the client at the forefront of the thought processes. Shortsighted opportunism has closed many a door and aborted many a career. Gavin, a sales manager for a large appliance firm, told me:

> "I'm constantly reminding our people that 'It's not about today—it's about tomorrow.' Spend more time trying to find out what they really need instead of just trying to get a deal done. When the buzz of a new purchase wears off, people must feel that they bought the right thing for the right reason and at the right price.
>
> If they don't feel this way, they'll blame the person and firm that sold it—they won't blame themselves for not being informed. It's hard to convince some people of this fact, but after 26 years, I know it's not about making a sale, it's about building trust. That principle must go beyond lip service. It must be gospel."

A study by the Securities and Exchange Commission revealed that 33 percent of clients left financial broker and advisor offices feeling like they had been talked into buying something they were not sure about. The fact that such a statistic exists is proof enough to conclude that many of these advisors lack empathy. The emotional ledger should be settled *before* the financial ledger—not afterwards. While such a statistic does not indict every advisor (as many clients are skittish about every purchase), it does implicate those who are selling a product for the sake of selling a product—with little or no regard for the clients' needs.

Manipulations of this sort are precisely the behaviors that sabotage all hopes of a long-term relationship. This sort of opportunism, for the sake of reaching today's sales goal, ultimately leads to a demise in client relationships and one's sales career. As empathetic sales professionals know, such tactics are not necessary if you have an eye and an ear for legitimate needs that can be resolved with your product or service.

PERSONALLY SPEAKING

"Find purpose in life so big that it will challenge every capacity to be at your best."

—DAVID O. MCKAY

Steven is passionate about motivating people to get their estate plans in order. He is the director of sales for an estate-planning firm and has seen firsthand the devastation that comes to families that are not proactive with their estate planning. He witnessed the compounding toll of long-term care, taxation, and, ultimately, probate on his own family's estate. Steven knows that procrastination and denial are the chief culprits, because most folks do not want to think about dying, much less plan for it. But he knows that the only thing surer than death and taxes are your death taxes, if you don't prepare ahead of time.

Steven's personalized story to potential clients is effective because he communicates empathy. One of his peers in the firm informed me that his close rate is twice that of the previous director of sales. This is due to his sense of conviction he communicates in his story. He is not selling a product; he is offering a solution.

Conviction in the solution that you bring to the table is the hallmark of highly successful sales professionals—the more personal the story the better. Empathy will keep you going after a thousand nos, if you know you have the solution to the problem. Think through the following questions as you seek to bring more personalization to your story.

- Have you personally benefited from the product or service you sell (or a similar product or service)?
- Is there someone close to you whose story you can tell?
- Other than for a paycheck, why are you doing what you are doing? How well do you communicate this to your clients?
- What is the greatest intangible, emotional benefit of buying your product or service? How well do you communicate those intangibles?

Steve Mikez, a former wholesaler, told me that one of his retail clients once said to him, "Steve I can't help but buy from you, you're so *evangelistic* about your products!" Steve was passionate about his products because he believed they were the best on the market, were right for the times—and were good enough to use himself.

The bottom line in long-term sales success is that the self-serving sales professional cannot keep pace in the race with the serving sales professional. Empathy is the tortoise, and opportunism is the hare. Empathy is the foundational motive that feeds the sales professional's sense of purpose and persistence in adverse climates and circumstances.

SELLING WITH EQ

- Make a difference in your clients' lives by taking an interest in their lives. Be extraordinary by doing the extraordinary.
- If you understand your clients' needs, you will not be easily dissuaded in your efforts.
- Consider the long-term emotional consequences before proposing a solution. More important than the immediate result is the subsequent impact on the relationship.
- Empathy is developed by identifying with the plight and problems of your client and is communicated by personalizing your story.

CHAPTER TWENTY-THREE

THE "LIKABILITY" QUOTIENT

"The most important single ingredient in the formula
of success is knowing how to get along with people."

—TEDDY ROOSEVELT

"Friendships are fragile things and require as much care
in handling as any other fragile and precious thing."

—RANDOLPH S. BOURNE

The Principles of Emotional Intelligence

- Clients place as much emphasis on "likability" as they do on ability.
- Relationships are dynamic in nature and are in a constant state of contraction or expansion.
- We must remain vigilant regarding the balances in our clients' emotional bank accounts.
- Some relational errors lead to irreparable emotional distancing.

Far too often in a selling situation, a tug-of-war develops between the rational and feeling sides of the brain. One side asks, "Does this make sense?" while the other side asks, "Does this feel right?" Ninety-nine percent of the time, the feeling side wins over the rational side, and if the deal doesn't feel right, it is usually the seller's fault.

Let me tell you about the easiest consulting assignment I have ever experienced. I was approached by a firm I will call XYZ Solutions. This was a company that had positioned itself pretty well in its industry. They seemed to have it all—the longest track record, high-quality products and services, an admirable service record, and representatives who were informed and accomplished. The question they wanted answered was this: "Why they were failing to pull highly desirable accounts from a certain competitor (ABC Solutions) that, on paper, was inferior to XYZ?"

My approach was to talk to the decision makers at these accounts and ask them, "Why do you do business with ABC?" I did not ask, "Why don't you do business with XYZ?" You can probably guess the answers I heard 90 percent of the time. These answers were not about product quality, pricing, or company history. The answers were about the human component. I repeatedly heard phrases like:

- "I *like* Mary."
- "Joe is *easy to work with*."
- "I have a good *relationship* with Rich."
- "We *enjoy* working with Susan. Everybody looks forward to seeing her around here, and if there's a problem, she takes care of us."

I gave XYZ the shortest report they have probably ever seen, "In future recruiting, give as much weighting to 'likability' as you do to ability."

Sales professionals are always looking for doors to open to bigger and better business accounts. Every firm has its own ideas about how to nudge or kick those doors open. Some do it with price, others with special features, others with positioning based on quality, service, etc. Ultimately, however, doors swing open or shut on the hinge of the *likability* of the person representing that firm. Give people reasons to like you, and they will find reasons to do business with you. Give people reasons not to like you, and they will find ways to make your life difficult and avoid doing business with you.

EMOTIONAL BANK ACCOUNTS

In his best-selling book, *Seven Habits of Highly Effective People,* Steven Covey introduced an analogy on building rapport called the "emotional bank account." Think of the interactions you have with clients or coworkers as either deposits or withdrawals from their emotional accounts. If you are sensing an undercurrent of resistance or you are getting "that look" from an individual, it is because you are in "overdraft" with that particular account. Emotionally intelligent sales professionals are keenly aware of the balance in their accounts, knowing that their success hinges on staying in the black.

It is important to remember that an emotional undercurrent is in every conversation and interaction. To practice emotional intelligence, we must pay as much attention to the nature of this undercurrent as we do to the facts, content, and agenda being discussed or interacted upon. This awareness will help you to keep a positive balance in all your accounts. It is important to be consistent in your behavior in and out of your organization. I have witnessed many sales professionals who work hard at charming the socks off of their clients but treat their home office support staff with ingratitude and impatience, thus sabotaging their own efforts.

The ledger for an emotional bank account might look something like Figure 23.1.

As you can see, this list could go on ad infinitum because an emotional debit or credit can take place in any interaction over any matter. We should practice vigilance regarding the emotional current we bring to every interaction. To form this habit may require that we mentally rehearse our approach to play out the possible emotional ramifications. I often rehearse conversations I am hesitant about with my wife so I can get her feedback on the emotional impact. Because of her high level of empathy, her feedback has often kept me from embarrassing myself and going into overdraft with business contacts.

THE LONGEST YARD

The distance between you and your client is dynamic in nature, meaning it is constantly in a state of expanding or contracting. Gary DeMoss, a career sales professional, calls the three feet of physical separation between you and your client *the longest yard.* Gary says we must be keenly aware of the emotional comfort level that dictates this physical distance. One wrong word, a testy tone, or a cross look can increase that distance. On the other hand, one good word, a comforting tone, or an encouraging look can decrease the dynamic distance.

Think of professional relationships in terms of this dynamic state of being, and you will suddenly become more aware of the emotional impact of your words, glances, tones, and questions. Relationships do not park often in a state of neutrality but instead move forward or backward (on the emotional level) at every intersection. Emotionally intelligent individuals work diligently at giving people a reason to like them.

GOOD MANNERS MATTER

"Good manners will open doors that the best education cannot."

—CLARENCE THOMAS

Two customers—a perfect contrast of one another—arrived at a business counter at the same time.

FIGURE 23.1 The Emotional Ledger

Debits	Credits
• Pushing to get something done • Hurrying them during a task • Showing up without an appointment • Taking too much of their time • Not allowing them sufficient opportunity to voice their concerns • Asking repeatedly for favors • Only acting friendly when they need something • Failing to show gratitude • Taking their efforts for granted • Asking them to do things out of their comfort zones • Asking them to perform tasks below their positions • Using an agitated, confrontational, edgy tone • Using a condescending, arrogant tone • Using a demanding tone of voice • Using an impatient tone of voice • Not following through with commitments • Not focusing on the speaker • Not listening to their directions and details • Shifting blame for your mistakes • Bringing an overintensive, uptight approach • Never smiling • Interrupting the person who is talking • Failing to communicate on critical issues • Avoiding them in negative or troubling circumstances • Talking negatively about others • Whining, complaining, moaning, and groaning • Being pessimistic • Being insensitive to others' time lines, pressures, and agendas • Invading their personal space • Acting overly familiar • Acting overly officious • Using inappropriate humor, making comments, bringing up past mistakes	• Asking for assistance • Asking for a time line • Calling ahead • Asking how much time they have • Patiently listening to concerns • Not asking for more than you give • Being sincerely friendly • Showing gratitude for every favor • Asking, not expecting • Checking their comfort levels first • Doing it yourself or asking for a special favor • Using a gentle, undemanding tone • Using a humble, approachable tone • Using an imploring tone • Using a calm, patient tone • Keeping your word; being on time • Focusing on the speaker • Taking notes when they offer help • "Owning up to" your mistakes • Lightening up in stressful situations • Smiling and bringing levity • Biting your tongue and listening to the person who is talking • Taking the time to sit down and talk out issues • Showing courage to confront • Speaking highly of others • Using a cheerful "can do" attitude • Maintaining an optimistic approach • Checking their time lines, agendas first • Keeping the appropriate distance • Earning the right to show familiarity • Using a personable approach • Keeping quiet when in doubt, and showing grace toward mistakes

The first was a man finely dressed, bespectacled, who possessed an air of self-importance. The second was a lady, somewhat plain, but neat in appearance, who possessed an air of humility.

The clerk addressed her first, "May I help you?"

Before she could respond, the man promptly cut her off. "Excuse me," he informed the clerk with perfect enunciation, "I believe I was here first, and I'm in quite a hurry."

The woman said, "That's fine," and politely stepped back.

Irritated, the clerk said to the woman, "That's OK, I'm sure I can help you in short order."

The clerk then turned to the man and crisply stated, "I'll be right with you."—*The Daily Dose*

The story reminds me of the observation made by Justice Clarence Thomas, "Good manners will open doors that the best education cannot."

Those who have gathered knowledge and credentials to the degree that they now believe they are above the laws of common courtesy have fallen prey to extreme stupidity.

People are more impressed with kindness than with knowledge. Doors open quickly—not to those impressed with themselves, but to those impressed with the importance of others.

How often have you seen an individual who has gathered knowledge, wealth, degrees, or credentials until they believe they are above the laws of common courtesy? These people have fallen prey to extreme emotional stupidity. They are ignoring the first commandment of EQ—*treat every person you meet with courtesy and respect.*

One day, as I was opening the door to the local mall with my teenage son, a rough, rather threatening looking young man walked up behind us. He was the kind of kid people would avoid—one who wore his animosity on his sleeve. I decided to open the door for him and greet him like I would any other person. He walked through the door with a stunned look on his face and looked at me in a way as if to say, "You're opening the door for me?" He choked out a "Thanks," and walked by us. Upon seeing his response, I suspected that no one had ever opened a door for him.

Treating the powerful and influential with courtesy and respect is common but often done only to obtain favor. It is uncommon to treat every person with VIP status, especially those gatekeepers who stand between you and the people you hope to do business with. In building rapport, the emotionally intelligent sales professional never underestimates the goodwill that comes from paying small courtesies to those who society would label "small players."

Many sales professionals become so intensely focused on the tasks at hand and their business goals that they neglect these small courtesies.

These small acts of neglect add up over time and can come back to haunt you—when you may need the help of one of the people you failed to treat courteously.

Recently overheard as a salesperson was leaving an office: "Don't you just love dealing with him? He is always so pleasant." If that's the only impression you leave with your clients, chances are you will come out a winner.

LIKES AND DISLIKES

As part of our study on selling with emotional intelligence, we asked clients who had regular, daily exposure to sales professionals the following questions: "What kind of salespeople do you like? And dislike?"

Listed are the six most common responses for each category. Generally speaking, people prefer those who pay attention to them much more than self-centered attention seekers.

I like people who . . .

- Pay attention to my opinions and ideas
- Talk to me on my level
- Show me respect
- Tell the truth
- Make an effort to connect with me
- Have a sense of humor

I dislike people who . . .

- Are disingenuous and manipulative
- Can't see past their own noses
- Pretend to be something they are not
- "One-up" and always shift the conversation back to themselves
- Use candor at the expense of others
- Are overly serious about everything

People naturally take a liking to those who are interested in others and who are unpretentious, honest, and respectful. It doesn't take a Ph.D. to figure out these aspects of human interaction, but obviously, from the feedback I've received, not all sales professionals have done the emotional math or exercised enough self-inspection to ensure that their conduct measures up.

BIG EMOTIONAL NO-NO'S

The next question we asked was, "What are the biggest mistakes you've seen sales professionals make?"

Following are three oft-repeated responses that I would characterize as "emotional time bombs."

Failing to Tell the Truth

Each year, the Heisman trophy is given to America's premier collegiate football player. In 1939, the winner of that coveted prize was the legendary running back from the University of Iowa, Niles Kinnick.

Kinnick's legend extended far beyond his exploits on the field. He gave his life in World War II and was posthumously decorated. Iowa's football stadium today bears his namesake.

Greater than all of his accomplishments, however, was this man's honor.

On the last day of Kinnick's award-winning season, the Hawkeyes were playing for the Big Ten Championship. With just seconds to go in the game, the Hawkeyes were driving to their opponent's goal line.

Kinnick took the handoff and headed to the end zone for what would be the winning score. Just as he hit the goal line, he fumbled. The officials could not decide if he had crossed the goal before the fumble—and everyone knew that the championship was on the line.

The officials then did something unheard of: knowing Niles Kinnick to be a man above reproach, they asked him if he had crossed the goal. Kinnick replied that he was 99 percent sure that he had not crossed the goal line.

Iowa lost the championship.

Why is Kinnick's legacy so great? In the words of William Shakespeare, "No legacy is so rich as honesty."—*The Daily Dose*

While every person's standard for truth varies in its rigidity, most would agree that the failure to speak truthfully about products and the level of service provided jabs like a thorn in the foot of the client's psyche. Once a sales professional gains a label for stretching the truth, misrepresenting, saying anything to get the sale—or any other phrase meaning *lying*—it is hard to shake.

Gay Hendricks, in her book, *Seven Secrets of the Corporate Mystic*, studied highly successful corporate leaders and distilled the basic personal characteristics these people had in common. The first shared characteristic was the belief in practicing absolute honesty. They had all come to the conclusion that it is better to sink with the truth than it is to float with a lie. The stock market troubles of 2002 are a macrocosmic picture of what happens to client trust when CEOs and companies like Enron decide to sell perceptions rather than realities.

It is best to practice absolute honesty for at least two reasons.

1. We respect ourselves more when we do. Misrepresentation chips away at our dignity and eventually draws us into poor company.
2. We gain the respect of others. People can and will tolerate the truth, but they will not tolerate deception. They may not like what we tell them, but they will respect our integrity for standing by the truth.

In the simple logic of one retired sales pro, "Once you lose trust, you lose. Period." Honesty not only makes you more trustworthy but more likable as well.

Constantly Pushing

"The decision-making process takes time. I wish it didn't take as much time in our organization as it does, but there's not much I can do to hasten the process. The vendors who shoot themselves in the foot with me are those who keep calling when I have nothing to tell them. They are in such a hurry and are so impatient that they end up being an annoyance, and I begin to question whether I even want to put up with their pushiness."—Regina Q., Director of Purchasing

Pushiness is a great turnoff and an emotional time bomb for those getting pushed. It may be one too many closing phone calls, an overly eager tone of voice, or insensitivity to a client's normal selling cycle. Some call it bully tactics, and others call it annoying, but most of us would agree that it is time to look for a place to hide (and are thankful for caller ID) when it comes to dealing with the pushy salesperson.

Pushy individuals lack the emotional competencies of both awareness and empathy—hence the ill-guided, bulldozing approach toward getting things done. They often seem oblivious to others' agendas, stresses, time lines, and concerns. They demand quick and instantaneous resolution to every impediment and have the illusion that applying "push" to the right person will get the deal done. Pushy professionals eventually wear down their clients and lose opportunities. And, because they lack awareness, they blame others for their failures.

The world of sales is fertile ground for aggressive and competitive individuals, but it is alluring for the overly aggressive as well. The trick is to temper one's aggression with diplomacy or, as one seasoned sales pro put it, "To be aggressive without appearing aggressive."

Leaning Too Heavily on the Relationship/Taking the Relationship for Granted

"We had this vendor who everyone really liked and the relationship was always smooth. It was so smooth that we let our guard down a bit and stopped doing our homework the way we should. One day, it came to our attention that he was charging us a very high price for a particular service. When we confronted him, he admitted that 'he had room to work' and would see about getting the cost down. When he left, we decided as a business that we were going to end this relationship, because we felt he had used his good rapport with us as a means to gouge us." —Vicki G., Vice President of Marketing

This story illustrates the fact that building rapport with a client is not a substitute for providing value to the client. At the end of the day, everyone is in business to make or save as much money as possible. The ultimate buying scenario is to receive the best value and to have a good relationship with the seller. But the trade-off between value and a good relationship has its limitations. People often will pay a premium to work with someone they know, like, and trust; however, that principle extends only so far. If, at any point, they feel they are being unfairly charged, their trust goes down the tubes.

You may feel that all your clients and accounts love you. You may be the most charming and likable sales professional on your side of the Mississippi, but that rapport will dissipate like vapor if your clients get the idea that you are not looking our for their best interests.

GIVE THEM A REASON TO LIKE YOU

"In my business, I'm often required to put together meetings for clients in hotels and must compete with all the other clients the hotel staff is catering to at the same time. I've witnessed how rude, abrupt, demanding, impatient, and insensitive some of these other clients can be, and I have always taken the approach that I simply need to give these people a reason to like me. I go out of my way to treat them with friendliness and respect and have always received great service and, I suspect at times, preferential treatment. It's not rocket science, but a lot of people fail to practice it."—Marian L., Sales and Marketing Training Director

The emotional parallel to your ability is your likability. In nurturing and developing your own likability, remember to follow these principles of selling with emotional intelligence.

- Pay attention to the little stuff. Little courtesies, small gestures of respect, paying attention, and words and tokens of gratitude go a long way toward likeability.
- Be aware of the balance at all times in the emotional bank accounts of the people you work with every day, as well as for your customers and clients. Consider the emotional impact of your words before you speak and the emotional impact of your actions before you act.
- Study people that you find to be likable and emulate the behaviors you observe. You will find that likable people possess the ability to make you feel good about yourself, to help you relax in their presence, and to pass on to you their enthusiasm about life.

SELLING WITH EQ

- Strive to keep a positive balance in every emotional bank account.
- Take no one for granted.
- Practice little courtesies in a big way.
- Try to give clients a reason to like you.

CHAPTER TWENTY-FOUR

REDUCING STRESS IN CONFRONTATION

"All problems become smaller if you don't dodge them but confront them. Touch a thistle timidly, and it pricks you; grasp it boldly, and its spines crumble."

—WILLIAM F. HALSEY

The Principles of Emotional Intelligence

- Confrontations do not need to be confrontational to be effective.
- Those who desire to fix the blame will have trouble fixing the problem.
- If people like your manner, they are more willing to help solve your problems.

When most people think of the word *confrontation,* they immediately associate it with negative emotions and the escalation of conflict. Yet confrontation, when handled properly, can be a positive emotional process that results not only in resolving the conflict but in preventing future conflicts as well. Your most crucial step is your first step—the *approach.*

I recently heard a story about a business owner who had an irate contractor pacing in his reception area. He fit the stereotype for his trade—a stout, muscular man with a stern demeanor that advertised the brevity of his patience. He told the receptionist that the business owner owed him $30,000 and he wasn't leaving the building until he had a check in hand. His tone was harsh enough that the receptionist figured he meant to become a permanent reception area fixture if not satisfied with payment. She called the business owner's office to apprise him of the situation. To her surprise and to the surprise of the contractor, he said, "Oh, send him right in."

Twenty minutes later, a stunned staff watched as the contractor exited the business owner's office a transformed man. He was wearing a jacket with the company's logo on it and holding a check for $3,000—and couldn't say enough about what a "great guy" the business owner was. He shared with the receptionist how the business owner was all smiles and handshakes and so glad to see him—the opposite of what he had expected. The owner listened to the contractor's complaint and assured him of how important their good business relationship was, especially as the business was growing. He told the contractor of the cash flow challenges they were experiencing with their growth and got him to agree to take $3,000 today and the balance in 60 days. He then fitted the contractor with a jacket and sent him on his merry way.

With a will to listen and some diplomatic charm, we can turn our worst adversaries into our greatest advocates. Study personalities who excel in the art of confronting difficult situations and note the patterns of diplomacy that they exercise. I have performed these observations over many years and have taken specific notes of the tactful approaches these winsome personalities employ. I would characterize these approaches as Confrontational Rules of Thumb.

If we heed the following rules in difficult, testy, and trying circumstances, we will experience the magic of emotional intelligence that capitalizes on conflicts rather than suffers from them. The wise sales professional recognizes the opportunities that await the captain who can successfully navigate through choppy seas. By following these simple but efficacious rules of confrontation, you will earn admiration, confidence, and trust.

Be Transparent

Our first challenge in a conflict scenario is to motivate the other party to work through the conflict. We can achieve this by starting with a clear and honest agenda. People often fail to work with us or to work things out because they are suspicious of our motives. They are thinking to themselves, "Yeah, this is going to be good for you, but what about me?" To obviate such problems, we need to address clearly why we are there by saying something like, "The reasons I want to work through this situation are . . ." When people are dishonest about their real motives, others will grow suspicious and try to detect our real angle. We are all aware that, "What's in it for me?" is the law of the jungle—and people rarely set out on a course of action without some hope of personal payoff.

Any attempts at confronting and resolving a conflict should commence with a transparent admission of why we are there. The payoff we seek may be emotional in nature such as, "I want to talk because I think I may have miscommunicated, and I don't want to have any tension or mistrust in our relationship. I was hoping we could talk through this matter and come to an understanding. I value you as a client and want this relationship to continue and grow."

The other party may retract their suspicions with this introduction, because we have laid our cards on the table. We have demonstrated that we want to keep their business and remove any tension from the relationship. If we were to tiptoe or circumvent the same situation with, "We need to talk about such and such a situation . . .", the client begins to wonder, "Why do you want to talk about this?" Without transparency in confronting conflicts, suspicions begin to fester, and communication erodes into a defensive jousting match.

Give the Credit, Take the Blame

> *"If things go really badly, I take the blame. If they go somewhat badly, we are both to blame. If things go really well, it's because of you."*
>
> —BEAR BRYANT, legendary football coach

The common narcissistic urge in most people is to gather glory when things go well and to spread blame when things go wrong. People within corporations and organizations often build up years of resentment based on these behaviors. People have an innate need to be recognized for their contributions and to be approached diplomatically and gracefully when they make mistakes. The secure and confident sales professional can sincerely accept responsibility when communication fails and processes falter.

Emotionally intelligent leaders understand that their leadership styles in times of tension establish a pattern for their entire organization. The individual who accepts blame and distributes credit recognizes the crucial importance of a team dynamic in organizational success. Motivation is quickly diffused when people contribute energetically and receive little or no recognition or gratitude. This demotivating spiral quickly accelerates when the leader harbors the credit for their efforts. Workplace history shows that such disingenuous and narcissistic behavior erodes relational trust and loyalty, leading to increased conflict and resistance to cooperation.

> *"When a person is always right, there has to be something wrong."*
>
> —ANONYMOUS

The world is full of people who want to take credit for what others do right, and those same people want to blame somebody else for everything they do wrong—which is the root of many business conflicts. Take a look at those people you work with who you just want to run away from. This second rule often defines what is wrong. Many people, because of insecurity, are living unconsciously by the rule, "Take the credit, give the blame." Sit back and observe the magic that happens when we start saying things like, "You know this situation fell apart, and I've got to look in the mirror first. I've got to ask myself where I screwed up. What did I neglect to look at?" If we are going to be emotionally intelligent leaders, we've got to be ready, willing, and able to take the blame for what happens on our watch."

"When you know you're going to be accused, accuse yourself first."

—ANONYMOUS

Herein is the magic of taking blame—it disarms our adversaries. By accusing ourselves, we remove the chief arsenal from our adversaries. We go from a metaphorical whipping to a metaphorical self-flagellation by saying, "I really screwed up here. Here's where I made my mistake. . . ." Now we're emotionally disarming our adversaries. We are literally disrobing our mistakes, and they're beginning to feel like, "Yeah, I agree, but hey, that's tolerable, we're all human." Take note of the phenomena that takes place when we accuse ourselves first. When we start saying, "Here's where I'm culpable," all of a sudden the client says, "Well, yeah, but it wasn't just you. I mean, I could have done . . ." Most fights are a Ping-Pong match of, "You did this" and "No, I didn't do that." Avoiding this frustration is simply a matter of taking the blame *before* it is offered.

Alternatively, when things go right, we can say, "Yeah, I was involved, but if you didn't do what you're doing and my staff didn't do their part, this wouldn't have worked so well. This is a team game we're playing here." Behind every great story is a team of people making it happen. When we start uttering these beneficent words, people are drawn to us because they want to be around secure individuals who are giving credit and taking blame.

Know When It's an *I* or a *We* Problem

In potential and actual conflict situations, we must pay close attention to the subtleties of our speech. If the problem is the result of our own making or negligence and we say to a coworker or client, "We've got a problem," we are implying that the problem is equally of their making—and now they share responsibility to fix it. There will either be outward or veiled resistance to this approach.

On the other hand, if there are equal and proportional contributions of negligence, then stating, "We've got a problem . . .", or "I've got a problem," is an emotionally intelligent approach, as it infers a team approach and a willingness to help.

If the cause of the problem is squarely on the shoulders of the other person(s), avoid saying, "You've got a problem," which isolates the individual in a negative spotlight. This approach is kind of like watching yourself do a belly flop in a slow-motion replay—a painful experience. The safest and best approach is to say, "We might have a problem here" or "We've got to figure out a solution." By using *we*, you are showing them they are not alone in this situation—and that we are there to help resolve the situation.

When we know we are the direct cause of the problem, the scenario is not a *we* problem, it is an *I* problem. "Because *I* caused a problem, it is my problem, not our problem." Then it is important to say something like, "I have a problem, I goofed up. Would you be willing to lend some help?" Or, "Unfortunately, I caused this problem by myself, but I can't fix it by myself. Is there any way you can help me?" How do most people respond to an approach like that? If they have half a heart, they will help you. If we are being blamed for a situation in which we've done nothing to cause the problem, treat it like a *we* problem anyway. As regrettable being blamed unfairly is, we can win friends by sharing and shouldering the responsibility, even when others cause the problem.

Use Self-Deprecating Humor

> *"Blessed is the man who can laugh at himself,*
> *for he'll never cease to be amused."*
>
> —ANONYMOUS

As mentioned in an earlier chapter, laughter and tension cannot occupy the same space at the same time. This idea translates into a good metaphor for the baggage people carry in the workplace, which often translates into interpersonal conflict. Approaching these conflicts with a self-deprecating sense of humor can diffuse the tension that prolongs the conflict.

If I had to pick out one rule in life for becoming a more likable person, I would keep this rule: learn to laugh at yourself. People are attracted to those who do not take themselves too seriously and can have a laugh at their own expense. People who can make fun of themselves are easy to communicate with and easy to be around. People are attracted to laughter and smiles, and self-deprecation indicates a secure and self-confident individual. The fact that we can joke about our shortcomings and foibles tells people that underneath the surface, we are confident individuals.

"A perfectionist is someone who takes great pains—

and gives them to others."

—ANONYMOUS

Why do so many people, especially those who take themselves too seriously, put up pretenses in conflict situations? Many people feel the need to keep up their image and are afraid of exposure. In psychology, this phenomenon is called the "imposter syndrome." Many people are afraid that others are going to find out what they really know (or don't know) and/or who they really are.

If we find ourselves in a situation where the potential for conflict exists, and we say, "I guess I was kind of a dope yesterday," that self-deprecating opening creates a loose and stress-free starting point. We disarm defensive instincts with this sort of approach. If they respond by saying, "Yeah, you were a dope all right," then instead of becoming defensive, you say, "At least we have agreement on that. Now, we're getting somewhere." Behind all this lightheartedness, a significant psychological shift is taking place. When we cease to take ourselves so seriously, our adversaries are inclined to lighten their own tension levels, because our self-deprecation has a disarming effect. Self-deprecation acts as a tension-releasing lever—once we pull that lever, the conversation takes on a more edifying tone.

A humorous approach works in your favor for many reasons.

- People who can laugh at themselves are easier to communicate with in conflict situations.
- Laughter releases tension and acts as a stress valve.
- People are attracted to laughter and smiles.
- A self-deprecating sense of humor indicates a secure and confident individual.

Use a Humble Approach

"It's what you learn after you know it all that counts."

—ANONYMOUS

A humility-based approach is indicated with these kinds of statements.

- "I may have messed up here."
- "I think I goofed."
- "Did I handle that properly?"
- "Do you think there's a better plan?"
- "I apologize."
- "I'll need some help for this to work."
- "Did I follow through the way we'd talked about on that project?"

People who are not accustomed to such an approach may struggle with such prefaces at first but will soon be convinced by the change in tone and response from the other party. In the TEAM Dynamics approach to conflict, each person recognizes both the natural strengths and flaws of each style. Once we realize that certain flaws or challenges are inherent in each style, we can more easily adapt a sense of humor and humble demeanor regarding those flaws. Chapter 25, "Masters in Conflict," shows what to expect and how to adjust to each personality type in conflict situations.

Tension and conflict build when we take the opposite path of accusation and self-justification. This path only breeds resentment—even when we are "in the right." Bjorn Borg's sporting maxim of "Win without bragging and lose without excuse" also serves well in the realm of managing conflicts.

Humility will bring you more success with people than stubborn pride. Humble people are grateful people. Humble people appreciate where they started and where they are today. A person who possesses humility doesn't need to make pretenses. Simply put, people connect with and trust those who possess humility. What's not to like about those individuals who are in touch with their own weaknesses as well as strengths? Their humility encourages a humble and responsible response on our part. Humility demonstrates that we value the relationship and have an open mind.

Some good words to practice are "I made a mistake" or "I could be wrong here" or "Please forgive me for what I said or did." Having the humility to say such words adds cohesiveness to our relationships. People are more at ease and want to deal with people who can articulate modesty. The articulation of this sort of humility indicates a secure, confident, and realistic person.

Here are a few of the many advantages of approaching conflicts with a humble demeanor.

- A humble approach is based on an open mind.
- A humble approach demonstrates an awareness of one's own weaknesses as well as strengths.
- A humble approach encourages a humble and responsible response.

- A humble approach demonstrates that you value the relationship at hand.

By practicing these five rules of thumb in confrontation situations, we'll find that others are more willing to work with us. These confrontational rules of thumb are emotionally intelligent methods for diffusing conflict situations. Too often, conflicts are intensified because of ill-advised approaches toward resolving the problem. It is important to have a people-smart approach to confrontation. People are more inclined to help you, when they find a reason to like you.

LET THEM HELP YOU

The story is told of a conflict that Ben Franklin was having with a member of the first Continental Congress. To move forward on an important idea, Franklin needed this individual's agreement; however, his foe would not move even an inch.

Franklin searched for a tactic to put himself in the good graces of this man. Franklin decided that this man needed to view him in a different perspective for any change to take place. He tried to think of some favor he could do for this gentleman and then came upon this idea: "To win another person over, it is best to allow them to give you a gift or favor than for you to give them a gift or favor." If he did a favor for the man, that favor could easily be misconstrued as a briberous act, but if he asked this man to do him a favor, it would only be interpreted as an act of grace.

Franklin learned that this man had in his possession a rare volume of a book that he desired to read, so he went to his adversary and implored him about the possibility of borrowing this rare book. The man was only too happy to extend this favor and display a more congenial side of himself. Once Franklin had read the book and they had discussed the author and contents, a more friendly dialogue had been established between them.

This amicability led to a compromise that helped Franklin move his cause forward. Ben Franklin's example helps to affirm our chief principle regarding confrontation, namely that people are most inclined to help you when they find a reason to like you.

WINNING FRIENDS, NOT ARGUMENTS

Emotionally intelligent confrontation skills come down to our ability to put relationships in their proper priority—above and beyond winning an argument or getting our way. What do we really gain by "winning" an argument, when the cost is a relational connection that could have contributed to our future prosperity? In laying out the confrontational rules of thumb, I do not intend to imply that these approaches or responses will be easy. We are all human, given to whims and occasionally carried far from logic by our own self-justifying emotions. Consequently, we will be tempted to plead our case, even if by doing so we pave the path to greater conflict. By practicing the principles laid out here, however, you will see the world of conflict through a different set of eyes. You will see that most people do not want arguments, disagreements, and the accompanying tension. You will see that people desire resolution and peace of mind. By following these principles, you can diffuse tension, bring clarity, and quickly move forward from negative situations.

People feel assured that their mistakes would be quickly repaired because the focus is on "fixing the problem, not placing the blame." Cooperation and teamwork flourish in such an environment, and the wise sales professional sets this *we* tone in conflict scenarios.

It is also important to make sure that your tone and your body language, as well as your words, communicate. Insincerity with team-building phraseology is more destructive than blaming and irresponsibility. Most conflicts find their roots in poor communication. Make sure every aspect of your communication—words, tone, nonverbal signals, and pace—convey the same message. "I value this relationship and I want to resolve this tension." Emotionally intelligent individuals understand this principle and work toward communicating that they are going to be easy to work with.

SELLING WITH EQ

- Avoid confrontational postures when confronting a problem. Your demeanor will set the stage for solving the issue.
- Let empathy be your guide. Always consider the other person's predicament and point of view.
- Don't take yourself too seriously and people will relax around you.

CHAPTER TWENTY-FIVE

MASTERS IN CONFLICT

"Persuasion, kind, unassuming persuasion should
be adapted to influence the conduct of men."

—ABRAHAM LINCOLN

The Principles of Emotional Intelligence

- Each personality possesses predictable behaviors in conflict scenarios.
- Knowing how to temper one's own biases and impulses prevents the escalation of conflict.
- An emotionally intelligent response acts as a catalyst for reversing a negative conversational climate.

Most of us would agree that much of the conflict we experience with clients, employees, and coworkers is personality based, hence the term *personality clash*. In this chapter, I reveal effective conflict approaches that reduce the clash dynamic by building an emotional bridge, giving the other party safety and comfort. I also highlight the personality biases that tend to surface in conflict scenarios and explain how to keep these biases from sabotaging the resolution process. Very specific compromises are effective for diffusing or preventing conflicts with each personality type. Finally, I discuss how to stay above the fray when encountering the surly, the arrogant, the defensive, and the many other negative approaches we are bound to run into.

THE POWER OF EMPATHY

The first and most crucial emotional competence necessary for resolving conflict is empathy—the process of identifying emotionally with another person. In fact, it safely could be stated that empathy is the cornerstone of all conflict management. Empathy is certainly a skill demonstrated by those who keep themselves disentangled from conflicts.

Because of our core personality, it can be difficult to force ourselves to feel events the same way another person does. However, we can, at the very least, understand that others feel events differently than we do, and that they are neither right nor wrong for the way they process events. The good news is that neither you nor the other party is wrong for seeing events as you do—the perception and response are rooted in core personalities.

If you hope to resolve conflicts, your first step is empathic identity with the other person's vantage point. Once this step is taken, defenses are brought down, and we are more willing to meet halfway.

THE LENS OF PERSONALITY

A good metaphor for developing understanding when dealing with opposing personalities is to realize that each personality sees the world through a unique *lens* (see Figure 25.1). The Togetherness personality sees the world through a wide-angle lens—always concerned about others in the process. The Enterpriser personality sees the world through a telescope and wants to keep moving toward a distant shore (goal). The Analyzer personality sees the world through a microscope and is constantly trying to get a closer, more detailed view. The Motivator personality sees the world through a kaleidoscope and captures the fun, spontaneity, and excitement of life.

Using these metaphorical lenses can help us to view a conflicted situation through the eyes of the other person, even if that person is our personality opposite. Understanding the perception of the other party is the great empathetic leap that makes most conflicts reasonable and many broken relationships reconcilable.

FIGURE 25.1 Personality Lenses

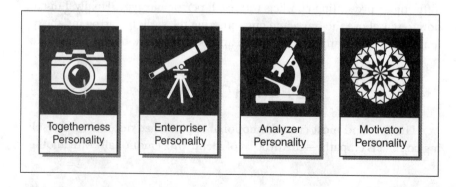

| Togetherness Personality | Enterpriser Personality | Analyzer Personality | Motivator Personality |

Parable—"Johnny Falls Down"

The following parable illustrates the phenomena of personality-influenced perceptions and their role in conflict.

> Johnny and his four friends were riding their bicycles, when Johnny fell down. Here is how his four friends responded to the situation.
>
> Togetherness Friend: "Are you OK? Can I help you?"
>
> Enterpriser Friend: "Where did you learn to ride a bike? Hurry up, we're going to be late!"
>
> Analyzer Friend: "You'd better not move. You could have an internal injury. You know, you wouldn't have fallen off if your shoe had been tied."
>
> Motivator Friend: "That was cool! Did you see that flip? Unbelievable!"
>
> The next day at school, Johnny's four friends gave their idiosyncratic accounts of what had happened.
>
> Togetherness Friend: "I really wonder if these are people I want to be friends with. Johnny falls off his bike. One person is yelling at him to get up, another is criticizing, and another is laughing at him. Those people have no sensitivity."
>
> Enterpriser Friend: "Johnny is such a klutz. Just because he can't ride a bike, we're late and end up with the worst seats. Next time he doesn't get invited."
>
> Analyzer Friend: "Johnny is so careless. I still think he should go see the doctor. Sometimes these internal traumas kick in late. I mean, I've heard of people dying."
>
> Motivator Friend: "It was hilarious! He goes flying, does a flip. I give him a '10'—Olympic quality. There was blood everywhere!"

Moral of the story: We often think that conflict arises because we cannot agree on a solution. Johnny's story illustrates that, because of our core personalities, we have trouble just agreeing on what happened—even when we all witness the same event.

THE OTHER PERSON'S PERSPECTIVE

Many of our conflicts are due simply to personality-based interpretation and response. The first and most powerful step in conflict management is to allow yourself to see the event through the vantage point of the personality you are dealing with. The chief question we need to ask in conflict is not "What do you think we should do?" but rather "What did you see happen?" or "What is the problem from your vantage point?"

Too often, conflicts escalate as we argue over the proper response, while we have not yet agreed on what happened (through one another's eyes). As the parable of Johnny and his friends illustrates, each person witnesses a different set of events within one event as biased by their core personality. Until we understand the other person's interpretation of the event, our attempts at resolution can be futile.

A large percentage of our continuing conflicts are rooted in these types of core-personality perceptions. Personality plays a substantial role in the amount of conflict we experience with coworkers, employers, and clients.

WHOSE FAULT IS IT? THE ROOTS OF STRESS IN THE WORKPLACE

Once it becomes clear that a person's actions and reactions can be traced to a core personality, our approach toward coworkers, employees, and clients can shift from blame and attempts at manipulation to negotiating compromises—or simply meeting at the "halfway point of our two personalities."

An individual's core personality is like the DNA that drives his behavior. Attempts at altering the DNA of an individual's core personality will be met with resistance, frustration, and even hostility. Certain modes of behavior are so far outside the comfort zone of their personality that they cannot enter those modes without becoming tense and stressed in the process. The individual who constantly forces these modes soon becomes the focal point for conflict.

Resolving core personality–based conflict plays a significant role in both production and management issues. Following are some examples of how core personality enters into our everyday affairs.

- *Scenario One.* The high *E* (Enterpriser) manager barks orders at a high *T* (Togetherness) sales professional, who is highly sensitive by nature of personality.
- *Scenario Two.* The high *E* sales professional frustrates a high *A* (Analyzer) client by pushing for closure on a project but not providing necessary details.
- *Scenario Three.* The high *A* manager takes an impersonal approach, focusing only on the process to the neglect of personal relationship. This manager alienates both the *T* and the *M* (Motivator) personalities, which are relationally focused.

- *Scenario Four.* A high *T* client is easily offended by the high *E*'s candor, and that same Enterpriser is frustrated by the high *T* client's indecisiveness.
- *Scenario Five.* The high *M* sales professional feels that the high *A* client impedes progress with pessimism, need for detail, and constant second-guessing.
- (*Note.* The inverse of the above scenarios would also be true.)

What is necessary to diffuse conflict in all of these scenarios is for each personality involved to meet the other halfway in establishing a comfortable mode of working and relating for both parties. For example, we have seen individuals in similar scenarios improve their workplace relations by:

- Tactfully confronting personality-based tensions
- Establishing halfway-point personality compromises

Negotiating Core-Personality Compromises

Scenario One: High *E* Manager and High *T* Sales Professional

Enterpriser Compromises	Togetherness Compromises
<ul><li>Find diplomatic ways to state case.</li><li>Ask—don't order.</li><li>Pause and inquire when you observe frustration.</li></ul>	<ul><li>Don't regard Enterpriser candor or abrasion as a personal attack.</li><li>Write directives down and reiterate.</li><li>Understand the Enterpriser's need for results.</li></ul>

Scenario Two: High *E* Sales Professional and High *A* Client

Enterpriser Compromises	Analyzer Compromises
<ul><li>Try to understand their need for thoroughness.</li><li>Wait for their input before pushing to completion.</li><li>State case in open-minded manner.</li><li>Demonstrate patience with tone and body language.</li></ul>	<ul><li>Find areas of agreement and restrain the impulse to judge.</li><li>Listen to and consider innovative input.</li><li>Play devil's advocate without being negative or cynical.</li></ul>

Scenario Three: High *A* Manager and High *M* Sales Professional

Analyzer Compromises

- Try to be more personal in approach.
- Understand that processes are most successful when people are enthused.
- Allow time for a little socializing.
- Ask for creative input.

Motivator Compromises

- Get help to organize your ideas before presenting.
- Prepare a plan for follow-through.
- Understand the Analyzer's need for detail to be comfortable.
- Stay focused (take notes) when the Analyzer is giving input.

Scenario Four: High *T* Client and High *E* Sales Professional

Togetherness Compromises

- Understand the Enterpriser's need for action and results.
- Keep a sense of humor regarding candor. (Enterprisers can take some ribbing.)
- Ask for the Enterpriser's input, and give a time frame for a decision.

Enterpriser Compromises

- Be mindful of high *T* sensitivity before responding.
- Talk through both options and consequences with the Togetherness personality.
- Temper an opinionated tone.

Scenario Five: High *M* Sales Professional and High *A* Client

Motivator Compromises

- Don't express ideas to the Analyzer that are not well thought out.
- Slow down your presentation and make a short outline.
- Regard pessimism as helpful troubleshooting rather than shooting down.
- Ask the question, "What will we need to do to make this work?" Take notes.

Analyzer Compromises

- Ask the Motivator where you can get the details you desire. Don't expect to get the details from the high *M*.
- Be prepared to hear big picture concepts.
- Be willing to play around with ideas.
- Make sure your expression is not communicating negativity or tension.

UNREASONABLE EXPECTATIONS

It was said of Alexander the Great that the more he got to know people, the more he loved his dog. It is unreasonable to expect everyone in our workplaces to adjust to all of the quirks and characteristics of our personality style. Those with patterns similar to ours will be more comfortable with our natural forms of relating. With these people, few compromises are necessary, and we can just be ourselves.

Diplomacy, restraint, and compromise enter in most often when we are dealing with people of opposite patterns. If we refuse to compromise when dealing with those of conflicting personality patterns, we will be met with equally powerful forces of resistance and resentment.

It is reasonable to expect that, if we are willing to temper our own personality impulses, then the other parties—sensing a step in their direction—will alter their responses. A reasonable expectation is to negotiate compromise first by *demonstrating* compromise. As these scenarios demonstrate, one party cannot negotiate compromise for both parties. True compromise involves both parties taking equal steps toward the halfway point of a working comfort zone.

PERSONALITY-BASED CONFLICT TENDENCIES

Because of the four different personality styles, we see radically different responses to conflict. It is important to understand these tendencies. By understanding these tendencies, we know exactly what to expect and are more likely to incisively diffuse the existing tension. People often become angry with one another because of the way they react—not understanding that many such reactions are programmed into the DNA of the core personality.

Following are some of the common conflict responses of the four personalities.

Common Conflict Responses: The Togetherness Personality

In conflict situations, high *T*s are likely to:

- Avoid interpersonal aggression
- Become quiet
- Freeze up (may flush with frustration)
- Become emotional and/or defensive

- Express frustration and feelings to people other than the offending party
- Give in or feign agreement to avoid losing approval

Recognizing the signs of escalating conflict or frustration with the Togetherness personality is important. They are often subtle in their methods of disagreement, and as a result, they are either overlooked, or attempts are made to superficially placate them. Conflict is building when the high *T* personality begins to clam up and/or flush, displays a lost or bewildered look, or responds in a defensive manner.

In conflict scenarios with Togetherness individuals, we should:

- Inquire about their thoughts and feelings in the situation
- Demonstrate concern and respect with good listening skills
- Outline the necessary steps in resolving the conflict

Common Conflict Responses: The Enterpriser Personality

In conflict situations, Enterprisers are likely to:

- Take a direct, aggressive approach
- Rapidly escalate the level of confrontation
- Create win/lose outcomes if there is a lack of cooperation (be competitive)
- Attempt to clear the air at one sitting
- Solve problems with more regard for closure than feelings
- Listen to creative input to solve problems

Because of their propensity for candor, Enterprisers will wrestle conflict head on. Some people appreciate their straightforwardness, and others find it offensive. Enterprisers often operate with a what-you-see-is-what-you-get mentality and abhor any pretense—especially in a conflict scenario. This personality style is not afraid of hurting people's feelings if they feel the resolution is right and are often heard saying, "They'll get over it!" in regard to emotional responses. Because of their intense desire for closure, however, Enterprisers will listen to creative input that solves the issue and will quickly move to resolve issues rather than stew and harbor resentment.

In conflict scenarios with Enterprises, we should:

- Avoid arguments. Listen to their complaints and ideas for resolution
- Ask for best ways to solve the conflict

- Own up quickly to any mistakes made (don't try to make up excuses)
- Be ready to put the situation behind and move forward

Common Conflict Responses: The Analyzer Personality

In conflict situations, Analyzers are likely to:

- Increase resistance and shift into passive/aggressive behavior
- Overpower others with facts and logic
- Become defensive
- Withhold information
- Respond with "what if. . . ?" questions and "prove that!" statements
- Judge their adversary and the situation in black-and-white (critical) terms

Resolving a conflict with Analyzers is going to be a different experience altogether than with the Enterprisers. While the Enterpriser wants a *quick* resolution, the Analyzer wants a *thorough* resolution. Analyzers examine all the events that led to the conflict, then carefully lay out the groundwork to prevent this scenario from recurring. Analyzers will not readily change their views without overwhelming evidence. The Analyzers' first response in conflict will be defensiveness, and they will quickly attempt to prove that they are right. Analyzers may withhold necessary input for solving the conflict or even refuse to participate at all in the resolution process.

In conflict scenarios with Analyzers, we should:

- Avoid forcing or pushing the resolution process (adopt a patient approach and move slowly and cautiously)
- Avoid debate and blaming
- Take notes and ask for their critique of the problem and their input for preventing future conflicts

Common Conflict Responses: The Motivator Personality

In conflict situations, Motivators are likely to:

- Avoid the scene when they sense negativity
- Try to dismiss or smooth over the situation (adopt a superficial fix)
- Become emotional and offensive—take criticism or conflicts personally
- Seek control or revenge by persuading others to side with them

- Openly joke about or trivialize the conflict (but be internally upset)
- Overwhelm their opponent with monologue

Motivators are quite uncomfortable in confronting conflicts, which go against the grain of their "take life in stride" nature. Motivators are good at rallying people to their cause and trying to win by virtue of a majority. They are also inclined to use superficial fixes by making light of the situation, restoring an air of amicability. Motivators avoid people whose tone communicates anger, frustration, or impatience. Criticism is often taken as a threat to their image, and they may respond by attacking the adversary or venting their frustrations. Motivators may also act as if the problem is solved (in hopes that it will pass), when there is still an undercurrent of conflict.

In conflict scenarios with the Motivator personality style, we should:

- Approach clients in a friendly and positive fashion
- Use self-deprecating humor to ease tension
- Frame a *we* approach to the conflict instead of an *I* or *you* approach
- Ask for their thoughts and ideas for resolution and listen without interruption

STAYING IN THE COMFORT ZONES

As illustrated in this chapter, much of the tension and conflict we experience with others is a result of a naïve and misdirected focus—we focus on *what* happened instead of *why* it happened. When we look below the surface of people's actions and reactions, we see deep-seated personality patterns. Learning to recognize these personality tendencies gives us a great deal of leverage in placating and resolving conflict situations.

The emotionally intelligent sales professional recognizes that each personality has an idiosyncratic comfort zone and that there will be conflict when those zones of comfort are violated. With such recognition comes opportunity. The opportunities are for us to demonstrate that we understand our clients' specific needs for security and to demonstrate our own flexibility to meet them at their point of comfort.

SELLING WITH EQ

- Throttle back your conflict impulses to squelch the conflict.
- Pay attention to personality quirks, especially in conflict.
- Take the high road and appeal to people's better instincts in conflict scenarios.

CHAPTER TWENTY-SIX

NEGOTIATING EMOTION

"The role of emotion or feeling, either positive or negative,
remains one of the least studied areas of negotiation."

—MAX BAZERMAN AND MARGARET NEALE, *Negotiating Rationally*

"If you don't know what you want, you might not get it."

—YOGI BERRA

The Principles of Emotional Intelligence

- We all bring a personalized style to negotiations based on individual emotional comfort zones.
- Empathy unlocks the motives and comfort zones of those we are negotiating with.
- The primary consideration when implementing negotiation tactics is the impact on the relationship.

Negotiation is an area where many of us feel emotionally vulnerable. We are afraid of being taken advantage of. We are afraid of looking foolish. We are afraid of selling ourselves short, and we are afraid of an impasse where nothing at all happens. In their book *The Power of Nice*, Ronald Shapiro and Mark Jankowski write that negotiations have been described as, "two SOBs locked in a room trying to beat the daylights out of each other, and may the biggest SOB win." Fred Jandt and Paul Gillette, coauthors of *Win-Win Negotiating: Turning Conflict into Agreement*, write, "Any fool can say 'take it or leave it,' and you don't have to be much smarter to say, 'Let's split the difference.' What separates the professional negotiator from the amateur—or from the nonnegotiator—is the professional's ability to find *creative solu-*

tions that help *all parties* obtain their interests." This level of skill requires both tactical savvy and emotional intelligence.

Shapiro and Jankowski write, "Despite all the clinical, logical, rational, psychological, data-sifting analysis, graphs, pie charts, methods, and techniques from MBAs, CPAs, CEOs, shrinks, mediators, mediums, gurus, and astrologers, *negotiation is not a science.*"

Negotiation is an art form where emotional reconnaissance and emotional radar meet tactical excellence. It is an art form where one is constantly swaying in the conundrum between self-interest and empathy, self-preservation and compromise, and self-absorption and emotional awareness.

G. Richard Shell, director of the Wharton Executive Negotiation Workshop and author of *Bargaining for Advantage: Negotiation Strategies for Reasonable People,* asserts six foundations for effective negotiation.

1. Your bargaining style
2. Your goals and expectations
3. Authoritative standards and norms
4. Relationships
5. Other people's interests
6. Leverage

I would classify three of these categories as tactical in nature (two, three, and six) and the other three as emotional intelligence issues (one, four, and five). Being aware of your bargaining style is as much *an emotional awareness* issue as being aware of your personality DNA. Relationships are an *emotional rapport* issue, while the other party's interest is an *empathy* issue.

In this chapter, I discuss the process of negotiation and its intercourse with emotion. The emotionally intelligent negotiator—aware that the other party must walk away with a good feeling if there is to be any hope of future collaboration—will address the awareness, empathy, and rapport issues in every negotiation.

NEGOTIATION AWARENESS—"GAME ON!"

Shortsighted negotiators view negotiations as a winner takes all contest, where they are willing to make only insignificant or phantom concessions. They show up with a take it or leave it attitude with little regard for the emotional consequences of their tactics. Many negotiators know only this hard-driving, adrenaline-charged win/lose approach.

On the other side of the equation are those individuals who hate confrontation and disagreements and are haunted by the sound of silent tension. These individuals often easily capitulate, overpromise, or altogether avoid the negotiation process. They do not like being put in a place where they have to negotiate.

Most people assume that they are not very good negotiators and feel a tinge of envy for those who are. Some people, even when they learn all the tactical tricks of negotiation, will still buckle under the emotional tension and overconcede their position. People are basically afraid of losing, and they view negotiations as an opportunity to lose rather than as an opportunity to gain.

MINI-MAX MODEL

One way to help gain your emotional balance in the negotiation process is to walk yourself through the mini-max model of negotiation preparation. This approach helps you sort out the emotional smog that can blur your thinking in a tense negotiation. While you do not want the other party to get everything, you do want them to walk away satisfied. You do not want to appear avaricious, but neither do you want to be exploited. Here are the mini-max questions you need to settle up front for your own emotional equanimity.

- What is the minimum that I can accept (without feeling regret and anger)?
- What is the maximum that I can ask for without getting laughed out of the room (without feeling embarrassment and shame)?
- What is the maximum that I can give away (without feeling exploited)?
- What is the least I can offer without getting laughed out of the room (without feeling greedy or usurious)?

EMOTIONAL TRICKERY

Before walking into any negotiation, it is important to be aware of the tactics, tricks, and techniques that more skilled negotiators will use to throw you off your game. These individuals treat negotiation as a contact sport and love it simply for the gamesmanship opportunity. Two specific assumptions you want to be especially careful about are:

1. They will be reasonable and do what you would do given their situation.
2. Their values are the same as yours (they may live by a radically divergent set of rules than you).

Be especially wary of the use of emotion in the negotiating process. Some negotiators will act like the teenager who uses melodrama to manipulate. Shapiro and Jankowski put it this way, "When the other side gets emotional, see their use of emotion for what it may well be: a negotiation play or tactic. It is simply a device to elicit a particular reaction from you, just as an opening low bid is meant to get you to drop your high asking price and eventually meet somewhere in the middle."

These authors warn to not regard emotional attacks as personal condemnations but as negotiation tactics meant to throw you off your game. You must possess discipline in that moment to neutralize the emotional response with the unemotional response, and the personal attack with the impersonal response. You can counteract negative emotional ploys with these responses.

- When they use *anger,* calmly ask why they are angry.
- When they act *insulted,* ask what kind of offer would not be insulting.
- When they use *guilt,* continue to focus on the issues.
- When they express *exasperation,* express understanding.
- When they use *false flattery,* offer thanks and bring focus back to the negotiation.

NEGOTIATION STYLE

People bring their own individual style and emotional comfort level to the negotiation process. One can make immediate parallels with the TEAM Dynamics personality profile (refer to Chapters 2 and 3) and a person's style in a negotiating scenario. Some of the most obvious personality tendencies in negotiations are as follows.

- *Togetherness Personality.* These individuals will be uncomfortable with tension in relationships and may overcompromise to preserve relationships. They are seen as easy negotiating prey by aggressive Enterprisers because of their inability to say no.
- *Enterpriser Personality.* These individuals are competitive and aggressive in their approach to negotiation. They are not averse to confrontation. They tend to drive to the bottom line as quickly as possible, and

because of their impatience, they may cave in on issues if the process drags on too long.

- *Analyzer Personality.* These individuals are rigid in their approach to negotiation. They have difficulty compromising on points. They research issues carefully and tend to bring an officious, agenda-driven, impersonal approach to the negotiation process.
- *Motivator Personality.* These individuals attempt to use their persuasion abilities and powers of charm to get their way in negotiation. If they meet an impasse (such as tension) in their negotiations, they tend to avoid the process, as they are not comfortable in hostile/disagreeing environments.

To characterize your pattern in negotiating specifically, I have developed a profile based on the dynamics of negotiating called the DEAL Dynamics Awareness Profile. Fill out the profile in Figure 26.1 to discover the style(s) you bring to the negotiation process. Then graph your results in Figure 26.2.

Following are the characterizations and brief descriptors adapted in The DEAL Dynamics profile.

- **D**ominating *(wants to win/hates to lose).* These individuals view negotiation as a contest of wills. They seek strategies to outfox their opponents.
- **E**qualizing *(works hard to get equal agreement and satisfaction for both parties).* These individuals look for equity. They are satisfied when both parties walk away happy.
- **A**cquiescing *(uncomfortable with the negotiation process).* These individuals desire an easy and personable resolution. They are quick to compromise to save the relationship from any strain.
- **L**aissez-faire *(avoids the situation when tension or disagreement enters the process).* These individuals prefer a hands-off style—not that they do not care, but they just do not want to confront a tense situation. They may insert someone else into the process to gain advantage of the situation.

As with all areas of emotional awareness, developing an understanding of our personal tendencies in negotiation will help us to become better observers within the process. We will improve at figuring out and predicting the other party's tendencies and emotional logic as well as our own tendencies and reactions. We all have varying emotional comfort zones that are acutely defined in a process with something tangible to lose and something significant to gain.

FIGURE 26.1 DEAL Dynamics Awareness Profile

Directions: *Place the appropriate number next to each descriptive phrase.*

1	2	3	4

← ——————————————————————————————— →

Least   *Most*

D ____ If I know I'm right, I won't back down.
E ____ I want to understand the other party's objectives clearly.
A ____ Halfway between us is the right solution.
L ____ I want others to feel comfortable around me.

D ____ I can usually get the deal I want.
E ____ I'm not averse to addressing disagreements.
A ____ I believe it's all about give and take.
L ____ I just want to get the process over with.

D ____ I don't mind telling people exactly where I stand.
E ____ I look at confrontations as challenges.
A ____ There is sensible middle ground between every opinion.
L ____ I cannot stand confrontations.

D ____ I do my best to make a good case for myself.
E ____ I work hard at understanding the other party's needs.
A ____ Sometimes what I want must defer to what others need.
L ____ Some things work themselves out when left alone.

D ____ It's all about the winning.
E ____ It's about making sure everyone gets the payoff they want.
A ____ It's all about being fair.
L ____ It's all about people getting along.

D ____ I can smell weakness a mile away.
E ____ I want both parties to walk away winners.
A ____ At times, I compromise more than I should.
L ____ Sometimes I give in to avoid tension.

D ____ I'm perfectly willing to walk if I don't get the deal I want.
E ____ I don't expect everyone to be reasonable in negotiations.
A ____ I'll make concessions to get the deal done.
L ____ I struggle with forceful, demanding personalities.

D ____ I use logic to get what I want.
E ____ I deal in a straightforward way.
A ____ I believe if we both give a little, we'll both get a little.
L ____ I get upset when people start playing games.

D ____ I just love to get deals done.
E ____ I want to know all I can about their goals, limitations.
A ____ I'll relax my demands to get agreement.
L ____ If I can't agree, I just walk away for a while.

D ____ I use a logical and persuasive approach.
E ____ The earlier I identify conflicts, the better.
A ____ I want the other party to feel good about dealing with me.
L ____ I try to avoid sore spots in a negotiation.

Add up totals for each and record in the box below.

TOTALS: D = [ ]   E = [ ]   A = [ ]   L = [ ]

FIGURE 26.2 DEAL Dynamics Awareness Profile Graph

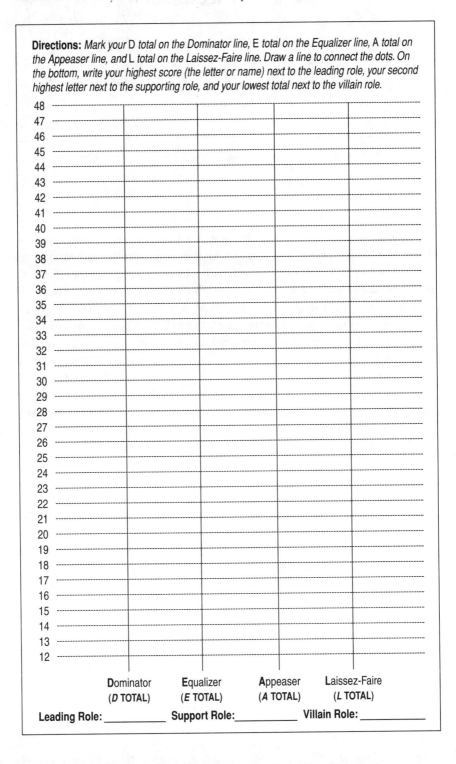

Directions: *Mark your* D *total on the Dominator line,* E *total on the Equalizer line,* A *total on the Appeaser line, and* L *total on the Laissez-Faire line. Draw a line to connect the dots. On the bottom, write your highest score (the letter or name) next to the leading role, your second highest letter next to the supporting role, and your lowest total next to the villain role.*

48
47
46
45
44
43
42
41
40
39
38
37
36
35
34
33
32
31
30
29
28
27
26
25
24
23
22
21
20
19
18
17
16
15
14
13
12

| Dominator | Equalizer | Appeaser | Laissez-Faire |
| (*D* TOTAL) | (*E* TOTAL) | (*A* TOTAL) | (*L* TOTAL) |

Leading Role: _____   **Support Role:**_____   **Villain Role:** _____

EMPATHY IN NEGOTIATION

"When I am getting ready to speak with a man, I spend one-third of my time thinking about myself and what I am going to say, and two-thirds thinking about him and what he is going to say."

—ABRAHAM LINCOLN

"Whenever two people meet, there are six people present. There is each man as he sees himself, each man as the other person sees him, and each man as he really is."

—WILLIAM JAMES

Individuals often carry hidden agendas into the negotiation process. There are the issues they tell you that matter, and there are the tacit issues that really matter. In my negotiations with a large national firm, I offered to give them the price they wanted, but I retained control of the process. While they never actually came out and said that they like to have total, in-house control over all processes, that attitude was implied in our conversations.

I was later able to get a higher price for my products when I agreed to grant them total control over the process, which is what they wanted all along (though it was not brought up as a focal point in the negotiation). The only way to detect the pivotal points that define winning or losing in negotiation is by having our emotional radar tuned in to tone and nonverbal responses—by asking good questions and listening with vigilance.

Many of us in the sales profession are, by nature, not very good listeners. We like to talk. Often we simply like to hear the sound of our voices waxing eloquent over some point, telling some story, or opining about a matter. Consequently, many of us have failed to nurture good listening habits and are chronic interrupters. We just have to speak our piece and cannot wait to hear out the other party.

If we do not let the other party completely finish their thoughts or if we respond in mid paragraph, however, we may lose the opportunity to learn something that could be valuable. They may have been ready to reveal something about their agenda, their emotions, or their needs—but we just cut them off. Valuable, critical information has just been lost, just as if it had been run through a shredder. Yet it was our impertinence that did the shredding.

If we overcommit to convincing our opponents to concede on our pet points, we fail to pick up telling nonverbal and tonal clues—responses where words don't match tone and body language—and further cement their resolve on their pet points. Most see negotiating as an opportunity to convince others and, consequently, talk more than necessary or prudent. Instead of listening, we are thinking of what we are going to say next. Yet empathy with the other party's point of view will hasten the resolution.

By clamping our mouths shut and allowing the other party to talk, we can pick up valuable pieces of emotional information, such as:

- Their comfort levels
- Their negotiating style
- Their mini-max limits
- Their perceptions of us

We learn none of these lessons while our mouths are moving. By listening, we learn to empathize with the issues that are important to the other party. This information may end up being your most valuable asset in getting negotiations done.

Max Bazerman and Margaret Neale, in *Negotiating Rationally,* write, "We have found that managers who take into account the other side's perspective are most successful in negotiation simulations. This focus allows them to better predict the opponent's behavior. Most people have a hard time thinking this way. Overall, executives in a negotiation tend to act as if their opponents are inactive and ignore the valuable information that can be learned by thinking about the other side's decisions."

By focusing on empathy, we learn the material and emotional issues that matter most to the party we are negotiating with. Maybe they are stuck on a point, not for material reasons, but because if they concede they will lose face with a superior. They may need a concession somewhere else to make this palatable. These valuable insights come through focused listening and the emotional radar of empathy.

EARNING RESPECT

"I was negotiating a contract with one of my top accounts, when the party I was negotiating with starting talking about what a pain in the butt another consultant was in their most recent negotiation. I just sat back and learned as they revealed how this person had taken a hard-core stance with no bend and had assumed an adversarial posture. They admitted that the consultant had gotten the better of them in the negotiation, but also confessed that they 'would dump him as soon as they could' because of the way he approached the process. It made me feel much better about my long-term relational approach and the importance of maintaining rapport through the negotiation process." —Andrew A., Consultant

Some people instantly think of confrontation when they think of negotiation. This posture diminishes any hope for rapport. These people are typically the dominator types, whose fatal flaw is underestimating the necessity of allowing the other party's ego and reputation to remain intact throughout the negotiation process.

For a negotiation to be successful, both sides need to get something they want both in material terms and emotional terms. Before entering a negotiation, it is helpful to answer the following questions.

- What am I trying to achieve?
- What kind of emotional environment do I want to create?
- What are they trying to achieve?
- What are the emotional payoffs they need?
- What problems are likely to arise?
- How will I approach these potential problems?

Negotiation tactics that fail to address the emotions of the other party are risky and sabotage the possibility of a long-term relationship. I once read a story about famed entrepreneur Wayne Huizenga. He liked to save a surprise request for the close of a negotiation. He supposedly would use this tactic knowing the other party was feeling a deal was close and would not want to jeopardize it by saying no. Using this sort of tactic may work, but it may also leave the other party feeling angry, manipulated, and exploited. Unless you have no need for future rapport, such a tactic should be avoided.

EMOTIONAL WISDOM

David Augsburger, author of *When Caring Is Not Enough—Resolving Conflicts through Fair Fighting*, wrote, "Maturity is knowing both how and when to yield, and where and why to stand firm. Never yielding and always yielding are both evils in human relationships." Emotional intelligence is regarded as wisdom when practiced in potentially contentious scenarios.

It takes not only wisdom but also persistence to work through a particularly tough negotiation. Effective negotiators do not try to win by upping the ante of anxiety but by affirming a foundation of confidence in their relationships with the other parties. By demonstrating genuine concern toward the other party, we raise their confidence in us. As a result, their needs—

as well as our own needs—will be met in the process. When negotiations get tough, you must prove this desire. In Augsberger's words, "Presence, not absence, is the real source of power. And an act of the will is the answer—I will work through until we break through. I'm here to stay."

SELLING WITH EQ

- Keep your eyes wide open to games, tactics, and maneuvers in the negotiation process.
- Never lose sight of the relational consequences in a negotiation.
- Know your negotiating style and tendencies as well as those of the person with whom you are negotiating.

CHAPTER TWENTY-SEVEN

SEVEN HABITS OF THE EMOTIONALLY COMPETENT

"Do not wait for extraordinary circumstances to do good;
try to use ordinary situations."

—JEAN PAUL RICHTER

"There is a proper dignity and proportion to be observed
in the performance of every act of life."

—MARCUS AURELIUS ANTONINUS

The Principles of Emotional Intelligence

- Individuals with high EQs place the emotional impact of their words and actions at the forefront.
- An individual's tone defines the emotional current for the message that is spoken.
- Emotionally intelligent individuals carefully rehearse the responses they utilize in emotionally charged or negative situations.
- The emotionally intelligent individual pursues personal growth as an end, not a means.

A man was riding in a train and saw another man eat a herring and put the head of the fish in his pocket. He asked the man why he did this.

The other fellow replied, "The head is the most valuable part of the fish—it's where the brain is. If you eat the head, it will make you smarter. I take them home and feed them to my children."

The man asked how much this fellow wanted for the head of the fish.

He replied, "One dollar."

So the man bought the head of the fish and ate it. After a few minutes had passed he became angry and said, "Wait a minute, I could have bought the whole fish for less than that!"

"See," the other fellow said, "it's working. You're smarter already."

I am grateful to people like Daniel Goleman (author of *Emotional Intelligence*) and Howard Gardner (author of the "multiple intelligence" theory), who have provided a great service to our society by expanding the definition of *smart*. In particular, Goleman's work on emotional intelligence has opened an awareness that most have understood intuitively but have had trouble articulating—that possessing a high IQ does not necessarily make an individual smart. In fact, some people with genius cerebral capabilities seem to severely lack limbic functions such as awareness, empathy, etc. Some individuals can be typed as simultaneously smart and stupid, depending on the section of brain activity.

Individuals who allow their facility with numbers and logic to lead them into pomposity and emotionally abusive personalities are in fact fools—maybe the greatest fools—because their abrasive manners cause those they meet to want to ignore their intellectual gifts.

Recently I heard a sportswriter talking on the radio about a well-known golf professional who has a reputation for being highly charismatic and dynamic with crowds. He is known as a crowd pleaser. This writer commented on how dazzling this man's personality was in the press conference with his use of witticisms and colorful commentary. He quickly added, "But in person, one on one, he is an absolute jerk, as rude and dismissive a person as you will ever find. I wouldn't give a plugged nickel to sit down with this guy, given what I've seen of his real side."

The litmus test of our emotional intelligence is how we handle the little matters and the isolated incident. Anyone can turn on the charm for public display. That doesn't require EQ, it requires showmanship. How we handle small tensions, little problems, and private conversations defines our emotional intelligence. People are taking emotional notes on how we treat them, how high of an opinion we seem to have of ourselves, and how we respond to annoyances, slights, and tension. Our emotional intelligence can be put to the test in almost any conversation.

In this closing chapter, I want to summarize with an evaluation of the responses and communication skills practiced by those who possess emotional intelligence—not just in word but in tone as well. In Figure 27.1, emotionally intelligent responses and behaviors are contrasted with low EQ responses. While by no means a comprehensive list of EQ competencies,

FIGURE 27.1 Evaluate Your EQ

Directions: *Rate your EQ in each of the sections below.*				
Signs of a Low EQ	**Signs of a High EQ**	**Rating**		
1. Can tell the details and thoughts of an event, but cannot tell feelings about it; becomes flustered when articulating emotions.	Expresses feelings clearly and directly.	1 Struggle with This	2 Back and Forth	3 Consistent Pattern for Me
2. Is insecure and defensive and finds it hard to admit mistakes, express remorse, or apologize sincerely.	Is not afraid to express insecurities and fears.	1 Struggle with This	2 Back and Forth	3 Consistent Pattern for Me
3. Cannot or does not want to interpret signals of emotional discomfort in others (are bullish with their agendas).	Is able to read nonverbal communication.	1 Struggle with This	2 Back and Forth	3 Consistent Pattern for Me
4. Lets things build up and then overreacts to something relatively minor.	Is able to articulate frustrations without offending other party.	1 Struggle with This	2 Back and Forth	3 Consistent Pattern for Me
5. Attacks, blames, commands, criticizes, and judges others.	Takes ownership of own fears, anxieties, and insecurities.	1 Struggle with This	2 Back and Forth	3 Consistent Pattern for Me
6. Is a poor listener, interrupts, invalidates.	Is interested in the fears, concerns, and ideas of others.	1 Struggle with This	2 Back and Forth	3 Consistent Pattern for Me
7. Misses the emotions being communicated; focuses on facts, rather than feelings.	Reads between the lines of communication for motive or controlling emotion.	1 Struggle with This	2 Back and Forth	3 Consistent Pattern for Me
8. Uses intellect to judge and criticize others without realizing they are feeling superior, judgmental, and critical, and without awareness of how their actions impact others' feelings.	Is cautious and tactful in giving feedback.	1 Struggle with This	2 Back and Forth	3 Consistent Pattern for Me
9. Locks self into courses of action against common sense.	Balances feelings with reason, logic, and reality.	1 Struggle with This	2 Back and Forth	3 Consistent Pattern for Me
10. Is easily manipulated into action by use of guilt or coercion.	Is independent, self-reliant, and morally autonomous; acts out of desire, not because of duty, guilt, force, or obligation.	1 Struggle with This	2 Back and Forth	3 Consistent Pattern for Me
11. Views failure as an affirmation of personal inadequacy.	Is optimistic; does not internalize failure.	1 Struggle with This	2 Back and Forth	3 Consistent Pattern for Me

this chart may be useful in helping you identify some specific areas of needed development within yourself.

These categories of emotional intelligence may also help explain why some people are such a frustration to you (at the emotional level). For some reason, when we can categorize or label the issue, we seem to have an easier time coping with it. Look at others only after you have taken an honest assessment of yourself. Which came first? The chicken or the egg? Are some people responding to me negatively because they lack EQ or because I'm sending the wrong emotional signals? To point fingers at the other party's issue before taking honest assessment of our own communication habits and patterns would indicate a lack of awareness. A lack of personal awareness leads to a critical spirit and, ultimately, duplicity—which was the point of Jesus' teaching of removing the log from your own eye before taking the splinter out of your neighbor's eye.

The terms *low EQ* and *high EQ* are not permanent labels, because EQ is not a static state like IQ. Instead, EQ is a dynamic state (demonstrated by the fact that many of us gave ourselves a 2 in many of the areas listed in Figure 27.1). This means that we bounce back and forth between low and high EQ in our responses to situations and people, depending on our emotional state at the time. The fact that EQ is a dynamic state should give us all hope for practicing higher levels of EQ in our communication. Awareness is the key to correcting our deficiencies.

Most people find strength in some areas, weakness in others, and vacillation in others. Often the demonstration of high EQ communication skills hinges on our emotional vulnerability at the moment. For instance, I may not be as cautious and tactful in giving feedback if I am under the stress of a deadline. This is why it is important to be honest with the above appraisal. For example, if I tell myself I am strong in an area where, in fact, I often offend, I only succeed in deluding myself and prolonging the pattern. Honesty with oneself is the anchor for awareness. On the other hand, if I am aware of the fact that when I am under a deadline, I tend to respond with a low level of EQ, that very awareness will act as the emotional border patrol the next time the situation arises.

CREATURES OF HABIT

"The chains of habit are too light to be noticed

until they are too heavy to be removed."

—WARREN BUFFETT

"Ever since I was a kid, I've had the habit of bullying people around. I've tried hard to rein in this pattern, because I've paid a price for it. But when I find myself under stress or strain, that pushy, abrasive voice seems to come flying out of my mouth before I can catch it. I immediately see in the eyes of my people that, although they are compliant with my directions, they resent my manner. It annoys me that I don't exercise more control with this pattern."
—Randy, Director of Sales

Each day offers manifold opportunities for practicing emotionally intelligent responses. Chances are good that, at some time during this day, you will be confronted with tension, stress, or negativity in a conversation. You will encounter an opportunity to offer feedback to another person's complaint. Take the conversational quiz in Figure 27.2 and write a response for each scenario that demonstrates tact and emotional consideration and awareness.

The two basic premises for emotionally intelligent communication habits that arise from this chart are:

1. Don't tell other people how to feel. Let them tell you.
2. Take ownership for how you feel. Don't blame anyone or anything.

DON'T TELL ME HOW I FEEL

A statement as innocuous as "You're really going to love this" may offend the party you are dealing with (an exception is the person you know like the back of your hand). A safer approach would be, "I thought you might like this idea, so I'd like to run it past you for your opinion." People bridle against others weighing in for them on opinions, likes, and dislikes. It is always safer to ask than to assume.

A tendency in strong and forceful personalities is to offer unsolicited advice. When people are told what to do, they often respond emotionally like a rebellious teenager (even if the advice is right on). In this case, the advice is not a hindrance but rather the manner in which it is delivered. It is always safer to use the Socratic method—asking questions that lead the individuals to discover the advice for themselves.

It is uncomfortable to be around a person who is venting negative emotions, because we feel we are being saturated with negativity while listening. Consequently, we often try to turn off the gushing fire hydrant with a big wrench that says, "Get a hold of yourself!" or "That's ridiculous." This sort of response tells people how they should feel about their predicament, which is of no value to them. Responding in such a manner is only for our

FIGURE 27.2 Seven Habits of the Emotionally Competent

Seven Habits of People with High EQ	Example Demonstrating High EQ
1. Label your feelings rather than labeling people or situations.	Instead of "This is ridiculous," you could say, "I get impatient in these situations."
2. Consider the feelings of others when you are sharing your thoughts.	Instead of "I don't think you know what you're doing," you could say, "Have you thought about doing this?" or "I feel like we may be missing the mark here" or "This is a good start, what else can we do?"
3. Take responsibility for your own feelings.	Instead of "You make me mad," you could say, "I'm feeling angry, upset, etc."
4. Show respect for other people's feelings, thoughts, and opinions.	Instead of "This is great, isn't it?" you could say, "How do you feel about this?"
5. Validate other people's feelings and fears.	Instead of "Don't worry about it" or "You shouldn't be upset," you could say, "Why are you so upset?" or "What are you afraid will happen?"
6. Practice getting a positive value from their negative emotions.	Instead of "Get over it" or "Get control of yourself," you could say, "What can you do to feel better about this?" or "How do we move forward from here?"
7. Don't advise, command, control, criticize, judge, or lecture others (rule of thumb: ask, don't tell).	Instead of "You need to _____," you could say, "Do you think _____ would be helpful?" or "How do you feel about _____ as a solution?"

own comfort and adds one more layer of frustration to the individual who is already bound and gagged with emotion. When we are confronted with over-the-top emotions, our safest route is to maintain a calm tone and ask a question such as, "What has caused you to be upset?" or "What are you afraid of?" Most people, when they describe their dilemmas, will begin to talk themselves down as the tidal wave of stress hormones ebbs out.

TAKE RESPONSIBILITY FOR YOUR OWN FEELINGS

When faced with negativity or emotional turmoil, we have the choice either to *transmit* or *transcend* our frustrations. When we fail to accept responsibility for our emotional reactions, we become transmitters and send the negative emotions (which are like viruses) to everyone we come in contact with. This is an area of EQ that many of us struggle with, because we can find plentiful reasons to justify our anger with another person's actions. This rationale, in our minds, then becomes a justification for negative behavior. "You'd be mad, too, if this had happened to you!"

Sooner or later we must confront the psychospiritual fact that acid eats away at its container and that we are harming our own emotional state by failing to forgive offense. Individuals who have not learned to respond with grace and understanding when offended become perpetual transmitters of their own personal frustration levels. This is what is meant by having a chip on the shoulder when referring to the individual who carries grudges.

While talking out your frustration with a trusted friend has therapeutic value, there is no value in talking it out with everyone who will listen. This beating a horse to death is nothing more than an exercise in vain self-justification. We continue to tell the story to make ourselves appear the hero (or victim).

The value in talking it out with a trusted friend or advisor is for emotional release and clarification. Some offenses will grow within us like a nest of termites, and we can feel them chewing away at our insides until we talk it out with someone. I know when I find myself in situations where I am wanting to blame someone else for my negative emotional state, that resolution comes only when I either just let it go or talk it over with someone— and then let it go.

Those who fail to take responsibility for their emotional states go into a relational sinkhole, and soon people start avoiding conversations for fear of being dragged down with them. These scenarios, where we are unjustly offended, may be the most challenging for our EQ, because both the offended emotion and the litigating logic have formed a tandem that can tie us up in knots if we fail to recognize it.

TONE-DEAF

How our efforts at communication are received have far more to do with tone than they do with content. Yet people often forge ahead with sending messages without paying attention to the climate in which they are delivering the message. It is kind of like standing outside and trying to have a conversation with someone during a hailstorm. They are going to be much more concerned with getting to safety than they are in listening to what you have to say. When we speak to people in condescending, patronizing, defensive, whining, austere, pessimistic, or otherwise negative tones, we generate a hailstorm in the limbic side of their brains, and they can barely focus on what we are saying. They are moving toward a state of self-preservation as soon as they pick up on the negative tone.

How aware are you of the offensive tones you deliver when you are stressed or upset? It takes maturity to want awareness in this area of EQ. I remember well the time I garnered the courage to ask my wife to critique the tones I use when I am in a negative emotional state (she didn't have to stop and think about it). She tactfully informed me that when I was upset, I used a condescending tone, which would deteriorate into a sarcastic tone, which would then cause so much offense that anything I said at that point was futile. She told me I had a tendency to "talk down" to people when upset.

This was not a pleasant message to hear, yet the awareness was a critical piece for my EQ development. I often catch myself slipping back into this pattern—and when I do, I am grateful for my wife's input. I remember wondering, after my wife informed me of this tonal flaw, about how many times I had offended her in this way and how many other people I had turned off with this poor habit.

Take inventory of your own tonal habits. Your tone is the current in which your message travels. Your tone can create a current like a gently flowing stream or a raging flood (or any current that falls between those two extremes). Even if you think you are aware of how your tone brings offense, ask someone who knows you well for input. They may bring a habit to light that surprises you. Are you susceptible to tones that are:

- Defensive
- Complaining
- Condescending
- Arrogant
- Flippant
- Disrespectful
- Impatient
- Agitated
- Bored

- Hostile
- Bitter
- Cynical
- Pessimistic
- Hopeless
- Over the top or sappy
- Overly familiar
- Obnoxious
- Haranguing

The list of potential tonal offenses is endless, as are the opportunities to offend. One of the great deterrents practiced by the emotionally intelligent is awareness of and restraint within the tone. Rehearse your tone before you formulate your message. We have the power to create a favorable climate for the delivery of our messages.

GROWING FORWARD

Like any goal in life, the development of emotional intelligence hinges on committing to an agenda that will produce the desired result. The question is, "What are the fundamental components that constitute an EQ growth agenda?" Authors Karen Stone and Harold Dillehunt offer such an agenda in their book *Self Science: The Subject Is Me.* Following are the main components of self science.

- *Self-awareness.* Observing yourself and recognizing your feelings; building a vocabulary for feelings; knowing the relationship between thoughts, feelings, and reactions.
- *Personal decision making.* Examining your actions and knowing their consequences; knowing if a thought or feeling is ruling a decision; applying these insights to deeply intimate issues.
- *Managing feelings.* Monitoring "self talk" to catch negative messages such as internal put-downs; realizing what is behind a feeling (e.g., the hurt that underlies anger); finding ways to handle fears and anxieties, anger, and sadness.
- *Handling stress.* Learning the value of exercise, relaxation, and distraction in managing stressful situations.
- *Empathy.* Understanding the feelings, concerns, and perspectives of others; appreciating the differences in how people feel about things.
- *Communication.* Talking about feelings effectively; developing listening and inquiry skills; distinguishing between what a person does or says and your own emotional reactions to that action; communicating your own feelings as opposed to sending blame.
- *Self-disclosure.* Valuing openness and the building of trust in a relationship; knowing when and how much to disclose about your private thoughts and feelings.
- *Insight.* Recognizing patterns in your emotional life and reactions; identifying similar patterns in others.
- *Self-acceptance.* Feeling a sense of dignity and healthy pride and viewing yourself in a healthy light; being able to recognize your strengths and weaknesses; being secure enough to laugh at yourself.
- *Personal responsibility.* Recognizing the consequences of your decisions and actions at the emotional and circumstantial levels; accept-

ing your feelings and moods as your responsibility; following through on commitments.

- *Assertiveness.* Being able to state your feelings, concerns, and opinions without anger, hostility, or passivity.
- *Group dynamics.* Cooperation and teamwork; knowing how and when to lead or to follow.
- *Conflict resolution.* Knowing how to fight fair; being able to disagree agreeably; using a win-win negotiating approach.

In large part, emotional intelligence is the result of self-discipline in an arena where we are fighting the raging bulls within ourselves. Positive intent can lead to practiced responses. Practiced responses can lead to behavior habits. Habits, as we all know, ultimately lead to what we call character—and our character defines our destinies.

At the end of every discussion about others, we assess those individuals on the basis of the emotional intelligence they display. We would all love to be thought of as smart or talented, industrious, or even unique, but, ultimately, we want to be thought of with affection. I once heard someone describe their friendship with a well-known individual in the following way, "As gifted as she is at what she does, she is equally as good as a human being." I remember thinking to myself, "That is the ultimate compliment. I could strive for no better than that."

I suspect that behind such a profound compliment is a human being who understands and practices emotional intelligence.

For more information on corporate training programs
or *Selling with Emotional Intelligence,*
visit <www.MitchAnthony.com>
or call 507-282-2723.

Acheson, Bill. "Facial Expression Notes." E-mail from Bill Acheson to author.

Anthony, Mitch. *The A.R.R.O.W. Program.* 1999.

Anthony, Mitch, and West, Scott. *StorySelling for Financial Advisors: How Top Producers Sell.* Chicago: Dearborn Financial Publishing, Inc., 2000.

Anthony, Mitch. *The Daily Dose.* Insights Press, 2002.

Augsberger, David. *Caring Enough to Confront.* Ventura, California: Regal Books, 1987.

———. *When Caring Is Not Enough.* Ventura, California: Regal Books, 1983.

Bazerman, Max, and Neale, Margaret. *Negotiating Rationally.* New York: The Free Press, 1992.

Borysenko, Joan. *Minding the Body, Mending the Mind.* New York: Bantam Doubleday Dell Publishing, 1993.

Bryce, W. *The Power of Consultative Selling.* Upper Saddle River, New Jersey: Prentice Hall, 1987.

Carnegie, Dale. *How to Stop Worrying and Start Living.* New York: Simon & Schuster, 1951.

Carter-Scott, Cherie. *If Life Is a Game, These Are the Rules.* New York: Broadway Books, 1998.

Covey, Stephen. *7 Habits of Highly Effective People,* New York: Simon & Schuster, 1990.

Crabb, Larry. *Connecting—A Radical New Vision.* Nashville: Word, 1997.

Damasio, Antonio. *DesCartes's Error—Emotion, Reason, and the Human Brain.* New York: Grosset/Putnam, 1994.

DeMaray, Donald E. *Watch Out for Burnout.* Grand Rapids, Michigan: Baker Book House, 1983.

Ekman, Paul, and Davidson, Richard. *Questions about Emotion.* Oxford University Press, 1994.

Epstein, Seymour. *You're Smarter Than You Think,* New York: Simon & Schuster, 1993.

Frankl, Victor. *Recollections.* Cambridge, Massachusetts: Perseus, 2000.

Friedman, Meyer, and Ulver, Diane. *Treating Type-A Behavior and Your Heart.* New York: Knopf, 1984.

Gardner, Howard. *Multiple Intelligences: The Theory in Practice.* New York: Basic Books, 1993.

Goleman, Daniel. *Emotional Intelligence.* London: Bloomsbury, 1996.

———. *Working with Emotional Intelligence.* London: Bloomsbury, 1998.

Gurney, Kathleen, and Srybnick, Mel. "Listen up," *Investment Advisor,* December 2001, p. 36.

Hendricks, Gay. *Seven Secrets of the Corporate Mystic.* Louisville, Colorado: Sounds True, 2002.

Jaffe, Azriela. *Starting from "No"—10 Strategies to Overcome Your Fear of Rejection and Succeed in Business.* Dearborn, Michigan: Upstart Publishing Co., 1999.

Jandt, Fred, and Gillette, Paul. *Turning Conflict into Agreement.* New York: John Wiley & Sons, 1985.

Jones, Stanley E. *The Unshakeable Kingdom, the Unchanging Person.* Bellingham, Washington: McNett Press, 1995.

Kabat-Zinn, Jon. *Wherever You Go, There You Are.* New York: Hyperion Books, 1994.

LaRouche, Loretta. *Relax—You May Only Have a Few Minutes Left.* New York: Villard, 1998.

Lasch, Christopher. *The Culture of Narcissism.* New York: Warner Books, 1979.

LeDoux, Joseph. "Emotion, Money and the Brain." *Scientific American,* June 1994.

——— *The Synaptic Self.* New York: Viking Press, 2002.

——— *The Emotional Brain: The Mysterious Underpinnings of Life.* New York: Touchstone Books, 1998.

Maxwell, John. *The 21 Indispensable Qualities of a Leader.* Nashville: Thomas Nelson, 1999.

McGinnis, Alan Loy. *Bringing Out the Best in People.* Minneapolis: Augsburg Fortress, 1985.

McLaughlin, Peter. "Catchfire!" *Professional Workforce Survey,* 1996. (As quoted in "Laugh it Up!" *Entrepreneur,* January 1998, p. 14.)

McMillen, S.I. *None of These Diseases.* Grand Rapids, Michigan: Fleming H. Revell, 1963.

Murnigham, K. *The Dynamics of Bargaining Games,* Upper Saddle River, New Jersey: Prentice Hall, 1991.

Nassar, Haya El. "Age Old Mystery." *USA Today,* December 29, 1997, p. 2A.

Pease, A. *Body Language.* New York: Harper Collins, 1981.

Peck, Scott. *The Road Less Traveled.* New York: Simon & Schuster, 1997.

Seligman, Martin. *Learned Optimism.* New York: Random House, 1990.

———. *The Optimistic Child.* New York: Random House, 1995.

Shapiro, Ron, and Jankowski, Mark. *The Power of Nice.* New York: John Wiley & Sons, 1998.

Shell, Richard G. *Bargaining for Advantage: Negotiation Strategies for Reasonable People.* New York: Penguin USA, reissue edition, 2000.

Spears, Larry. *Insights on Leadership.* New York: John Wiley & Sons, 1998.

Spranger, E. *Types of Men.* Halle, Germany: Max Niemeyer Verlag, 1928.

Stocker, Steven. "Finding the Future Alcoholic," *The Futurist Magazine,* May–June, 2002, p. 42.

Stone, Karen, and Dillehut, Harold. *Self-Science: The Subject Is Me.* Goodyear Publishing, 1978.

Sternberg, Robert. *Beyond I.Q.* Cambridge University Press, 1985.

Taurus, Carol. *Anger: The Misunderstood Emotion.* New York: Touchstone, 1989.

Tice, Diane, and Bauerster, Roy. *Handbook of Mental Control.* New York: Prentice Hall, 1993.

Visser, Martha. "Ire Extinguisher: How to Get a Grip on Your Anger," *Success Magazine.* December 1997, p. 10.

Walker, Michael, and Harris, George. *Negotiation: Six Steps to Success.* New York: Prentice Hall, 1995.

Wright, Norman H. *Helping People in Crisis and Stress.* San Bernardino, California: Here's Life Publishers, 1985.

INDEX

A

Accumulation, 118
Accuracy, 16, 28
Acheson, Bill, 149, 150
Achievementality, 41, 52
Adams, George Matthew, 135
Adaptation to Life (Valiant), 86
Adversity, 108–9, 113–14
Advice, unsolicited, 246
Aging, 91, 94
Alcholics Anonymous, 59
Alcoholism, 87
Amygdala hijack, 55
Analyzer personality, 16, 19, 28–30,
   156, 161
   areas of improvement, 29, 30
   challenges, 28–30
   conflict and, 222, 225–26, 229
   critical selling adjustments,
     170–73
   negotiation and, 235
   strengths, 28, 29
Anger, 54–61
   see also Conflict; Confrontation
   chill chart, 80, 81
   containing, 78–82
   facial/body language and, 146
   physiology of, 64–65
   restraint and, 54–61
   self-sabotage and, 62–70
   venting and, 68–69
Anthony, Mark, 49–51, 114–15
Anthony, Mitch, 176
Appearances, 37–38
Arrogance, 129–30, 131
ARROW
   profile, 2–5
   restraint, 60–61
   stress exercise, 90, 92
Assertiveness, 251
Assumptions, challenging, 46–47

Attitude
   aging and, 91, 94
   -behavior-control, 59
   of gratitude, 122–23
   optimism, 100, 103–4
   sales ability and, 101–3
Augsberger, David, 67, 240, 241
Awareness, x, 1–9, 245
   ARROW profile, 2–5
   body language and, 147
   developing emotional radar,
     154–63
   empathy and, 7–8
   goals and, 2–5
   identifying stress, 90, 92
   negotiation and, 232–33
   personal, 5
   personality adjustments and, 23
   pushiness and, 209
   rapport, building, 8
   resilience, 6–7
   restraint, 5–6
   of self, 250
   stress and, 63–64, 91

B

Babyak, Michael, 86
Bazerman, Max, 231, 239
Bellin, Andy, 154
Berra, Yogi, 231
Billings, Josh, 164
Bitterness, 111–12
Blame, 80–81, 82
Body language, 7, 145–53, 220
Borg, Bjorn, 218
Borysenko, Joan, 90
Bourne, Randolph S., 202
Boyenga, M.V., 10
Brain physiology, 55–58, 76, 145
Brennan, Peter, 101–3
Brooks, Bobby, 122–23

Bryant, Bear, 214
Buffett, Warren, 245

C

Cacioppo, John, 128
Cancer, 89
Change, reluctance and, 140–41
Chicken Soup for the Soul, 104–5
Chill chart, 80, 81
Clarke's Law of Revolutionary Ideas,
    140
Client Conversation Profile, 156–58
Clients
    discovering history of, 193–94
    questioning, 185–94
Cloninger, C. Robert, 87
Closing, 141
Cluckhom, C., 188
Coachability, 48
Comfort zone, 17
Communication, 250
    body language, 7, 145–53, 220
    facial/body language and, 145–53
    listening skills, 180, 238
    miscommunication, anger and, 82
    personality and 12, 19
    tonal language, 7, 248–50
Competencies, building, 42
Competitiveness, 39–41, 40, 52,
    119–21
Conflict, 20–21, 221–30
    see also Anger
    comfort zones and, 230
    empathy and, 221–22
    personality and, 222–23, 227–30
    perspective and, 223–24
    resolution, 251
    stress in workplace, 224–26
    unreasonable expectations and,
        227
Confrontation, 212–20
    see also Anger
    credit and blame, 214–15
    grace and, 219
    honesty and, 213–14
    humility-based approach to,
        217–19
    relationship priorities, 219–20

self-deprecating humor and,
    216–17
    team approach, 215–16
Control, 118
Core personality, 11
Covey, Steven, 96, 203
Critical mass, 36–37, 40
    applied, 44–53
    interviewing for, 51–52
    report card, 45
Culpability, 80–82
Curiosity, 122, 176–84
Curran, Dolores, 85–86
Cynicism, 7, 100, 101

D

DEAL Dynamics Awareness Profile,
    235, 236–37
Decision-making, 139, 250
DeMoss, Gary, 204
Diffusion, 62, 78
Dillehunt, Harold, 250
Dimberg, Ulf, 127
Dimitrius, Jo-Ellan, 146–47
Disappointment, 108–9
Discouragement, 107–15
Distraction, 78, 79

E

Egocentric focus, 12
Einstein, Albert, 34, 36
Ekman, Paul, 150
Emerson, Ralph Waldo, 145
Emotional bank accounts, 203–4, 205,
    211
Emotional Intelligence (Goleman), ix, 58,
    74, 126, 128
Emotional quotient, evaluating, 244
Emotion(s)
    body responses to disturbing,
        64–65
    brain research and, 63
    changing a negative climate, 131
    emotional agenda, 134
    facial/body language and, 146
    intentionality and, 127
    managing feelings, 250
    mood dance, 127

negative, expressing, 73, 78–82
negotiation and, 234
positive intent and, 126–34
taking responsibility for, 248
viral spiral of, 71–77
Empathy, 7–8, 152, 195–201, 250
client values and, 194
conflict resolution and, 221–22
empathy rubic, 183
negotiation and, 238–39
sales presentations and, 189
self-assessment, 180–82
Energy, 16, 30
Enterpriser personality, 13, 16, 19, 156,
159–60
areas of improvement, 26,
27–28
challenges, 26, 27
conflict and, 222, 225–26,
228–29
critical selling adjustments,
168–70
negotiation and, 234–35
resiliency and, 142
strengths, 25–27
Excellence, desire for, 121–22
Expectations, 101–3, 227

F

Facial language, 145–53
Failure, 41, 108–9, 136–37
Fear, 135–37
Feedback, 79
Feelings, 13
Flexibility, 30
Fortgang, Laura Berman, 79
Foster, Larry, 34–39, 47
Frankl, Victor, 178
Franklin, Benjamin, 62, 219
Friendships, building, 123–24
Friesen, Wallace, 150

G

Gardner, Howard, 243
Gillette, Paul, 231–32
Goals, 124–25
Goleman, Daniel, ix, 55, 57, 58, 71, 74,
85, 126, 128, 243

Gratitude, 122–23
Group dynamics, 251
Growth, desire for, 122
Gurney, Kathleen, 179

H

Habits, 242–51
Halperin, Stephen, 198
Halsey, William F., 212
HALT, 59
Handbook of Mental Control, The
(Zillman), 65
Harvard Medical School study, 91
Health, stress management and, 86
Helping People in Crisis and Stress
(Wright), 83
Hendricks, Gay, 208
Hiring process, 37–38
Holmes, Oliver Wendell, 116
Holtz, Lou, 70
Honesty, 208–9, 213–14
Huizenga, Wayne, 240
Humiliation, fear of, 137
Humility, 217–19
Humor, 41–42, 94–95, 216–17

I

If Life Is a Game, These Are the Rules
(Scott), 109
Impulsiveness, 31, 55
Insight, 250
Intangibles, 34, 37, 39
Intentionality, 127, 128, 130, 133
Interview process, 35
Introspection, 5, 49, 82
Intuition, 146

J–K

Jackson, Phil, 1
Jaffe, Azriela, 136
James, William, 238
Jandt, Fred, 231–32
Jankowski, Mark, 231, 234
Johnson, Edith, 22
King, Frank, 185
Kinnick, Niles, 208
Koppen, Angie, 42

L

Leading role, 17
Ledoux, Joseph, 55–56
Likability, 8, 202–11
    developing, 210–11
    emotional bank accounts, 203–4,
      205
    emotional time bombs, 207–10
    good manners, 204, 206–7
Lincoln, Abraham, 221, 238
Listening skills, 180, 238
Living Your Best Life: Discover Your Life's
    Blueprint for Success (Fortgang),
    79

M

McKay, David O., 200
McMillen, S. I., 62
Marcus Aurelius Antoninus, 242
Microexpression, 151
Mikez, Steve, 201
Minding the Body, Mending the Mind
    (Borysenko), 90
Motivation, 116–25
    extrinsic (materialistic)
      motivators, 7, 116–18
    intrinsic motivators, 7, 119–25
Motivator personality, 16, 30–32, 156,
    162–63
    areas of improvement, 31, 32
    challenges, 31–32
    conflict and, 222, 226, 229–30
    critical selling adjustments,
      173–75
    negotiation and, 235
    resiliency and, 142
    strengths, 30–31
Multitasking, 26
Murray, H., 188
MVP Model, 11

N

Narcissism, 8
    overcoming. *See* Curiosity
Neale, Margaret, 231, 239
Negative behavior, 129–30
Negotiating Rationally (Bazerman and
    Neale), 239

Negotiation, 190, 231–41
    awareness and, 232–33
    emotional trickery and, 233–34
    emotional wisdom and, 240–41
    empathy and, 238–39
    foundations for effective, 232
    respect and, 239–40
    style, 234–37
Nonverbal signals, 145–53
Norris, Chuck, 69–70

O

Observation, 154–63
Optimism, 7, 30, 97–106
    attitude and, 100, 103–4
    expectations, 101–3
    mental barriers to, 104
    reacting to discouragement with,
      98, 109–11
    self-saboteurs, 104–6

P

Paine, Thomas, 126
Pavlov's Trout (Quinnet), 143
Peale, Norman Vincent, 99
Peale, Ruth, 99
Pearsall, Duane, 133
People pleasers, 137
People rules, xi
Personal awareness, 5
Personality, 22–33
    see also Personality profile; *specific*
      personality type
    analyzer type, 28–30
    centenarian, 91, 94
    core, 11
    enterpriser type, 25–28
    fear or rejection and, 136
    motivator type, 30–32
    reading and adjusting, 32–33
    recognizing style of, 155–63
    stress and, 86–87
    togetherness type, 23–25
Personality profile
    awareness graph, 15
    axis, 13, 16
    discovering, 13–15
    leading role, 17

polar opposites/conflict origins,
    20–21
predictability and, 18–19
roles defined, 16–18
sample patterns, 17
supporting role, 18
team dynamic, 12–16
villain role, 18
Personal responsibility, 250–51
Perspective, 223–24
Pessimism, 7, 100–101, 106
Peter McLaughlin Co., 94
Polar opposites, 20–21
Post, Robyn, 89
Posttraumatic sales syndrome,
    137–38
Power of Nice, The (Shapiro and
    Jankowski), 231
Power of Positive Thinking, The (Peale),
    99
Precision, 16
Presentations, 164–75, 182, 187–88
Pressure, 18, 40
Professional Work Force Survey, 94
Pushiness, 209–10

Q–R

Questions, 185–94
    qualitatve discovery, 191
    quantitative discovery, 189–91
Quinnet, Paul, 143
Rapport, 8
Rationality, 65–66
Reading People (Dimitrius), 146–47
Recognition, 118
Rejection, risking, 135–44
    analyzing "no," 138–39
    comfort zones and, 141
    fear and, 136–37
    price objections, 139–40
    reluctance to change, 140–41
    resiliency and, 135–36, 141–43
Relaxing, 87
Resiliency, 6–7, 41, 72
    optimism and, 97–106
    resilience reactor, 98
    risking rejection and, 135–36,
        141–43
    sense of purpose and, 124–25

Resourcefulness, 39
Respect, 239–40
Responsibility
    personal, 250–51
    restraint and, 58
Restraint, 5–6, 54–61, 64, 74
    introspection and, 82
    lack of, 71–75
    negative outbursts/containing,
        78–82
    preparing for restraint exercise,
        90, 93
Results, achieving, 13, 16, 25
Richter, Jean Paul, 242
Roosevelt, Theodore, 202
Rosenthal, Robert, 152
Rubenstein, Steve, 145
Ryan, Jim, 89

S

Sales presentations, 187–88
Sarcasm, 100
Satisfaction filter, x
Schweitzer, Albert, 124
Scott, Cherie Carter, 109
Screening tests, 35
Secret Power Within, The (Norris), 70
Self-acceptance, 250
Self-awareness, 250
Self-centeredness/self-absorption, 178,
    179–80
Self-confidence, 40
Self-control, 60–61. *See also* Restraint
Self-deprecation, 216–17
Self-disclosure, 250
Selflessness, 178, 195–201
Self Science: The Subject Is Me (Stone and
    Dillehunt), 250
Selling adjustments, 164–75
    analyzer personality, 170–73
    enterpriser personalities, 168–70
    motivator personality, 173–75
    togetherness personality, 165–68
Selye, Hans, 83
Seneca, 54
Sensitivity, 13, 23, 152–53
Setbacks, 41
Seven Habits of Highly Effective People
    (Covey), 203

Seven Secrets of the Corporate Mystic (Hendricks), 208
Shakespeare, William, 208
Shapiro, Ronald, 231, 234
Shell, G. Richard, 232
Silver, Margery, 94
Skepticism, 100, 101
Smiles, 151–52
Socrates, 74, 195
Spurgeon, Charles H., 44
Srybnik, Mel, 179
Stevenson, Robert Louis, 143
Stone, Karen, 250
Stress, 5, 66, 83–88, 250
    confrontation and, 118, 212–20
    feeling of helplessness, 89–90
    humor and, 94–95
    lack of restraint and, 54–61
    management, 84, 89–96
    self-healing, 85–86
    sources, identifying, 90, 92, 224–26
    supporting role and, 18
    susceptible personalities, 86–87
    three elements in, 83–84
    villain role and, 18
Stress and the Healthy Family (Curran), 85
Success, 38–42
    achievementality, 41
    awareness and, 2
    competitive drive, 39–41
    fear of, 137
    persona of, 38
    teachability, 41
    wit, 41–42
Sullins, Ellin, 127
Sullivan, Harry Stack, 67
Supporting role, 18

T

Teachability, 34, 41, 46–48, 49, 52
TEAM Dynamics, 12–16
    personality awareness profile, 13–15
    personality axis, 13, 16
Tension, 5, 18

Tests, screening, 35
Thomas, Clarence, 204, 206
Thoreau, Henry David, ix
Tice, Diane, 68
Time management, 50–51
Togetherness personality, 13, 23–25
    areas for improvement, 24, 25
    challenges, 24–25
    conflict and, 222, 225–26, 227–28
    critical selling adjustments, 165–68
    negotiation and, 234
    recognizing, 156, 158–59
    strengths, 23–24
Tonal language, 7
Training process, 35
Truth, 208–9
Twain, Mark, 159

V

Valiant, George, 86
Value, 139–40, 210
Vansickle, John R., 22
Venting, 68–69, 72
Villain role, 18
Viral spiral, 6, 71–77, 127
Voice pattern, 159, 160, 161, 162–63
Voice tone, 79, 220, 248–50
Vulnerability, 59

W–Z

Ward, William Arthur, 69
Weaknesses
    awareness of, 49–51
    finding/addressing, 48–49
Wenzel, John, 123
When Caring Is Not Enough—Resolving Conflicts through Fair Fighting (Augsburger), 240
Win-Win Negotiating: Turning Conflict into Agreement (Jandt and Gillette), 231
Wit, 41–42, 52, 94–95
Wooden, John, 5
Worry, 85
Wright, H. Norman, 83–84
Zillman, Dolf, 65, 75, 79

Emotional intelligence can increase sales.

Start developing and using the skills you need to succeed in today's competitive market by enrolling in a new seminar offered by Dearborn and Mitch Anthony.

Selling with Emotional Intelligence is a new, instructor-led program based on Mitch Anthony's *Selling with Emotional Intelligence* book. Students will learn the "art" of selling by explaining the soft science that underpins effective relationship building in advisor-customer relationships. Selling with Emotional Intelligence addresses five key emotional competencies critical to sales success:

- Awareness
- Restraint
- Resilience
- Empathy
- Building Rapport

Contact us today to learn more about how emotional intelligence can help build your business!

Financial services organizations, call: 1-800-824-8742
All other organizations, call: 1-507-282-2723

Dearborn™
Financial Services
A **Kaplan Professional** Company